LET IT BE TOUGH

LET IT BE TOUGH

TRAIN YOUR MIND TO PERFORM UNDER PRESSURE

ANT WILLIAMS

SIMON &
SCHUSTER

New York · Amsterdam/Antwerp · London · Toronto · Sydney/Melbourne · New Delhi

LET IT BE TOUGH: TRAIN YOUR MIND TO PERFORM UNDER PRESSURE
First published in Australia in 2026 by
Simon & Schuster (Australia) Pty Limited
Level 4, 32 York St, Sydney NSW 2000

10 9 8 7 6 5 4 3 2 1

New York Amsterdam/Antwerp London Toronto Sydney/Melbourne New Delhi
Visit our website at www.simonandschuster.com.au

NATIONAL LIBRARY OF AUSTRALIA

A catalogue record for this book is available from the National Library of Australia

ISBN: 9781761638565

Cover design: George Saad
Cover image: ADVENTURE photo courtesy of Apple TV+
Typeset by Midland Typesetters, Australia
Printed and bound in Australia by Griffin Press

FSC www.fsc.org MIX Paper | Supporting responsible forestry FSC® C018684

The paper this book is printed on is certified against the Forest Stewardship Council® Standards. Griffin Press holds chain of custody certification SCS-COC-001185. FSC® promotes environmentally responsible, socially beneficial and economically viable management of the world's forests.

For whoever needs permission to take
the risk they want to take.
Here it is.

PROLOGUE

At the edge of the Bermuda Triangle, Long Island in the Bahamas is a splinter of land barely 6 kilometres wide at its broadest point. One side is buffeted by the roaring surf of the Atlantic, the other lapped by the neon blue of the Caribbean, with the two halves conjoined by a tropical coastline scalloped with rocky coves and stretches of pristine white sand. Yet tucked in a hidden nook of this beach-bum paradise is an underwater cavern that locals claim is a direct portal to hell.

Islanders believe that Dean's Blue Hole was dug by the devil himself. Most flatly refuse to swim there out of fear that Satan will emerge from the depths to drag them down to their doom. This sense of dread is fuelled by the sinkhole's freaky geology. Positioned just 20 metres off the beach, Dean's Blue Hole consists of a long, vertical cave that looks like a bottomless pit. The limestone shaft extends down and down to a depth of 202 metres. For superstitious locals, that leaves plenty of room for demonic forces to lurk.

The scare stories are backed with a body count. Three tourists from Nassau drowned at the Hole a few years ago, while six months back, a 19-year-old lobster diver vanished while his family enjoyed a picnic on the beach. The teenager's body has never been found and his white bones are now believed to lie somewhere in the Hole's black abyss.

Personally, this folklore doesn't faze me. The only demons I'm worried about are the mental ones that could sabotage what I've come here to do. I've travelled more than 15,000 kilometres to the Bahamas from my Sydney home to compete at Vertical Blue 2012, an invite-only competition for the best freedivers in the world. But as I squeeze into my hooded wetsuit and walk barefoot towards the sea, I'm aware of the fear that's starting to flicker in my stomach.

'All set? How're you feeling, mate?' says Dave Knight, my support partner and childhood friend, as I limber up with a few last-minute stretches.

'Yeah, pretty good,' I lie in a vain attempt to convince myself that it might actually be true.

Nerves are to be expected today. Vertical Blue is a big deal in this sport with the event often described as 'the Wimbledon of free-diving'. The aim in today's 'Constant Weight' discipline is to dive as deep as you can with no breathing apparatus and just a monofin (a single swimfin a bit like a whale's tail) to propel your descent. Due to its depth and accessibility from the beach, Dean's Blue Hole is one of freediving's top destinations. Today, I'm hoping to nail something I've never done before: dive to a depth of 100 metres on a single breath. Before I got here 15 days ago, I'd never managed more than 82 metres.

I've got 15 minutes until my dive time at 2 pm. In the water, Dave tows my floating body out towards the competition zone; I don't swim as I need to conserve all my energy for the dive. As we slowly drift over, I notice the sky has become overcast with a ruffled layer of cloud obscuring the sun. That means it'll be even darker when I venture underwater. At 30 metres, I'll be unable to see my arms in front of my face. Then it will get darker still, with my world eventually reduced to a smothering black. Engulfed in that gloom, it's easy to get spooked as the door of your imagination opens to worst-case scenarios. Except the dangers with freediving are very real.

Right now, my fellow competitor Miguel Lozano is under the surface navigating that darkness alone. Hailing from a fishing village north of Barcelona, he's a rangy Spaniard whom I've got to know a bit in the lead-up to this competition. Friendly and outgoing, Miguel's easy laugh conceals a formidable mindset. One of world's truly elite freedivers, yesterday he reached a gobsmacking depth of 117 metres. Today, he's targeting 122 metres. If he succeeds, he'll be only the third person in history to have gone that deep.

Dave and I slowly paddle to wait just outside the dive zone where the competition platform is set up. It's marked by a set of white PVC pipes that are connected to form a 6-metre square above the Hole. Three judges sit on a floating platform alongside a photographer and videographer. In the water, five safety divers are primed for action. These veteran professionals are entrusted to chaperone the athletes in the last 30 metres of their ascent. Nearing the surface is where problems are most likely to arise.

Jutting off the end of the platform is a miniature crane that's operated with a counterbalance system that a diving rope is spooled through. Last night, every diver had to submit their proposed depths to the judges. Before each competitor's attempt, a metal plate covered in Velcro is lowered down to the diver's specified distance. That plate is affixed with a tag that you have to pluck off at the bottom of your dive to prove you've reached your target.

When it's your turn, you attach the lanyard on your belt to the rope via a carabiner. Being loosely tethered like this has two purposes. First, it stops you from swimming off in the wrong direction in the pitch black, but second, it could also save your life if something goes wrong. The safety team have a sonar-powered device that tracks your movement. If it detects your body is motionless – suggesting you may have lost consciousness – the rope can be used to winch you back to the surface. Hopefully that won't be necessary today.

I start some positive self-talk to try to get myself into the zone.

Come on, Ant, it's game time now. This is your time to shine . . .

My pep talk is interrupted by a flurry of yells and splashes. Recovery divers and medics are scrambling to help a figure in the water. It's Miguel, but it's immediately clear that something is very wrong. A safety diver pulls his head out of the water, but it instantly flops back. His eyes are shut tight; he's blacked out. Is he okay?

'Safety! Here, now!' yells an official. 'We need oxygen, fast!'

Still unconscious, Miguel's face is blue, his mouth twisted into a leer. Then his head jerks forward and he starts to cough up blood. Medics haul his convulsing body up to the platform as he continues to violently retch.

'Don't look, mate! Don't look!' warns Dave.

Not wanting to freak out, I avert my gaze. Turning my head to the clouds, I try to ignore the evil hacking noise erupting from Miguel's chest. I think I know what's happening and it's not good.

Water is almost a thousand times denser than air. The deeper you dive, the barometric pressure from the weight of the water builds and builds until there comes a point where something has to give. At 10 metres of depth, the pressure is strong enough to crush a beer can. Internally, that force causes your lungs to shrink. But at the same time, your body launches into emergency mode, diverting extra blood from your limbs to your chest in a bid to deliver oxygen and stop your lungs from collapsing. As the pressure intensifies, it may cause damage to the lung tissue, resulting in small leaks or tears. I suspect this is why Miguel is coughing up blood.

Unable to help myself, I glance over at him. He's still unconscious on the platform, his body twisted into the recovery position to stop him from choking. A regulator attached to an oxygen tank has been stuck between his lips. But as I'm watching, it falls out and more blood spills from his mouth, the drops bright red against the white of the platform.

Fear suddenly hijacks my mind. Blackouts are an occupational hazard in this game, but this one looks bad. How did it happen to such an experienced diver? Did Miguel bring it on himself by going so deep on successive days? And if so, what does that mean for me? I've also just backed up my deepest ever dive without a rest day and my lungs still ache from yesterday's practice. Will pushing myself to 100 metres – a depth far beyond anything I've done before – put me at similar risk?

I recall the email I got yesterday from Tanguy, a training partner back in Australia. After hearing of my progress during the week, he pleaded with me not to get reckless. 'Don't be an idiot,' he wrote. 'You've already got your PB, don't try and go deeper or you'll kill yourself.'

I'm aware of my heart pumping faster, the prickle of panic at the back of my throat . . .

'Williams 100-metre Constant Weight, New Zealand! Three minutes till dive time!' shouts an official.

Three minutes. That's 180 seconds to turn panic into calm. How I use those three minutes will determine if my dive is successful or if I'll end up in a state like Miguel. In freediving, adrenaline is the enemy. You have to stay relaxed in order to slow your heart rate and reduce your oxygen consumption. Stress results in loss of focus and bad decisions. I need to recover my composure fast. This is a mental game that's won or lost in the buildup.

Okay, mate, get a grip, right now. You can't afford to tense up. Get rational and process the facts. You've witnessed heaps of blackouts. Yes, Miguel's is a bad one, but at least it happened on the surface and he's getting medical help. On balance, he should be fine. He's in good hands and you can't do anything to help. Compartmentalise the incident and move on.

To centre myself, I concentrate on bringing all my attention back to the present moment. I focus on my physical senses: the bobbing motion of the sea, the breeze on my face, the briny tang of the water on my lips. Then I zoom out to gain a bigger perspective. Looking towards the shoreline, I observe my environment with fresh eyes: the crystalline waters, the palm trees, the untouched beach. Over to the right, I see my Kiwi compatriot, Will Trubridge, watching the action from a clifftop. I force a smile and give Will a friendly wave while consciously relaxing my shoulders and unclenching my jaw. When I get anxious, I start to tighten up. By smiling, I'm manipulating my facial muscles to lull my brain into a more positive state. Opening my posture, I slow my breathing until I'm gently inhaling and exhaling just four times a minute.

The mind follows the body. Non-verbal cues will shepherd your mind into a calmer state.

'Two minutes to go!' barks the official.

I slot on my nose clip and goggles. The action triggers a mental switch. I'm no longer Ant Williams, sport psychologist, business consultant and married father of two. I'm an elite freediver about to set a new personal record. The tone of my inner monologue cranks up to become hyper-positive. Self-belief is everything now.

Come on, this is your moment, Ant. You've trained hard, there's no reason not to be supremely confident. This is your chance. It's go time!

Closing my eyes, I visualise myself snatching off the Velcro tag at 100 metres and coming out of the water triumphant at the end of my dive. I imagine the praise from the judges. The pride rippling through my chest. The buzz of satisfaction at achieving my goal.

'Sixty seconds to go!'

Mentally re-engaged, I switch my attention to my lungs as I take my final breath. Slowly I draw in an immense quantity of air. After ten seconds I'm still inhaling while moving my shoulders back and forth to load every last chamber of my lungs with as much oxygen as I possibly can. Once my lungs feel completely inflated, I begin 'packing', a special technique used to force in even more air. I take another huge gulp, then close my glottis – the space between the vocal cords in my larynx – to ram the air down into my lungs. Then I do it again and again to complete 30 'packs', opening my glottis for a microsecond to cram in even more air. By the time I've finished, I've increased my lung capacity by around 4 litres.

An official gives me a final countdown: five, four, three, two, ONE!

Rolling into the water, I'm enveloped by the blueness of the ocean. The water offers plenty of resistance as my lungs are so full of air that my body is unusually buoyant. I kick assertively with my monofin to propel myself downwards, but I'm careful to keep the movement fluid and relaxed. Down I swim with my arms above my head while kicking with a smooth undulation of my legs and hips. Every 2 metres, I 'equalise' by making a forceful exhalation with my mouth shut to blow air into my middle-ear canals and neutralise the pressure.

At 20 metres, the vast mass of water bearing down on me turns my body into a negative weight. Instead of holding me up, it now starts pushing me deeper. That means I can stop using my legs now and begin to freefall. Tucking my chin into my chest, I glide downwards effortlessly, giving a small kick every 5 metres or so for extra momentum. At the same time, I start to bring the air from my lungs up into my cheeks that I puff out like I'm blowing up a balloon.

Metre by metre, the colour of the water darkens, changing steadily from aqua to navy to midnight blue. At 30 metres, I'm consumed by blackness – holy crap, it's dark down here – and soon there's no visibility at all. I shut my eyes and proceed on sensation alone. There's nothing to see now and your eyes require oxygen to function, so swimming blind conserves your supply. I pull my arms down by my sides leaving my index finger and thumb lightly gripping the rope to gauge the speed of my descent. By my estimations, I'm descending at the pace of a light jog.

At 40 metres, I'm aware of the growing tightness around my chest and throat. The pressure is starting to build. But instead of fighting the sensation, I relax into it.

It's totally normal. Everything is unfolding as expected. Keep going. Stick to the plan.

Burrowing further into the darkness, I focus on retaining a streamlined position and preserving the mass of air that I've trapped in my mouth and throat. I equalise the air pressure as gently as I can using my tongue to push the air into my eustachian tubes – the narrow passages that connect the middle ear to the back of the nose and throat.

With no visual or auditory stimulus, my sensory awareness starts to shift inwards. All my consciousness is directed towards the 2 centimetres of air between my tongue and the roof of my mouth. My entire universe is reduced to that tiny cavity and the sensation of the rope between my fingers. Apart from that, I'm untethered from the world, plummeting into a boundless void. The pressure and the urge to breathe is building now, but I try to surrender to the discomfort.

Just let go. Let go.

The alarm on my watch beeps to tell me that I'm at 70 metres. My lungs are now the size of tennis balls. But while my cheeks have deflated significantly, I've got a bit of air left. That's a good sign – I'm still in the game and can keep on pushing deeper.

At 90 metres, things start to get ugly. The pressure in my chest is cranking up with visceral intensity. It feels like an elephant is sitting on top of me. Is that deep enough? Should I turn back?

You still have some air. Keep going, Ant. You've got this!

Can I trust this inner voice? Or is my judgement addled by narcosis, an inevitability at these depths as nitrogen dissolves in the bloodstream and starts to anaesthetise the brain. Evoking a dreamlike state like huffing nitrous oxide, narcosis prevents you from thinking straight. Can I afford to ignore the thumping pressure, the rippling convulsions in my chest? Because it's getting really gnarly now. Like someone is trying to wrench a cricket ball through my sternum. Every atom in my body is getting crushed.

You're okay. You're still okay. Go! Go! Go!

Out of the blackness, the alarm on my watch beeps again. It's a welcome sound. I'm at 93 metres. Only seven more to go! Slowly I twist my body into the turn position. My cheeks are empty of air now. But there's still the tiniest space on the very back of my tongue. I think I've got a pea-sized morsel of air left. Root it out, use it to equalise.

Then my outstretched hand strikes the 100-metre base plate. My head is still tucked into my chest and I resist the urge to look up. If I straighten my neck, the weight of the water risks crushing my larynx. Carefully, I spin my body around until I'm horizontal. The torch under the base plate is illuminated. I need to rip off the tag. But my dexterity is compromised by the lack of oxygen and I fumble it. Shit! Frantically, I grope for it again. Got it!

There is no flicker of satisfaction and I immediately turn around and start kicking hard. Reaching 100 metres is only half the battle. It's taken me almost two minutes to get to this depth. I'm fast running out of air and have to fight my way back up to the surface. The real danger starts now.

All at once, I'm aware of the reality of my predicament. I'm so alone down here, so far from help, my safety divers still 70 metres above me. My weakening body will have to muster a colossal effort to slog through the ten atmospheres of water pressure that are pinning me down.

For a second, the cavernous depth becomes overwhelming. The solitude of the void feels impossible to breach, the darkness too dense to escape.

Snap out of it! Don't let the panic in. Stay in control.

Arms up to streamline my body, I start swimming uphill as fast as I can – I've got the equivalent of a 30-storey building to climb. But after lulling myself into that state of relaxation during my descent, making my body fire up is hard with the lack of oxygen. In the blackness, I can't gauge my progress.

I'm kicking and kicking and kicking, my body arrow-straight, arms outstretched. My eyes are open, but I still can't see anything. There's a desperate edge to my kicking now. My legs are tiring, but the darkness remains as impenetrable as ever. I should be able to see by now. What's gone wrong? Am I even moving? Has the narcosis befuddled my brain?

Keep kicking.

Is my lanyard tangled around the 20-kilogram base plate at 100 metres? Or is the lack of oxygen disrupting my vision? Am I making any headway at all? I'm on fumes of oxygen now, lungs burning, chest convulsing, a silent scream in my throat. Have I swum the wrong way? Gone off course? Still the clutching blackness refuses to yield.

Keep kicking. Just keep kicking. If you're snagged on the base plate it can't be too heavy – you can pull it to the surface. Fight the darkness. Kick away the panic. Just bloody kick!

Then, from a direction I can't quite fathom, I hear three blasts of the 'groper call', the communication sound my safety divers make to flag they're nearby. But I can't see them! Surely I should be able to if they're stationed at the 30-metre mark? Where are they? That must've been a warning call, urging me to hurry the fuck up. My divers must know I've been down here too long. What the hell has gone wrong?

Reach for the surface. Keep pushing. Just another ten kicks.

Suddenly, I explode through the water and into the light. I can't see anything through my clouded goggles and I flail my arms reaching for the rope that I somehow manage to grasp. I'm disorientated and wildly dizzy, struggling to stay afloat.

'Breathe! Breathe!' someone yells.

Woozy from three and a half minutes underwater I can't think straight. Then, through my gasping haze, I realise that Dave is shouting my name. But I can't process his words.

'Surface protocol!' he screams. 'Five seconds left!'

Finally, my brain makes sense of what he's saying. Hands shaking, I rip off my mask and the world lurches. Whoa! Then I tear off my nose clip, before flashing the okay sign to the judges. There's a 30-second wait while they check my motor control and make sure I'm not about to black out. Then one of them holds up a white card to validate my dive.

I've done it! I've bloody done it!

Emotions flood my brain. A tidal wave of adrenaline spiked with naked relief that I've escaped that choking darkness. The primal delight of survival collides with pride that I've finally done it. I've reached 100 metres at last after years of trying.

Grant Graves, the official judge, leans over the platform. 'Well done, Anthony. So you're number 23. That's your number.'

'What's that?'

'Only 23 people in history have ever reached 100 metres in competition. You, my friend, are number 23.'

The implications of the words make me reel. Last year alone, over 600 climbers summited Mount Everest. By diving to a depth of 100 metres, I've joined an exclusive crew.

Dave swims over and grabs me in a clumsy hug that accidentally dunks us both. There are tears in his eyes. 'How did you manage that? I was shitting myself! Thought seeing Miguel black out might've psyched you out. But you did it, Ant! You stayed so cool. Did you grow up with balls of steel or something?'

I respond with a grin, but I know that what Dave said isn't true. I was never a brave kid growing up. In fact, I was fearful and meek, a lifelong rule follower too timid to step out of line. The difference is that my work as a sport psychologist exposed me to an armoury of mental tricks to stop fear from holding me back. Tactics that anyone can learn to perform under pressure.

For a minute, I just float on my back and chuckle quietly to myself, marvelling at the life-giving wonder of every breath. Then the reality of my achievement hits home and I'm blinking back tears. Things got hairy down there, but I didn't buckle. By diving to 100 metres, I've achieved a decade-long goal and survived.

Eventually, I compose myself and roll around to face Dave.

'Miguel is okay, by the way,' he says. 'He came around pretty quick. Didn't even want to go to hospital although they talked him into it.'

'Thank God, it looked like a bad one.'

Together, we bob side by side, taking in the craziness of what just happened. Finally, Dave breaks the silence. 'So you didn't see the devil then, hanging out down there in the Hole?'

'No, I didn't and that's a good thing, too. I've heard he's a pretty bad guy.'

PART 1

CHAPTER 1

It's May 1997 and I'm in my share house in Auckland when the landline rings. On the other end is a gruff Afrikaans accent.

'Finally tracked you down. Do you know that you're the only prick in Auckland who does sport psychology?'

'Sorry, who is this?'

'Eh? Oh. It's Ian McIntosh. Coach of the Natal Sharks.'

Instantly I grip the phone tighter. Despite being a Kiwi, I'm no rugby tragic, but Ian McIntosh is a well-known name. He's the former coach of the Springboks and the man who many credit with laying the foundations for their 1996 World Cup triumph.

'Good to hear from you, Ian. What can I do for you?'

'Look, mate, I'll cut to the chase here. You got anything on right now?'

'Nothing I can't shuffle around.'

'Good, because we need some help and don't have much time. Get yourself down to the Centra Hotel on Queen Street where the team is staying. Be there at 2 pm. Will fill you in on the details then.'

McIntosh hangs up and I stand there in a baffled state of excitement. I'm 24 years old and only a few months out of university after doing a double major in sport and cognitive psychology at the University of Otago. On paper, I'm supposedly now working as a sport psychologist. In reality, my clients so far have consisted of one surfer mate and a climber who suddenly developed an inconvenient fear of heights. The upshot is that I'm mainly supporting myself by working as a barman at the Chill Bar on Ponsonby Road. Now I've apparently been hired by an internationally respected rugby coach. What on earth does he want?

Trying to get myself up to speed, I flick through the sports section of a day-old copy of *The New Zealand Herald* that Brian, my flatmate, has left crumpled down the side of the sofa. Quickly, things start to make sense. McIntosh's team, the Natal Sharks, are over from Durban ahead of a semi-final against the high-flying Auckland Blues. The Super 12 match is taking place this Saturday at Eden Park. That's in just three days' time.

Hastily, I get ready. Keen to project some authority despite my rookie status, I figure dressing up is probably a good idea. I iron a shirt, chuck on the suit I wore to my high-school formal and rush out the door to get into town.

When I arrive at the Centra, McIntosh is prowling the lobby. He's dressed in a Sharks tracksuit with a cap pulled down low and tufts of grey hair poking out the sides. After a bone-crushing handshake that makes me audibly gasp, he sizes me up and frowns. 'Shit, you're a fair bit younger than I expected, eh? Oh well, you better come and meet the management team.'

McIntosh leads me down a corridor into a foyer. Over in one corner is a large oval table with about ten burly guys sitting around it. They're all wearing tracksuits and I instantly regret my decision to wear a suit. Waving me into a seat, McIntosh introduces me to the Sharks' inner circle – the assistant trainers for the forwards and backs, the strength and conditioning coach, the team manager, the physios, and so on. Unfortunately, I can't take in any of the names because all my attention is directed towards the head of the table where the team's skipper, Gary Teichmann, is sitting. The towering forward also captains the Springboks national team and is viewed, even in New Zealand, as one of the best number eights in the world.

'Right, first up,' McIntosh says, 'let's get one thing straight. We've never used a sport psychologist before. And I don't want word getting out that we're using one now. Don't want anyone thinking we're weak in the head.'

As he's speaking, a troop of hulking men built like refrigerators walk past our table and into the hotel ballroom next door. I recognise the colossal prop, Ollie le Roux, and his Springboks' teammate, the hard-tackling fly-half, Henry Honiball. This is the Sharks team I'll be working with.

'So here's the thing,' McIntosh continues. 'We're playing the Blues on Saturday and the bloody media keep saying we're going to get fucking walloped. That we're going to lose by 30 points or more. Forget the fact that most of those chumps never even played the bloody game. The problem is all this nonsense has got into the boys' heads.'

He sketches out the background to the hoodoo. Last year, the Blues comfortably beat the Sharks in the 1996 Super 12 final. Propelled by the freakish power of Jonah Lomu, Auckland rampaged to a 45–21 victory at Eden Park, the same venue the teams will play at in three days' time. 'To be fair, the score could've been a lot worse,' McIntosh admits.

Psychologically, though, the real damage happened a few months later. That Blues side who beat the Sharks in the final contained 11 All Blacks who then toured South Africa for a test series. They included the Brooke brothers, Zinzan and Robin, Michael Jones, the formidable lock, and Sean Fitzpatrick, world rugby's front-row strongman. Over three games, the All Blacks came out on top and became known as 'the Incomparables' for their feat of winning a test series in South Africa for the first time.

Subsequently, the Sharks faced the Blues this season in Durban and came off second best in a bad-tempered clash. McIntosh now feels his team have lost their belief.

'The energy is low, the morale is shot, the team lack intensity in training. Now the media is beating us up. Look, I know it's been a bloody long season. But this is a semi-final, for Christ's sake, and it's like no one wants to be here. It's clear from the boys' attitude and body language that they're sick of travelling and just want to go home. What I need you to do, Anthony, is fix their heads. Restore some pride. Get the boys up for this game. Reckon you can help us?'

'I'm sure there's heaps we can work on,' I say.

'Alright, then you better come and see the lads. We've got a team meeting now. Let's go.'

Everyone gets up and walks through to the ballroom. I trail behind Teichmann, marvelling at the girth of his neck and shoulders. Inside, the 30-man Sharks squad are sitting at several tables, joking around or flicking through the local papers. I opt to pull up a chair at the back of the room. I'll keep a low-profile today, I figure, watch McIntosh's session and gather some intel. Presumably, he'll want me to brief the team tomorrow and start to gee them up.

Another tracksuited member of staff – I think it's one of the physios – takes a seat alongside me. 'You've got a hell of a job on your hands here, mate,' he whispers. 'God knows what you can do, because the boys' confidence is at rock bottom. Talk about getting a hospital pass . . .'

As I'm processing all this, McIntosh walks up to the front of the room where a makeshift stage has been assembled. 'Right-ho,' he shouts. 'Listen up. I'm going to get straight into it. I wanted to introduce you to an old mate that I've just run into. His name's Ant Williams and we caught up last year – went for a jog together when I was visiting Auckland. Anyway, he's a top sport psychologist and he's going to come and have a few words with you. Over to you, Ant . . .'

Whoa! What the hell? I had no idea I'd be addressing the team today. I'm totally unprepared and have nothing to go on. Now an entire room full of grizzled players – many of whom are veteran internationals – are staring at me, waiting for me to do something. Oh shit.

Trying to look confident, I puff out my chest and walk to the front of the room in my shiny suit. McIntosh passes me on the way and nods. 'You've got them for the next two hours,' he says, patting me on the shoulder. 'Don't waste our time.'

From the stage, I recognise a bunch of faces from TV. There's Gary Lawless, the fullback who scored 50 points in a game against Otago earlier this season. Next to him is André Joubert, who turned in a heroic performance against the All Blacks in the World Cup final despite playing with a broken hand. All these hardened pros are eyeballing me with a mixture of suspicion and disdain. And I have no idea what I'm meant to say.

Smiling nervously, I size up the room while wracking my brain for my opening salvo. Just as I'm about to utter my first words, someone yells out. It's the Springboks' lock Mark Andrews, a 6′7″ ogre of a man. 'So what are we supposed to be focusing on then, eh? Are we meant to be focusing on ourselves and our game? Or concentrating on these Blues pricks?'

Instantly, the room erupts. Players start venting about the dirty tricks they've experienced at the hands of the Kiwi players. Names of Blues' players ring out amid tales of eye-gouging, testicle-pulling and worse in the depths of the mauls. Andrews is the most voluble, ranting about how Zinzan Brooke ground his studs into his ankle when he was stuck at the bottom of a ruck.

'He told me I was a disgrace to the jersey,' he says incredulously. 'And as for that niggly Sean Fitzpatrick, he's a devious one alright . . .'

Now there's some energy to work with. At least people are engaged, even if they're worryingly combustible.

'Okay, that's a great question,' I say. 'A great question. Just to recap what Mark said there: are you supposed to be focusing on your game? Or focusing on your opponents? And we'll get into all of that, I promise. But first up, let me start today by asking you all a question. Are you guys going to win this weekend?'

No one speaks. Some players cross their arms and look sullen, while others avoid eye contact and stare at the floor. The silence hangs heavy after the preceding clamour. Looking about the room, I decide to try again.

'I don't know if you heard me. But if you believe you're going to beat the Blues at Eden Park in the Super 12 semi-final on Saturday, can you stand up right now.'

All eyes look towards the top table of Teichmann, Honiball and Lawless. None of them moves. I didn't anticipate this at all . . .

Eventually, one young kid who barely looks out of his teens gets to his feet. The reaction isn't positive. He's instantly heckled by his teammates who yell at him to sit down. To the kid's credit, he stands his ground.

'No, fuck off. I'm standing up – we can bloody win this game.'

Then, on the next table, a shaven-headed youngster with a broken nose that looks like a heavily chewed dog toy also stands up to further jeers.

'So why are you two standing up?' I ask them.

'Boys!' cries the shaven-headed youngster. 'We can win this! What's all this negativity crap about, eh?'

The kid's remark ignites more scrappy debate between the different tables. But at the end of it, there are still just two players standing up. Two people out of 30 who honestly believe they can beat the Blues. I'm staggered by this pessimism and glaring lack of belief.

Still, at least there's a consensus. What I have to try to do now is reframe the narrative in a more positive way.

'Okay. So the votes are in. Clearly most of you don't reckon you can get a result on Saturday. But let's park that for a second and look beyond the game. When you boys get back to Durban next week, I want you to think about what'll happen when you land at the airport. Your friends, your families, your kids will be there to meet you. There'll be a load of reporters. Maybe even some Sharks fans to welcome you home. My question to you is this: what would success look like if you *didn't* win?'

'Mate, it's a semi-final!' shouts a guy who must be a prop judging by the mangled state of his ears. 'It's win or lose.'

'Haven't you read the paper?' another Afrikaans voice calls out. 'This journo predicts we're going to lose by 30 points.'

'Yeah, I get that the Blues are the bookies' favourites,' I say. 'What I want to know is what needs to happen for you guys to walk into that airport in Durban and still be able to hold your heads up high. How can you retain your sense of pride even if things don't go your way?'

There's a glum silence that I allow to fester for a good 20 seconds as I look around the room.

'Well, we'd have to have played some football. Give a good account of ourselves, eh?' someone eventually offers.

'Yes, that makes sense,' I say. 'But how do we quantify that in a tangible way? What does playing well and losing actually look like?'

'Got to keep the score down. Keep it tight,' Teichmann says.

For the next few minutes, I probe a bit deeper to ascertain what a respectable losing scoreline would look like. The debate rumbles on for a while. Last year, the Blues beat them in the final 45–21. Everyone agrees that an improvement on that performance is required. This time, the Sharks can't meekly surrender. They have to play some attacking rugby and put some points on the board. After a lot of cajoling, I eventually get the players to agree on an acceptable scoreline. The winning margin, they decide, cannot be more than 20 points. If the players can fly home having lost by 19 points or fewer, the verdict is that they'll have salvaged some pride.

What I'm hoping to do here is to reframe the team's mindset in a more helpful way. In physically threatening situations, we naturally default to the negative as a survival mechanism. It's a way of priming our defences to keep us safe. But that's rarely beneficial in sport as it's liable to make athletes tighten up or freeze rather than playing with freedom and belief. By establishing a more achievable goal, I'm trying to get the team to buy into a more positive narrative.

'So we're all agreed then, yes? You are not going to lose by more than 20 points. But if that's going to happen, if you're going to succeed in keeping things that tight, what will that involve?'

'Defence! Tight defence!' someone at the back table shouts.

'That makes sense. To keep the score down at Eden Park, you'll have to maintain an incredible defence. And you'll have to do that against a team packed full of All Blacks, who are playing in front of a capacity home crowd who'll be cheering every mistake you make. To do that you need to have each other's backs. You need to support each other. You need to put your bodies on the line and you need to be totally united in that goal to stand firm and not collapse in the face of the Blues' attack.'

Glancing around the room, I feel like I've got the players' attention now, even if many of them are still eyeing me warily. I push on.

'To help you all stick together and have each other's backs, what we need to agree on is some collective self-talk that you're going to use to rally yourselves when things get ugly. I'm talking about the moment when you're gasping for air in the fifth phase of play and you're getting hammered by the Blues forwards, who've pinned you back 5 metres from your try line. In the midst of that pressure, when you're copping some heavy punishment, what you need to do as a team is to stay staunch. To keep putting your head in where it hurts, to keep tackling. Because if you're right and the Blues are the stronger team, that scenario is going to play out over and over again on Saturday. It's going to get bloody tough out there. During those moments, we need to find a keyword that you'll say to your teammates. A word of solidarity that'll encourage you all to stay united and strong. So what is that keyword going to be?'

There's a bit of discussion before a cackle of laughter erupts from one table. Suddenly, a word starts to reverberate around the room. It sounds like 'lem'. Soon it becomes a chant: 'lem, lem, lem.' I have no idea what they're talking about.

'Sorry, fellas, can someone help me out here? Maybe translate?'

Everyone looks to Henry Honiball. He's the Springboks' fly-half, a tall man for the position and a notoriously fierce tackler. So far, he hasn't uttered a single word; now he stands up to tower above his seated teammates. 'They call me "Lem",' Honiball grunts. 'It's an Afrikaans word. It means to cut down the middle with a razor.'

'Lem', the Sharks agree, is going to be the team's defensive keyword. It'll be their war cry to dig deeper, and maintain their defence with thundering tackles that cut their opposite number in half. The players will use it to fire each other up when protecting their line and hopefully keep the score down in the process.

Having established some collective self-talk, I split the squad into groups of six. Pads of paper and coloured crayons are circulated as we start an hour-long workshop. Now we've got a team language, I want to draw out the players' individual sources of motivation. I want to identify what they're really competing for and remind them why they signed up for it in the first place.

Presently, the sheets of paper are scrawled with gung-ho slogans. One bruising flanker has written 'PRIDE OF NATAL'. Another forward jots down a rambling message about his determination to 'show my kids you NEVER give in, however tough things get'.

When I've deciphered his handwriting, we condense that message down to 'NO SURRENDER'. Once each of the players has settled on their personal calls to action, I get them to write them out again and again on smaller bits of paper.

'Those individual mottos are going to become your private mantras,' I say. 'When you go back to your rooms, I want each of you to stick them up next to your bed so they're the first thing you see in the morning. I want them on the bathroom mirror so you're reading them when you're brushing your teeth. Those words need to be at the front of your minds 24/7 until the final whistle blows on Saturday.'

By the end of the workshop, the atmosphere in the room has lightened. The mood is no longer that of a pending execution – there's more laughter now and even a flicker of excitement among the younger players. Broadly speaking, I'm happy with how it's worked out, given the off-the-cuff nature of the workshop. At this stage, it's hard to know how much the session will help, but at least I've acquitted myself okay in my first big professional gig. But there is one thing that's still bugging me and, as the session breaks up, I go and seek out McIntosh.

'Early days,' he nods at my approach. 'Still, looks like you're getting a response.'

'Some promising foundations,' I agree. 'But there is something I need you to help me with.'

I explain that I've noticed how the really senior pros – the Sharks' most respected players – were notably aloof during the session. They're only participating with grudging reluctance and still seem suspicious of the process. Privately, I'm pretty sure that I haven't won them over yet and, given their influence on the rest of the team, that's a major problem. With no time to win their trust, I need to tackle the issue head-on.

'I need a private session with that leadership group. We've hardly got any time here and we need to get them on board.'

McIntosh nods. 'Anthony, remember back in the day when you used to get on the school bus? Remember the cool kids that everyone else looked up to? Where did they always sit?'

'Gee, we're going back a fair bit, Ian. But in my day they always sat in the back row.'

'Exactly. It's a universal thing. The cool kids always sit at the back of the bus. There's always a backseat crew in a rugby team, too.'

'Well then, I guess what I need is a session with the backseat crew.'

McIntosh claps me on the back, partially winding me in the process. 'Leave it with me. I'll sort it.'

At 8 am the next day I'm back at the Centra for my meeting with the backseat boys. Weirdly, although I'm more prepared this morning, I'm more nervous, too. That's because I'm about to sit down with some of the best players in the game, men who've won hundreds of caps, lifted the World Cup and have the facial scars to prove it. I'm nervous because, quite honestly, overnight I've been wondering what I can really teach these guys about how to approach this match, given I haven't played rugby since high school. These blokes have competed at the top level for years. Why should they listen to me?

The reality is that I'm straight out of uni and have no credibility beyond my degree. I've never worked with a professional sports team and have limited first-hand experience of managing team dynamics. Everything I know about sport psychology is purely theoretical. The only reason they've heard me out so far is that I've been sold to them as an old mate of their coach. The younger players are more open-minded. Having not experienced so many of life's disappointments, they're less disposed to self-doubt. My audience this morning, however, will consist of gnarled veterans who know all the motivational tricks and dark arts. They're going to be much harder to convince. On the positive side, at least I now look more like I'm part of the set-up: yesterday I was handed a Sharks tracksuit so I've finally ditched my suit and tie.

When I walk into the conference room, the four players are already sitting down. There's the skipper, Teichmann, Honiball, Joubert and Lawless. As soon as I enter, their banter turns to silence. No one even offers a 'hello' until Teichmann eventually nods at me. 'Heard you needed some help?' he grunts.

'That's right, Gary. I absolutely do. One thing, though – I thought Mark Andrews was coming along to this session?'

Teichmann sighs. 'We had some bad luck during training. Mark buggered his shoulder and needs some physio. Touch and go as to whether he'll make the game.'

Potentially, that is a big blow. Andrews is the Sharks' enforcer, a powerhouse of aggression and the focal part of the line-out. His absence will leave a gaping hole in the team.

'Oh well,' I say as brightly as I can. 'Hopefully he'll come good. But if not, it'll make what I want to say even more important.'

I take a sip of my water.

'The thing is we're really close to the game now, only two days to go. I honestly believe that I can help your team and give you some mental tools to improve your performance. But there's no way that'll work unless I get the full endorsement of everyone in this room. Young players look up to the senior pros – they always have and always will. They dream of emulating you and achieving the same kind of success that you've enjoyed. I've been parachuted in at the last minute here and I'm trying to peddle some ideas to help your team prepare. Some of these ideas might be new to you. Some of them you might think are a crock of shit. But I've shared them because I know they can help you to raise your game on Saturday. The fact of the matter is, though, that they'll only work if you four – the most senior and respected guys on the team – visibly buy into them.'

I look around the table. No one speaks, in fact there's no reaction at all. Doggedly, I push on.

'Here's what your "endorsement" needs to look like. In training, I need each of you to go to your closest teammates and echo some of the messages we've gone through. Henry, that means you go up to the half-backs, to the centres and repeat the importance of the "lem" stuff. Gary, I need you to have a quiet word with each of the forwards and emphasise the importance of keeping the points margin below 20. Hammer home the value of not surrendering an inch. Say whatever you think is going to land with them. If these young guys see that you're buying into these messages, that will convince them to follow through. Without your endorsement, none of this will work.'

Once again, I look around the table for a reaction. Honiball is staring at the wall, Joubert is scratching a scab on the back of his hand. Eventually, Teichmann gives a tiny nod of his head. 'Alright, we'll do it,' he says.

The four players rise up out of their chairs and walk out of the room. After barely ten minutes, the meeting is over.

Over the next two days, I try to implement every motivational tool that I know. I put a blanket ban on the team reading the papers or watching the news. The Kiwi press is confidently predicting a battering and I don't want the team exposed to that message. That editorial line runs directly against the narrative that I want to instil, so we need to shut it down.

I speak to Ian McIntosh about the possibility of getting Nelson Mandela on a video call to deliver a morale-boosting team talk. In the end, it doesn't eventuate – Mandela is travelling on state business – but the fact the management team attempts to make it happen reassures me that they're backing me up.

The coaches group the players into their tactical cliques – separating the forwards and backs – and run through their strategy and approach for the game. We analyse their opponents in detail, highlighting their biggest weapons and most effective plays, while reflecting what we can do to neutralise these threats.

Feeding into all that, I run two hour-long workshops each day. One of the main areas we explore is what the team will do if things start going wrong and our plans misfire. Momentum is crucial in rugby and it cuts both ways. Often a one-off error – a mistimed pass or a bad kick – will lead to the opposition scoring. But if you allow your heads to drop and lose your composure, more blunders will follow, leading the game to get away from you at terrifying speed. Every player will make mistakes, but they can't afford to dwell on them. We come up with contingency plans so that when things do go awry, each player will quickly regroup and regain his focus.

Speaking to the forwards, we imagine a scenario where they bungle a line-out and miss tackles leading to an Auckland try. In the minutes that follow, when the team is standing on the try line awaiting the conversion, I talk about the value of taking ten deep breaths to mentally reset. I then explain how the players can dramatically amplify that effect just by tweaking their body language in simple ways.

'If you slow your breathing while pulling your shoulders back and standing in a wide, balanced stance, internally you're reframing your immediate situation. When your posture is confident and relaxed, it transmits reassuring messages from body to brain. Your spinal column, your gut, your heart – all these vital areas will translate that physical info in a reassuring way. Sure, you're still in a really stressful situation, but physically you feel more confident. Those body-to-brain messages are powerful and can bolster the standard brain-to-body self-talk.'

I also tell them about the value of 'centring' to manage the transition in skillsets that many players have to perform on the fly. Kickers like Honiball, for example, might be involved in a play where they've just run the length of the field to score a try with their adrenaline and heart rate spiking. During that all-action sequence, their focus has to be external. Where's the ball? Where are my support runners? Where are the gaps in defence? Seconds later, however, when attempting the conversion, that focus has to move internally. You have to place the ball down and ignore the baying crowd to concentrate on your kicking routine. The precise number of steps before striking the ball. The angle of your run-up. The redirection of energy to the task in hand.

To help with that, we work on the 'one breath technique' that's done just before the moment of truth. Standing on the grass, you inhale and imagine all the tension coming into your body like a bright green laser beam that travels down through your chest and into your limbs. Then as you exhale, you imagine the release of that tension, leaving your body relaxed and free to perform.

Gradually, I see glints of positivity. In one training session, during a break in play, Teichmann shepherds the back row through a defensive manoeuvre that's punctuated by loud cries of 'lem'. When I walk into the locker room after lunch, Honiball is sitting in a corner talking to several junior players and I catch a line about how they have to keep the defensive line 'tighter than a warthog's backside'.

I know that I've started to get properly accepted into the fold when one Springbok player takes me aside to share a private fear that's been troubling him. Back home in Durban, the player suspects that his best mate may be shagging his wife. We organise a one-on-one session to discuss how he can block the negative thoughts and park his concerns until after the game. The poor guy looks understandably tortured and admits he's been struggling to sleep. It's a reminder that behind the hero worship, all these players still have their own private lives and problems off the pitch.

CHAPTER 2

Come match day, Eden Park is rocking. Taking their seats ahead of the game, the Auckland Blues fans seem jubilant and relaxed. Victory has become the expectation at the spiritual home of New Zealand rugby. For visiting teams, it's become one of the world's most treacherous grounds.

The fans' confidence isn't misplaced when you look at the team sheets. For the Sharks, the big news is that lock Mark Andrews has been ruled out due to his shoulder injury. It's a hammer blow for the team. The Springboks' mainstay is a genuine hard man and a galvanising presence when things get tough. Frankly, he's impossible to replace.

The Blues' line-up, meanwhile, is frightening. Mercifully, there's no Jonah Lomu anymore, but the team is still packed full of talent and a worrying number of All Blacks. The back row features New Zealand skipper Zinzan Brooke, a number eight with the build of a forward but the skills of a back; openside flanker Michael Jones, a dynamic and punishing tackler; and Mark Carter, a marauding blindside force. The front row is entirely comprised of All Blacks too. Tighthead prop Olo Brown is rock-solid, loosehead Craig Dowd is a 114-kilogram monster, while sandwiched between them is Sean Fitzpatrick, the most feared and respected hooker in the world. Eyeing that contingent, I begin to understand why the Sharks' morale was so low.

Auckland's backs aren't too shabby either. Threats include the giant winger Joeli Vidiri who combines power and pace with a muscle-bound frame. There's fly-half Carlos Spencer, who marked his All Blacks debut this year by scoring 33 points, and Junior Tonu'u, who's just breaking through into the national team. The weather looks ominous for their running game; under an overcast sky, there's not a whisper of wind and conditions are perfect underfoot.

As I climb the steps of the stadium to take my seat, I feel apprehensive. It's clear that, on paper, the Blues are a much stronger side with a home advantage behind them. They're definitely capable of dominating this game and I'm praying the result isn't too one-sided.

I've only been drafted in at the last minute and I fear that I haven't had enough time to instil my mental fitness tactics in any meaningful way. Being called up to help was an amazing opportunity, but whether I've made a positive impact will soon become brutally clear.

Spotting a spare seat a couple of rows below the coaches, I make a beeline for it, when McIntosh, who looks visibly tense, calls me over. 'No, Ant, over here. You're sitting next to me.'

All I can think of as I take a seat on McIntosh's left is how the cameras always cut to close-ups of the coach at moments of high drama. Despite being an Aucklander born and bred, I'm about to be publicly embedded with the enemy. Oh well, at least my brothers will see my face on TV.

'Start fast, unsettle the fans,' mutters one of the Sharks' coaches under his breath as Honiball kicks off to begin the match.

The Sharks players seem to heed his message. Less than two minutes after kick-off, they win a line-out midway into the Blues' half and work the ball out wide for André Joubert to free up winger Shaun Payne to score the opening try. It's a dream start for the Sharks. Hopefully that will finally inject some belief into the team.

Instead, the try merely riles up the Blues. Less than three minutes later, Vidiri shows why he's the fastest man in Super 12, pouncing on a long pass from Eroni Clarke to zip past three players and score under a post. Soon after, the Blues score again, as Zinzan Brooke shows his wiles, taking a quick penalty to bundle the ball over the try line. Now the home team are flying. Vidiri scores another try and two more follow as the Blues seize control.

By half-time, the Blues are leading 38-5. Hopes of keeping the score to within 20 points look increasingly fanciful now. In fact, unless the Sharks mount an immediate response, this could turn into a humiliation. The players' fears that they'd be unable to live with the Blues' fast, expansive football are now starting to feel menacingly prescient. Their worst nightmares are coming true in front of 50,000 spectators.

Trudging down the stairs, McIntosh's face is grim. We've agreed that the dressing room is a sacrosanct place and that it'd be unsuitable for me to speak there at half-time. But walking alongside me, he also seems unsure how to tackle the team talk.

'Any ideas?' he asks.

'In terms of your messaging, stay calm and keep a check on your emotions – no industrial language. Absorb pressure from players, don't add to it. Right now, the boys need lifting up not dressing down. Allow them to rest and rehydrate. Avoid information overload – they're not going to take much in now. Instead try to lean more towards inspiration.'

McIntosh nods and we enter the room.

Inside, the atmosphere is quiet and tense. Having walked straight off the field, the players have steam pouring off their hulking bodies. Most are sitting down on the benches gulping down fluids, while certain players are having their war wounds tended to by the physios. André Joubert has his head in his hands and is rocking back and forth as if trying to wake up from a bad dream.

McIntosh walks around, patting backs. He stops to have a quiet word with Teichmann about the line-outs and then with Honiball about how the backs can try to contain Vidiri. Then he stands in the centre of the room and addresses the team.

'Look, boys, we knew it would be tough out there today. Truth is they're not a bad team. Here's the thing, though: I know that you are, too. I picked each of you today because I believe in your capability. So show what you can really do in the second half. Let's not walk away from this semi-final with any regrets. Now Gary has got a few words for you.'

I have no idea what Teichmann is going to say. He's more a lead-by-example type than a Churchillian orator, but he also commands genuine respect. As he steps into the centre of the room, I see the Sharks' giant prop look up towards him like a child seeking advice from his dad.

'Yeah, we're a few tries down. But if we stick together, we can fight our way out of this hole. This second half is an opportunity for us. An opportunity to show who we really are. Remember what you're playing for. Remember the mottos you wrote down. Remember you're putting your bodies on the line for your teammates. We're not out of this, yet. Pride is at stake; the pride of Natal and the pride of South Africa. We said we'd keep them within 20 points. There's one way that we can do that: "Lem!"' Teichmann thumps his fist into his open hand and the volume of his voice rises. 'Lem! Lem! LEM!'

From the restart, the Sharks begin to play with more purpose. They battle their way to a decent spell of concerted pressure and work the ball into the Blues' territory. This is looking good! But then André Joubert fumbles the ball and Clarke snaffles it up to run from his own 22 to score a break-away try. McIntosh covers his eyes. Surrendering that opportunity was a sickener. After the try is converted, the Blues lead by 45–5. Morale could seriously crumble now.

Instead it stings the Sharks into life. Centre Pieter Muller makes a scything run down the middle, before quick support allows the ball to be pinged out wide for Payne to get his second try. A minute later Joubert follows up with a second. And then, astonishingly, the Sharks make it three in a row! A long Honiball pass finds Muller, who sends Joubert over in the corner once again. It's now 48–22.

On 76 minutes, the Blues finally wake up and score a converted try that puts the final result beyond doubt. But even now, the Sharks keep going. Honiball takes advantage of a mistake to pounce on a wayward Blues pass to score the Sharks' fifth try of the game.

Going into injury time, the score is 55–29, yet still the Sharks continue to push. They've lost the game but their targeted points margin remains in reach. In the dying seconds, Honiball launches a huge up-and-under. It looks like he's overhit it as the ball lands behind the try line, but the fullback flubs the catch and Errol Stewart swoops on the ball to score. Honiball converts, the ref blows for full time, it's over.

The Sharks have lost the game convincingly and their season is over. But somehow it doesn't feel like a gut-punch defeat. In the second half, the team rallied to outscore the Blues and fought their way to territorial dominance. Crucially, the final score line of 55–36 means they snuck in under the 20 point total they'd set themselves. Given the debacle of the first half, it's a respectable result.

In the dressing room, there's an atmosphere of quiet satisfaction. Scoring six tries at the home of the reigning champions is an achievement of sorts. While limbs are bandaged and cuts stitched up, Teichmann wanders over. Peering down at me – he's about a foot and a half taller – he extends a shovel-sized hand. 'I wanted to thank you, Ant. We wouldn't have got to this point without your help.'

And I do feel a sense of pride. Yes, the Sharks lost, but then I was only brought in three days out from one of the most challenging fixtures in club rugby. You can't expect to turn everything around in that time frame. Mental fitness tactics are the same as physical skills. They have to be honed over time.

What we managed to do was to find a tangible and realistic goal to set for them. The Blues were undeniably superior and fully deserved their win. But my brief wasn't to make the Sharks a better rugby team. It was to lift their motivation and get them playing to their full capacity.

As Teichmann wanders off to get the physio to look at his swollen hand, I bump into McIntosh.

'How are you feeling, Ian?'

'Look, I hate losing. Just hate it,' he sighs. 'Still, we scored six tries at Eden Park. That's something to build on, I guess.'

That night I'm invited out to their post-game dinner and drinks. I'm chuffed to be asked and delighted that I've gone from being viewed as an enemy outsider to being accepted as part of the broader set-up.

Things quickly descend into full-blown alcoholic carnage. Countless beers are sunk as we stumble and lurch between venues. After 9 pm, recollections become hazy. Someone falls down the stairs. A chair is thrown in a pub. I have to stop the reserve team flanker from squaring up to a huge Māori bouncer.

The last thing I remember is being forced to stand on a table in my undies, my trousers around my ankles, while being surrounded by the entire team. I have to chug a pint of lager before they finish singing an Afrikaans war song. When I can't neck it in time, I'm made to do it again.

The room starts to sway, but I can't stop grinning. It's not just the booze but the realisation that this could be my launch pad into the world of elite sport. Not only am I getting to work with the calibre of athletes that I've always looked up to, now I'm part of their tribe – they come to me for advice! At last, after years of study, I'm reaching the professional destiny that I've always dreamed of. I feel like I've finally arrived.

CHAPTER 3

It's a Thursday night and the bar is chaotically busy, the air shuddering with yelled conversations, howls of laughter, clinking shot glasses and pounding dance music. A gaggle of shrill girls is celebrating a 21st birthday with bottles of multi-coloured alcopops. A cricket team is having a bonding knees-up in fancy dress. There's an office party full of braying salesmen in bad suits, plus muddled through it all is the usual mishmash of yuppies, backpackers, ravers, deadbeats and booze hounds. I'm working frantically to keep up with the tide of orders that crash across the bar, scooping ice, clearing spills, pulling taps and cracking jokes to appease the impatient punters hustling for service.

I may have just done a job for the Natal Sharks, but I'm still only getting occasional work as a sport psychologist. That's why tonight, once again, I'm working at the Chill Bar, shaking cocktails and pouring shots.

By 11 pm the crowd has finally thinned out. One of the cricket team dressed as Superman is smooching a girl in a very short skirt over on a corner banquette. I guess he's found his Lois Lane. Two giant Māori dudes are swigging pints by the window while hospo workers trickle in for a nightcap at the end of their shifts. A barrage of Sambuca shots has finished off most of the office party, but one bloke remains at the middle of the bar. Red-faced and dishevelled, with his tie at half-mast, he nods his head dozily to Stevie V's 'Dirty Cash' that booms over the sound system.

Two women, a pretty blonde and a waif-like brunette, come in and grab a seat at the bar where they order large glasses of white wine. They look to be in their late thirties, a bit older and more sophisticated than our usual clientele. The drunk guy at the bar pounces on the opportunity.

'Ladies! Get you a drink?'

'Thanks for the offer,' the blonde woman replies. 'But we're good right now.'

Unperturbed, the man blunders on trying to make a couple of slurred attempts at conversation. The women are polite but curt; it's clear they don't want to encourage him. But the man refuses to pick up the signals and keeps interrupting with his drunken prattle. Eventually, the blonde woman gets impatient.

'Look, mate, I don't want to be rude. But my best friend here just got back from London. We haven't seen each for ages. I just want to catch up with her tonight, if that's okay?'

Forced to wade through the torrent of booze sloshing through his bloodstream, it takes a while for the knockback to permeate the man's brain. When it does, he's not happy.

'What's the matter? You think you're too bloody good for me?'

Back turned, the blonde woman's body stiffens at his tone. Her friend shoots a nervous glance over her shoulder.

'So you're not going to answer me now, you fucking slut?'

I place my hands on the bar and lean over. 'Easy, mate. These ladies just want to have a quiet drink and be left in peace. They didn't mean any disrespect.'

The man glares at me belligerently. 'Yeah? And who the fuck are you? What gives you the right to tell me what to do?'

Quickly, I look over to the door where our two bouncers are usually positioned outside on the pavement. But there's no sign of

Coolah, our huge Samoan doorman, or the new bouncer, Shane, who started just this week. The drunk guy is standing up now. His red eyes are glassy and he's swaying slightly. But he's a big unit, at least 6′4″ and heavily built.

'Come on, mate,' I say trying to defuse the situation. 'Don't be like that. Tell me, how's your night been?'

'Fine, apart from all these stuck-up bitches!' he yells in the direction of the two women, who've grabbed their drinks and scuttled over to a table by the far window. 'Oh well, at least they've fucked off. Gimme another bourbon and coke.'

'I'm sorry, but I think you've had enough.'

'Had enough? Had enough, have I? I'll tell you when I've fucking had enough!'

With the back of his hand, he swipes his tumbler glass towards me. It slides off the bar and shatters by my feet. Shane, the new bouncer, suddenly materialises by the bloke's side.

'Okay, time to go home now,' he says.

The drunk cackles at the idea, throwing his head back in a performative laugh. Then he grabs the glass ashtray from the bar and smashes it down towards the bouncer's head. Instinctively, Shane catches his wrist and yanks it into an armlock. The man yelps with pain and the ashtray clatters to the floor. Shane twists his arm behind his back and marches him out of the bar.

'Like I said, mate, it's time to go home.'

Outside the bar, Shane releases the man and waves him off. The drunk responds by throwing a wild haymaker that Shane side-steps as if it's coming towards him in slow motion, before delivering a calf-slicing kick behind his knees. The man lands heavily on the pavement.

'Go home. Now!'

Watching from the doorway, I'm in awe at Shane's control of the situation. That drunk must've been 20 kilograms heavier and at least a head taller than him. Despite the mismatch, Shane handled him with laughable ease.

At the end of the night, after shutting the doors, Shane and Coolah walk over to the bar. After his intervention this evening, I'm sizing Shane up with fresh eyes. He doesn't have the physical might of Coolah. Nor does he carry himself with the usual tough-guy swagger. Softly spoken, he's a wiry 5′9″ with the leanly coiled physique of a middleweight boxer. What he does have is an air of quiet capability.

'Shane! Thanks for your help earlier. That guy was a real prick. Can I get you a beer?'

'No thanks, mate. I'm in training.'

'Oh yeah? What for?'

'I do a bit of a cage fighting, eh. Got a fight next Friday.'

'Go on then, ask him,' urges Coolah with a grin.

'Yeah, so the thing is, Coolah said you did a bit of sport psychology on the side.'

'Well, to be honest I'm trying to make the bar work my sideline. But yeah, I've just started out as a sport psych.'

'The thing is I've got this big fight coming up. It's going to be a tough one. I was hoping you could help me out with some things.'

Coolah interjects. 'You should see my brother fight, man. He's a stone-cold killer, I'm telling you. Pulls off some real Jackie Chan shit in that cage. He's an animal, trust me. Come to the fight next Friday, Ant. My man is going to put on a show.'

Shane replies with a bashful shrug and shakes his shaven head. He looks slightly embarrassed. We arrange a time the next day for him to come and see me ahead of his next shift.

'The session is on the house,' I say. 'Thought I was going to cop a face full of ashtray back there, for sure.'

*

Sitting in my inner-city office the following day, up close Shane does, in fact, exhibit the telltale hallmarks of a semi-professional fighter. The knuckles on his sturdy hands are swollen, his nose is dented, while patches of skin around his eyes are discoloured by pink scar tissue. Right now, however, Shane doesn't exude much warrior spirit. Dressed in a black T-shirt and grey trackpants, he sits quietly in the chair with his head down and shoulders slumped. Staring at my threadbare carpet, it's like he's questioning his decision to come.

I don't feel that confident myself. I'm only vaguely familiar with cage fighting, a sport that's still in its early days in New Zealand, where newspapers largely condemn it as 'human cockfighting'. All I really know is that it's a raw, underground spectacle designed to answer the hypothetical question: which fighting style is the most effective in a blood-splattered tear-up?

'So Shane, what's the story? How can I help?'

'Yeah, well, I got this big fight coming up, see. I'm up against this Polish dude, Aleksy.'

Aleksy, it turns out, is a highly rated middleweight. Nicknamed 'the Anaconda' for his wrestling prowess, he specialises in taking his opponents to the ground before overpowering them with evil chokeholds. Ominously, Shane points out that Aleksy is also known for his 'ground-and-pound' knockouts.

'What's "ground-and-pound"?'

'It's kinda when they pin you down and then just batter you with fists and elbows.'

'Yeah, you probably want to try and avoid that one. But Shane, is there something you'd like to talk about?'

Shane swallows hard and looks to the ceiling.

'Well, it's just . . . I've had a bunch of fights, yeah. My win/loss record is 9/2. But y'know, every time in the build-up, I just get so, I just get so fucking nervous . . .'

There's a long pause where I think he's searching for the right words. But then I notice Shane's jaw is clenched and his eyes are screwed shut. He takes a sharp intake of breath through gritted teeth, before a choked, guttural sound escapes his throat. Then he begins to cry. He hides his face in his battered hands as if despairing at this betrayal of emotion.

I'm totally thrown.

Shane, after all, is a super-tough weapon of a man. I've watched him disarm violent punters as if they were toddlers. Now, this shaven-headed fighting machine is openly weeping in my office and I'm not sure what to do. In New Zealand, men rarely cry in public. But Shane isn't just crying now, his shoulders are heaving in great wrenching sobs. I hand him a box of tissues.

'Hey, it's okay to be upset. In fact, it's a logical response – a fight like this is an emotional thing. But let's try and break down what's causing you to feel this way. Take a moment there, get your breath.'

I fetch a glass of water and he takes a big gulp and then sighs.

'I'm sorry, I don't know what it is,' he says at last. 'But every time I fight, I get so scared and anxious. I have nightmares of being knocked out. I'm constantly asking myself why I'm putting myself through it all. It happens to me before every single fight and I fucking hate it.'

'Well, let's try and figure out the source of all that. Is it because you're scared of getting hurt?'

'Nah, I'm not scared of pain. When I get into the ring, I'm so geed-up and full of adrenaline. Even if I was hurt, I wouldn't know.'

'So are you scared of losing?'

''Course, I want to win. But I wouldn't say that I'm scared of "losing", that's kinda part of the game. Anyone can get on the wrong end of a lucky punch. There's a saying my coach has about fighting: "Some days you're the dog, some days you're the tree".'

'So do you think you're scared of letting people down, then?'

Shane considers the question. 'Maybe, I guess. My coach has always been good to me and I owe him a lot. The guys at our gym, we're a tight crew, eh. They'll all be there for this fight next week. My brothers will be there, my dad is coming a long way. I don't want to embarrass myself or let them down, for sure.'

'Okay, well then let's just unpack these fears a bit and see whether they're legitimate or not worth worrying about.'

I quiz Shane about his fitness and whether he's carrying any injuries. I ask about his training and whether he's coming into this fight well-prepared or undercooked. The answers are reassuring. Shane has just come out of a long training camp, he's fully fit and has zero concerns about making the weight.

'Everything you're telling me leads me to believe that you're in excellent shape for this fight. So what am I missing?'

He offers a forlorn shrug in reply.

My opening move is to try and dial up Shane's sense of self-worth. To step into the cage in front of a big crowd, any fighter needs to completely back their ability. Self-belief provides a vital form of mental armour that helps you deal with that heavy pressure. Right now, Shane doesn't seem massively confident, so I want to try and shift his perspective and get him to view himself through a more objective lens.

'Shane, how would your coach or sparring partner describe the way that you train?'

'They'd say I was a hard worker, for sure. That I'm dedicated. Never miss a session.'

'Doesn't sound too bad. Those are all valuable qualities. And what do you think they'd say about you as a fighter?'

'They'd probably say that I'm not the strongest or the most explosive fighter. But everyone knows that I'm relentless. I've got a real gas tank on me so I just keeping coming and coming and coming. That pressure style is a big part of my game.'

'And when someone recognises those qualities how does it make you feel?'

'Yeah, pretty good, I guess.'

I get Shane to consider the characteristics he's listed. To reflect on how valuable they can be amid the hammer fists and guillotine chokes in the fight. There's been a perceptible change in energy now and Shane doesn't seem quite so despondent. We agree that, when viewed from the outside, he should be feeling optimistic, given his training, fitness and all-round preparation.

'But I still get so bloody stressed out, though. The days leading up to the fight, I can't sleep, I struggle to eat, I just start freaking out, man. I'm thinking about the fight 24/7. It's fucking horrible.'

'What we've got to do then is establish a way of stopping that flow of negative thoughts.'

The first strategy I offer is a written technique for cognitive restructuring. I hand Shane a notebook and get him to divide the page into three columns. I then ask him to think back to his last fight, which took place in Christchurch two months ago. Shane has to imagine himself wrapping his hands ahead of that bout and his step-by-step moves until the bell rings for the start of round one. I push him for specifics on the dressing room, getting him to recall the tiled floor, the bright strip lighting, the blood-soaked tissues in the bin from the previous fight. I ask him to describe the mood of the crowd and their drunken yells and heckles. He talks me through the long walk towards the cage and his battle to conceal his nerves behind his swagger.

Then, in the left-hand column of the page in the notebook, I get Shane to write down some of the worries swarming his mind as he steps into the ring.

- This guy looks like one mean son-of-a-bitch.
- He's built like a tank!

- What am I doing here?
- Much taller than I expected, he's going to have serious reach.
- Is my dodgy shoulder going to hold up?
- Stomach is in knots, please don't throw up now.
- My arms feel heavy, my legs feel heavy. Have I overtrained?
- Don't get knocked out in front of everyone. Please don't let that happen.
- Do I really belong at this level?

After that brain dump, in the middle column, I tell Shane to write the word 'STOP' in huge, block capitals that run vertically down the centre of the page.

'The reason we've listed these fears explicitly is to try and make them easier to identify. That's because these thoughts are trying to sabotage you and so what you have to do is outmanoeuvre them. Whenever any of these thoughts arise, recognise them for what they are and say that word "STOP" out loud. You need to short-circuit that negative loop and cut off those thoughts at the root.'

In the third column, I explain to Shane, we need to establish some positive alternatives and reminders of why he's such a formidable competitor. Previously, in successful fights, what were the winning characteristics – both physical and mental – that gave him the winning edge?

We kick this about for a while. Shane, it turns out, has been doing some form of martial arts training since the age of five. That experience gives him an intuitive understanding of the mechanics of violence. He knows the best moment to throw a hook or feint a kick. How to negate a height or reach disadvantage. Whether to take evasive action or shoot for a takedown. After ten minutes of discussion, we distil these plus-points down to a hit list of reasons why he's actually in a great position to win.

- I'm mentally tough.
- I never quit.
- No one trains as hard as me.
- I'm strong, injury-free and in killer shape.
- Years of experience have given me an advanced fight IQ.
- I'm a well-rounded fighter who can strike and grapple.
- I've got the game plan to win.
- My courage is stronger than my fear.

'What you're trying to do here, Shane, is turn your inner dialogue from a critic into a coach. As soon as a negative thought enters your head, you're going to stop it dead in its tracks. Then you're going to start reeling off those positive affirmations.'

'Kinda like a counterpunch?'

'Yeah, but make that *punches*, plural. You're going to destroy that self-doubt with a flurry of high-speed combinations. It won't know what the hell's hit it.'

Shane seems a bit more upbeat. His posture has straightened and he looks slightly less glum. Quizzing him about his training, I'm surprised by the physical workload. He's been doing two three-hour training sessions a day for the past six weeks, on top of working nights as a bouncer.

'That sounds like a lot.'

'Physically, I can handle it, but mentally yeah, it's a grind. At this stage, I get tunnel vision. I'm thinking about the fight 24/7 from the moment I wake up to the moment I fall asleep. Sometimes I dream about it too.'

'Does that feel overwhelming?'

'Totally! Anything I eat, I'm thinking, *How is this going to affect me tomorrow?* In any conversation I feel like I'm only half-present because I'm obsessing about the fight. There've been times in the past that it's got so full-on that I've even thought about faking an injury to pull out to get a bit of a mental breather.'

Shane recognises that his fixation is sapping his energy, but I'm concerned it may be affecting his preparation, too. Sometimes he tells me that he finds himself struggling to fully engage in his training or listen to his coach. At night, his brain keeps automatically jerking back to the fight and the prospect is so harrowing that it's affecting his sleep.

Talking it over, we agree that it's hard to do two things at once really well. What I want Shane to do is to compartmentalise his stress to limit its impact. To do that we're going to methodically break down his remaining time before the fight, chunking it up into 30-minute units. Each of these blocks needs to be filled, because idle time will inevitably be consumed with stressing about the fight. Among all these time slots dedicated to training, stretching, recovery, food and relaxation, I also want Shane to block out designated 'thinking time'. Every three hours, I tell him he can devote ten minutes to mull over the fight in any way he likes. During that time he's allowed to agonise over his strategy, fret over his opponent's chokeholds or catastrophise in whatever way he chooses. But he can only do it for ten minutes.

'If you start stressing about the fight at any other time, just make a note of it and tell yourself that you'll park that anxiety until later when you can unpack it at length in your "worry window". You can't afford to let stress consume every minute of your day. You have other things you need to focus on right now.'

Regrettably, I can't attend Shane's fight as I've got another shift at the Chill Bar. But as I'm pouring beers and mixing drinks, I keep wondering how he's faring against the Anaconda. I plan to text Shane afterwards, but then I worry that if things haven't worked out it won't be appreciated. Instead, I figure I'll get the news from him in person at work the following night.

The next evening as I approach the bar, I can see Shane and Coolah already standing by the door. The sight of Shane's face makes me wince. His left eye is swollen shut. A livid crescent of purple bruising has erupted from his eyebrow down to his cheekbone, engorging the lid into a puffy slit. His lip is also puffy and split while his left hand is bandaged up. He sees me walking down the street, grins and waves.

'Bloody hell, Shane, that eye doesn't look too clever.'

'Should've seen what happened to the guy he knocked out in round three,' interjects Coolah with a dark chuckle. 'I'm tell you, Ant, this dude here, he's got a sledgehammer arm. Seriously, he throws like a truck!'

CHAPTER 4

Standing trackside against the barrier at Phillip Island, it's a screaming cacophony of noise. As the MotoGP riders hammer their bikes down the straight, the engines wail with bloodcurdling intent. If it wasn't for the foam plugs, my eardrums would surely melt.

I've never experienced MotoGP before and just thought of it as Formula 1 for motorbikes. But what I'm witnessing today is a high-torque strain of bedlam, and these are just the practice laps.

The acceleration of the bikes is astonishing. They explode from nought to insanity in barely a few seconds. Right now, one rider barrelling along at about 300 kilometres per hour edges himself on the inside line of another rider and they hurtle along side by side in sickeningly close tandem. As the challenging left-hand corner of Lukey Heights looms, neither seems willing to apply their brakes first. Another second passes. Fear grips my throat . . . Then they're swooping into the curve, bikes virtually horizontal, elbows and knees grazing the asphalt, bodies millimetres from oblivion. Then they're thundering away from the bend, yanking their machines upwards, already plotting a fresh line of warp-speed attack.

My jaw is clenched and I've got a white-knuckle grip on the barrier. Just watching these riders scares the whimpering shit out of me. I can't imagine what it's like actually riding one of these crazy-fast bikes.

But that's the mindset I've got to tap into. I've been invited here in a professional capacity through a friend of a friend. Dave Stewart runs a small MotoGP team, BSL, that's making its debut this year in the 1999 Grand Prix Motorcycle Racing World Championship.

It hasn't proved a smooth baptism for the team. The team's bike is the BSL 500 V3, a 500cc two-stroke machine that was made in New Zealand. From what I can gather, it was essentially built to showcase the mechanical nous of Buckley Systems Limited, a highly successful electronics and engineering firm in Mount Wellington, whose initials give the team its name. Taking a new bike into MotoGP's big league has proved a daunting technical challenge. The motorcycle has been so beset with problems that most of the season the team has had to rely on a hastily leased Modenas KR3 instead.

Dave's concern right now though is less on the bike than its rider. Mark Willis is a highly rated young prospect. In 1996 he was named Australian Rider of the Year and in 1997 he finished fourth in the Australian Superbike Championship. Last year, the 23 year old was a wildcard ride at the Superbike World Championship here at Phillip Island. Mark came sixth in Race 1 and ninth in Race 2 on a private Suzuki, beating both factory Suzuki riders along with many other world superbike regulars.

Dave believes Mark has serious potential. But right now he's more fussed about his current performances. 'The kid is riding too slow,' he tells me. 'I need you to make him go faster.'

So far, I've only had a couple of fleeting interactions with Mark and neither has gone well. Yesterday, after landing in Melbourne, I met him at the airport car hire where we were picking up our vehicles to drive to Phillip Island. When Dave introduced us, Mark was already sitting behind the wheel of his rented Falcon, an unsmiling presence in a pair of wraparound sunnies.

'Pleased to meet you, Mark,' I said, extending my hand towards the window.

All I got in response was a dismissive nod. Then he revved the Falcon into a burnout right there in the car yard and screeched off at speed with the stereo blaring AC/DC's 'Back in Black'. It's not the most positive of introductions.

The second meeting wasn't much of an improvement. A couple of hours ago, I'd approached Mark in the garage, hoping we could grab a coffee and have a chat ahead of practice. Those hopes were quickly dashed.

'How you going, Mark?' I say.

'Fucking shithouse, mate.'

'So what's up?'

'What's up?' he laughs. 'Tell you what's up, mate. This bike they built in New Zealand is a piece of shit. Every time I ride it, it tries to kill me – that's why we had to lease the Modenas. But now they're making me ride the Kiwi bike.'

It turns out the millionaire owner of the BSL team, Bill Buckley, is in town for the race. Not only that, but he's rented a 737 to fly all his mates from New Zealand to see his bike in action. Consequently, Dave is making Mark ride the BSL.

'It's fucking bullshit, mate. All year I've been trying to get my head around all these new tracks, having to learn all these different curves and chicanes, while riding different bikes. Finally I get to come back to Australia and race at a track that I actually know – that'll enable me to have a fair go – and now I've got to do it on this joke of a bike! I'm telling you, mate, this bike cannot produce enough horsepower. And when it does, the engine seizes up and it tries to hurt me. Trust me, I'll be lucky to get through practice.'

From my trackside position, I'm now about to watch Mark in action. I'm intrigued to see whether there's any substance to his claims or whether he's trying to divert the blame for his poor performances. Approaching the end of the season, he's barely placed in a single race.

Unfortunately, Mark's assessment of the BSL bike seems fair. For the first couple of laps, he rockets along fairly comfortably, but then on the third he slows and then dismounts before pushing the bike about 100 metres up to the pit lane. Judging by the way he's shaking his head, something has gone horribly wrong.

By the time I wander off, there's a full-on slanging match going on. Mark has confronted Dave and one of the engineers. One hand is violently prodding the air while the other is clenched by his side. It looks like he's ready to take a swing.

'Mate, I'm telling you – the piston's seized up. Again! I told you this would bloody happen. I warned you. Now the bike's overheated already and I've only done three laps. I've had it with this shithouse bike full stop. I'm riding the other one. Get it ready for me now.'

'Alright, you've made your point,' Dave says. 'We'll sort the other bike. But you need to get a grip and calm down a bit before you ride.'

Mark storms off hissing a series of F-bombs and kicking a metal bucket that clatters across the concrete floor. I consider going over to talk to him, but I figure I've got no chance of a positive conversation with him right now.

It takes 15 minutes for the Modenas bike to be prepared. By the time Mark gets on, it's clear he's still quietly seething. He doesn't acknowledge the mechanics as he mounts the bike. Instead, he slams the visor shut on his helmet and then screws the accelerator back to shoot off at alarming speed.

'Got a lot of attitude, this kid,' sighs Dave.

Mark zooms around the first lap as if propelled by the intensity of his rage. It's like he's taking out his anger on the throttle. Zipping around again, he approaches the second turn very fast, but his angle of entry looks off. Suddenly, the front wheel goes into a death wobble. Mark battles to control the bike, but it skitters off the track, sending him straight for the barrier. With the impact looming,

Mark bails and is rag-dolled through the air before landing heavily. The bike slides along the ground and smashes into the barrier.

Medics rush over to Mark who's lying motionless on the ground. Mercifully, he's soon back on his feet, but he's clutching his left shoulder and looks hurt.

'Is he okay?'

'Looks like he'll live,' Dave says. 'But I've never seen anyone crash in practice before. The kid won't be happy with that. I'll take him to hospital, get him checked out.'

There's no way to gloss over it: this is a disastrous build-up to the race and I still haven't spent any meaningful time with Mark. Unsure what to do with myself, I figure I'll hang with the mechanics and see if I can get some intel from them.

Inside the garage there's a flurry of activity and the strong whiff of two-stroke petrol. BSL's three mechanics are busy trying to repair the two bikes. But the chief mechanic, Roy, is happy to chat away as he tinkers about with the spark plugs and brake pads. Despite all Mark's criticism, it's clear the mechanics are proud of what they've achieved with the New Zealand bike. 'It took three years of development and we built it pretty much from scratch,' Roy says.

He explains that Bill Buckley, the owner of Buckley Systems Limited, had always dreamed of racing his own bike at the 500cc Grand Prix. Really wealthy people, of course, have the power to indulge their craziest whims. So Buckley assembled a team of Kiwi engineers who used his company's CNC milling machines, lathes and industrial machinery to make the bike. Soon, Roy is regaling me with technical details about the bike's construction that I barely follow. The engine, he says, was designed in 3D CAD and manufactured using a special patternless casting method. 'Basically,' he explains, 'it massively reduced the time and expense.'

He concedes there've been problems with both pistons seizing and overheating. Roy blames the fact that New Zealand racetracks have a 95-decibel noise limit that meant all testing and exhaust development had to be done overseas. 'Logistically, that made life tricky. We didn't have the chance to fine-tune everything and iron out all the gremlins.'

When I ask Roy about what the mechanics think of Mark, he shakes his head. 'Honestly? He's an ungrateful little shit. He doesn't appreciate what we've managed to do here in difficult conditions. Yes, there've been a few issues. But he's not as shit-hot as he thinks. I mean, who crashes in practice, for God's sake?'

Clearly, the mechanics feel underappreciated and that Mark is using them as scapegoats for his poor season. The relationship has become strained and is taking a toll on the team dynamics. Mark's abrasive personality isn't helping. But as I drive back to my lodgings, I can also see the issue from Mark's side. As the team's rider, he just wants to be able to focus on his own performance rather than fretting about the technical issues holding him back. As I pull into the driveway of the motel, I get a call from Dave.

'How's Mark's shoulder?' I ask.

'Not broken, thankfully, but pretty sore,' he says. 'But we've got another problem now. He says he won't get back on the bike. You're the sport psychologist; this is your job. When we get back in an hour or so, you need to go and fix this.'

What Dave is overlooking is that Mark has zero desire to talk to me. As a country kid full of macho bravado, he's not receptive to psychological help and certainly isn't about to spill his vulnerabilities with me. It's clear he views me as being a tool of the management team he openly loathes and, by extension, one of the bad guys. After texting and calling Mark several times with no response, I decide to try a more direct approach.

When I knock on his door, he doesn't answer initially but I persevere and keep banging.

Eventually, he opens the door, looking haggard and pale. 'Look, mate, I know you want to help. But I don't want you mucking around in my head, alright?'

'I'm not here about your head – believe me, I don't want to get into that can of worms,' I joke. 'I want to help with your shoulder. I do a bit of massage and I know you've got some heavy bruising. Let's see if we can work some mobility back in that area.'

Mark shrugs. 'You can have a go, but I'm not going back on the bike today. I'm too bloody sore. My shoulder is fucked.'

At the mobile clinic, I persuade Mark to strip down to his waist and submit to the massage. To be fair, his shoulder does look painful. The bruising is a deep crimson and envelops most of his deltoid before extending down to his triceps. His shoulder is so tender that he flinches at a gentle touch. But he grits his teeth and doesn't complain as I carefully knead the surrounding muscles.

'Been in this mess before,' he says when I mention his high tolerance for pain. 'Must've broken my collarbone now at least four times.'

Gradually, he begins to open up. As for the crash, he recognises that he took the bend too fast and acknowledges he was reckless. 'It was the red mist,' he admits. 'I was just so pissed off that I had to change bikes. After everything I'd said to them . . .'

Mark claims the pain isn't the reason he doesn't want to race today. Instead he feels his shoulder will compromise his range of movement, forcing him to adapt the way that he rides. Reading between the lines, it's clear he fears his shoulder injury will hamper his performance and, given his pitiful form going into this event, he can hardly afford a dip. The real reason he doesn't want to race today it seems is that he's scared of disappointing the team and wants to avoid further humiliation.

'At the end of the day, it all rests with me, y'know?' he says quietly.

As I continue the massage, we come to an agreement. We'll do a mobility test on the stationary bike to see if he's got enough strength with half a shoulder to safely handle racing.

'If you don't pass that,' I reassure him, 'obviously you're in no fit state to race.'

Glumly, Mark agrees and we arrange to meet in an hour at the team garage to do the test. In the meantime, I call Dave to organise a team meeting, the plan unbeknown to Mark. Ideally, I should be talking to him but, given how unreceptive he is to sport psychology, I need to use the broader team to implement the messaging indirectly.

In the garage, the mood is earnest as the mechanics work to get the bikes track-ready again. When Dave calls them over for a debrief, I can sense their reluctance – I'm interrupting and holding them up. These guys understandably see their jobs through their mechanical prism. What I need them to realise is that their contribution can be far more profound.

'Fellas, thanks for your time. First up, I just wanted to say that I know it's been a tough season, I know you're a small team with limited resources, and I know that Mark can be a bit of a prima donna at times. But what I've also noticed is the team has developed a real "us and them" mentality. Results haven't gone the way you wanted them to. Mark blames the bike and points his finger at you lot. Meanwhile, you guys blame him for not doing the business on the bike. Honestly, I don't care who's right or wrong – I'm not looking for a scapegoat here. What we all want to do is finish this season on a high. But what I see with Mark is a young kid who's scared about letting you down. That performance anxiety is intensified by the group negativity.'

'Jeez, he's a handful, though,' one of the mechanics says.

'Either way,' I continue, 'what I need you to do in this mobility test, and in the lead-up to the race, is to back Mark in a really visible way. Show him that you're invested in his performance and want him to do well. Convince him that you're on his side. He's not a robot – right now he's a scared kid with a buggered shoulder. Trust me, if you all get behind him, I believe it'll make a tangible difference.'

That evening in the pit lane, the engineering team, to their credit, follow the plan, despite their misgivings. There's no sniping about the crash or about the fact they've had to work non-stop to repair the two bikes and ready them for action. Instead, Roy expresses fatherly concern for Mark's shoulder and listens intently to his worries about how it could limit his ability to corner. The team put him on the bike and lean it this way and that to see how his mobility copes. One engineer comments on how well he's managing the pain and acknowledges his courage for putting it to the test. Gradually, Mark's surly attitude begins to thaw. By the end of the session, he's reluctantly agreed to compete in the qualification rounds the next day.

'So I'll be riding at 50 per cent,' Mark tells me. 'Roy says I'll have to ride smooth and not do anything to make the bike buck and snort. Dunno how I'll get on. But I've ridden through pain before. I'll give it a go.'

'Mate, you know these guys are all rooting for you. They've been worried sick about your shoulder. They all really want you to succeed.'

'You reckon?'

'Bloody oath, and they know you can do it, too. Look, I get you've had some bad luck this season. But don't dwell on the potential negatives. Focus on all the positives that'll come when you qualify.'

'I do have a few mates in the crowd today, eh.'

'Well, they'll be right behind you, too. Just give them something to cheer about.'

*

The next day, Mark still looks uneasy as he lines up for the second qualifying session. When the lights go green, they'll take off en masse and have 15 minutes to set the fastest possible lap time. Despite his crook shoulder and his horrible run of form, Mark turns in a surprising performance. I know he's worried about the Southern Loop, the toughest turn on the circuit that's super-fast and requires a smooth line and meticulous throttle control. But he handles it comfortably and as qualifying goes on, his confidence grows and his lap times get progressively quicker. He eventually qualifies within the required time gap.

Back in the garage, the mood has lifted. The mechanics are clearly delighted that the bike has held up. With its long, undulating curves, Phillip Island is a demanding track for any bike. The circuit features plenty of fast left-handers, so riders have to lean hard and use a lot of throttle, which heaps strain on the rear tyre.

There's now real excitement ahead of the main event and I want to encourage those shoots of positivity. Mark is back at the motel resting, so I decide to take the opportunity to have a powwow with the rest of the team.

After congratulating them for qualifying, I thank them for supporting Mark in the way we discussed. 'Repeat that tomorrow and he's got every chance of turning in a performance your team can be proud of. But fellas, there is just one other thing . . .'

I explain how I've noticed how serious they all seem. The garage is a place of quiet industry and hard work where the mood is grimly earnest. 'I get you're all under pressure and crazy busy,' I say. 'But I'm convinced that Mark will ride better if we can just change the vibe.'

For an athlete, I explain, a state of heightened arousal doesn't usually equate to good decisions. Mark's accident in the practice session was a classic example. High emotions chew up your mental bandwidth, stealing your attention and hijacking your senses.

Relaxation, on the other hand, improves self-confidence and concentration. It lowers your heart rate and decreases tension and anxiety, thereby resulting in better performance.

'In this team, no one smiles, no one cracks jokes. You're all bloody serious and while that signifies your professionalism, I want you to mix it up. Mark's a larrikin and he clearly enjoys a bit of banter. I know relations have got a bit strained at times this season. But ahead of this race, I want you to try and have fun. Make him laugh, goof around, distract him from the pressure. The more relaxed Mark is, the faster he'll ride.'

Credit to the team, they listen once again. When Mark walks into the garage, the radio is blaring the Venga Boys. The mechanics, and even Dave, do a great job of jollying him along and generally taking the piss. There's an exchange of truly filthy jokes and a very involved discussion of the celebration plans should Mark finish on the podium. Before he closes his visor, I can see he's smiling. He looks to have finally regained his swagger.

It's lucky that he's got his head back in the game because the race is absolute carnage. Anthony 'The Go Show' Gobert, a mad kid from rural New South Wales, ends the first lap abruptly with a crash that Mark has to swerve to avoid getting tangled up in. That sets the tone for the mayhem. By the sixth lap of the 27, five riders in total are out.

In the early stages, Mark is riding conservatively. But by lap ten, he's picking up the pace as his confidence grows. As the race progresses it becomes less about speed than guts and attrition. Suzuki's Kenny Roberts dominates nearly the entire course until, with five laps to go, a chunk of his rear tyre crumbles away because of the mounting heat and he's forced to back off. Immediately he's passed by a three-bike convoy of riders who zoom ahead to fight it out for the win. Mark is never in contention, but he keeps plugging away to eventually finish 15th. It's not spectacular, but it's his best result of the season. Given his dodgy bike and injured shoulder, it feels like an oversized triumph.

Getting off the bike, Mark is clearly relieved that he's put on a reasonable show, but he disguises his satisfaction behind his usual bravado. He walks into the garage and tosses his helmet over to me. 'I knew I was better than half of those clowns,' he says.

On a personal level, I'm satisfied too. Trying to help a bloke who's suspicious of all authority and openly derides what I do as 'airy-fairy bullshit' hasn't been easy, but we managed to connect in the end. Behind the posturing, I can see real glimpses of Mark's talent. Now we just have to try and bring that through.

CHAPTER 5

The Ardennes region in eastern Belgium is renowned for its dense forests and swooping river valleys. Its lush beauty draws hikers from all over Europe. Right now, we can't see any of that. On the motorway, the rain is relentless. Hammering down on the windscreen of our rental car, it reduces visibility to the confines of the waterlogged road.

'Bloody rain,' Mark says from the driver's seat. 'Shame we're not going to be racing jet skis.'

We're heading to compete in the Spa-Francorchamps Motos, a 24-hour endurance race that takes place on a fast, undulating track. Competing in teams of three, swapping riders every time you need to refuel, the race starts at three o'clock in the afternoon and finishes at the same time the following day. The winning team is the one that completes the most laps during that 24-hour period. Mark has never ridden in a 24-hour race before, but we've decided to enter him into the 2000 event in a bid to salvage something from another disappointing MotoGP season. This time, it's got nothing to do with his temperament.

Mark stuck with the BSL team, but barely managed any track time due to the bike's ongoing mechanical woes. Frustrated by the limitations, Dave, the BSL team leader, is now in the process of setting up a new MotoGP team called Pulse GP for the coming season and recruited Mark as one of the team's two riders. More surprisingly, Dave also hired me to help him run the new team and, while the new season is still months away, I've already begun laying the groundwork.

This has necessitated a move to the south of France in order to be better placed to manage the logistics, given most Grand Prix races are held in Europe. As a start-up team, we don't have the spare cash for endless flights to and from New Zealand. My official role at Pulse has the grand title of 'director' but is essentially a hybrid position that involves managing the human resources side of the business along with the odd bit of sport psychology. Admittedly, it's an unexpected career move, but it seemed liked too good an opportunity to turn down.

Given Mark's key role for Pulse, Dave and I are obviously keen to do whatever we can to help him return to top form. So when France Yamaha reached out to ask if they could borrow Mark to join their three-man team for Spa, Dave and I were happy to allow it. Our hope is that he'll enjoy a much-needed boost of confidence after a couple of frustrating years.

'You've got to chaperone him, though,' Dave warns. 'Make sure he doesn't get into too much strife with that bloody temper of his.'

Ever since Phillip Island I've got to know Mark pretty well. Dave has had me working more closely with him in a bid to unlock his potential. During the pre-season, I even spent a couple of weeks with him up in the Gold Coast, training twice a day with him, going for runs and hitting the gym. Until that trip, I hadn't appreciated just how fit MotoGP riders have to be. I soon learned that these guys are serious athletes. No rider can compete effectively without a serious base of cardio endurance. They also need to build enough strength to be able to control a 130-kilogram bike rounding a corner at speeds of more than 200 kilometres per hour. But they can't stack on too much muscle or the excess weight will compromise their overall speed – during race season, Mark typically competes at 65 kilograms. Core strength is vital to maintain balance and a good body position on the bike, while flexibility is also key for control and to minimise the risk of injury. Despite enjoying the odd beer, Mark is disciplined about staying in shape, viewing it as the necessary cost of entry to the sport that he loves.

The more time I've spent with Mark, the more he's warmed to the possibility that sport psychology may not, in fact, be a 'total crock of shit'. Initially, I felt he was focusing too much on his competitors' form, rather than concentrating on his own performances. Mark has now agreed that his number one opponent is actually himself. We've worked hard to shore up his weaknesses (emotional regulation/anger management) and hone his strengths (determination/self-belief). Along the way, we've examined what he needs to do mentally in order to shave off another half a second per lap, and we've worked on his confidence to brake later and be more aggressive in his turns.

The sad truth is that Mark hasn't really had the opportunity to capitalise on these tactics because of the ongoing problems with the bike. Nevertheless, he's bought into the idea and, in the process of working with him, we've also become mates. I admire his defiant optimism and self-belief despite the fact he's been plagued with so much bad luck you'd think he was the victim of a voodoo curse.

When we get to Spa, it keeps raining and raining. I'm expecting the event to be called off, as surely it's unthinkable to compete in weather like this. Even in the sunshine, the Spa-Francorchamps Motos is commonly viewed as one of the most challenging motorcycle endurance races on the planet. A 24-hour contest on two wheels is always a punishing ordeal, but in these sopping-wet conditions it seems like a kamikaze mission.

The track has always had a tough reputation. They stopped holding MotoGP here in 1991 after it was concluded that it was too dangerous, with the circuit not having enough gravel safety zones and barriers to match the speed of the track. But even stopping the fastest bikes from competing hasn't put an end to a death toll that's seen 44 fatalities since 1925.

Last year, Belgian rider Luc Van Haver died here during a practice session for another 24-hour race. Van Haver lost control at Blanchimont, a high-speed left-hand corner that's notoriously challenging. But it's by no means the sketchiest of the bunch. Another contender is the scarily tight hairpin bend of La Source, and then there's Eau Rouge and Raidillon, a viciously steep right-hander that directly follows a long straight, tempting riders to attack it flat out. Throw in this rain and the reflex-sapping fatigue of 24 hours in the saddle and the Spa-Francorchamps Motos is a special form of madness.

Maybe it's this danger factor that draws such a crowd. The Europeans are crazy about endurance racing and more than 20,000 are braving the grim conditions to camp out and watch. Despite the rain, many have somehow managed to light bonfires around the campsite and a fug of smoke mixes with the scream of bike engines and the insistent drumming of the rain. It all feels very *Mad Max*.

'They admire the valour of the pilotes,' Christian Sarron, the head of the Yamaha Motor France team, explains when I comment on the size of the crowd. 'To ride for 24 hours. C'est a brave thing to do, non?'

Mark, meanwhile, seems bizarrely unfazed by the prospect of competing in his first-ever 24-hour race. The other members of his team are both Frenchmen. Fabien Foret is a friendly but intense rider from southwest France who only graduated to the Supersport World Championship this year. Jean-Marc Delétang is far more experienced and a previous winner of another 24-hour race, the Bol d'Or, but there are doubts over whether he's physically up to this challenge. In May, at the French Superbike Championship, he crashed into a guardrail at over 200 kilometres per hour, sustaining a double pelvic fracture and broken fibula. Given that accident happened barely two months ago, I can't believe he's fit enough for an ordeal like this.

After watching their practice laps, Mark is characteristically dismissive of his teammates' ability. 'To be honest, mate, they're both pretty shithouse,' he tells me in worryingly close earshot of Fabien. 'But I reckon I can guide them through okay.'

As the only one of the team who's raced MotoGP – albeit with limited success – Mark is being treated by France Yamaha as the team's star rider. He's responding to the attention well and is clearly relishing the extra responsibility. The morning of the race, there's a group meeting between the riders, team managers, mechanics and physios as we go over our race strategy once again. The plan is for Mark to start first and push fairly hard in the early stages without doing anything that'll endanger the bike.

Having picked up a bit of French since moving to the country earlier this year, I translate the bullet points of the meeting for Mark. 'The main point is to stay focused, be cautious and stay out of trouble for the first four to five hours of the race,' I say. 'We just want to make sure we're in one piece for the final hour. It's a marathon event, so you need to pace yourself and avoid mistakes that will cost us time if we need to repair the bike. Consistency beats intensity, okay?'

'So basically what you're saying, mate,' Mark replies while fiddling with his glove, 'is don't fuck up the bike.'

It's still raining as the race begins, with the riders of the 63 teams having to sprint in full leathers and helmets for 20 metres across the track to reach their bikes. After hastily mounting, the engines roar into life in a chorus of howling exhausts.

Mark gets away intact and negotiates the first few laps without any drama. But even by the end of the first lap, there are already casualties, with three riders sliding out of control off the wet track. I see one poor bloke pushing his half-mangled bike back to his mechanics, his leathers scuffed beyond recognition.

After 55 minutes the bike needs to refuel. That signals the moment for a change in riders, with Fabien taking over to do the next stint. 'Allez! Allez! Il arrive!' someone shouts and our pit explodes into life.

The second Mark stops the bike it's surrounded by ten crew members. One mechanic grabs the handlebars to hold it steady while Mark dismounts in a stiff-legged hobble. An engineer is already filling the gas tank, four more are changing the tyres, while the chief mechanic is adjusting the chain. Before the gas cap is snapped shut, Fabien is sitting astride the bike, primed for action. Then the stand is pulled out from the rear wheel and he starts the motor, glancing over his shoulder for traffic entering the pit lane before splashing through a puddle to launch us back into the race. The whole pit stop is completed in under 30 seconds.

Meanwhile I've helped Mark into a chair and thrust a bottle of water into his hand.

'It's crazy out there,' he says. 'The surface is so wet, the tyres can't get any grip.'

Team reps from Yamaha and the tyre supplier Michelin come over and we hastily debrief as the scale of the challenge becomes clear. From what Mark is saying, the conditions are a total nightmare.

The Spa track is 7 kilometres long and that distance complicates matters because it encompasses a range of subtly different micro-climates. Riders face multiple obstacles from slippery puddles of water where it's easy to skid out of control to drier sections where the wet-weather tyres don't offer as much grip. Mentally, that makes it extremely demanding. You're having to concentrate doubly hard on the whims of the track as you adapt to the changing conditions at speeds of up 300 kilometres per hour on some of the long straights.

Yet Mark is handling it all with hard-headed poise. He's already completed 20 laps of the daunting track and catapulted Yamaha France into an early lead. The team boss wanders past and claps Mark on the back of his sodden leathers.

'Your rider – he's fast, non?' he says to me with a smile.

In endurance car races, drivers can manage stints of up to three hours between pit stops. The benefit of that is their rest periods can stretch out to six hours before they have to return to the track. Bikes have smaller fuel tanks, necessitating more frequent rotations. With shorter rest breaks, the cumulative fatigue takes its toll. That's why, until his next stint in just a couple of hours' time, Mark's job is to shovel down some chicken and pasta to refuel, drink a gallon of Gatorade for hydration and try to recover as best he can. There's a primitive caravan for the riders to rest, but sleep is an unlikely prospect when you're buzzing with adrenaline and there's a constant backdrop of roaring bike engines. By 5 pm, Mark is back on the bike. Somehow, it's raining even harder.

Despite the apocalyptic weather, it's meant to be the Belgian summer and the sun doesn't set until almost 10 pm. As the light fades, the team are still faring well. Mark is the quickest rider by a considerable margin and a pattern has emerged whereby he extends the team's lead during his ride, before we're pegged back slightly when Fabien and Jean-Marc take over. After three cycles of rotation, it looks like a promising formula, but the strain of the effort is beginning to tell on the riders.

Riding a motorcycle at speed on a racetrack is a full-body workout, even in dry conditions. Accelerating strains the legs as you squat on your bike pegs while squeezing the tank with your knees, but your core is also working overtime to stabilise your body position. Cornering targets the same muscle groups even more fiercely, while braking engages your forearms, triceps and chest. The only respite comes on the track's straights when, for short periods, the riders can relax their bodies as they crouch down and prepare for the next turn. The faster you ride, the more strenuous all this becomes. Now, as darkness falls, a new challenge emerges.

Riding in the dark, visibility is compromised and lap times drop off. The track at Spa is unlit, with riders primarily guided by their headlights. But when cornering at high speed with knees almost brushing the ground, the angle of the bike's headlight is out of sync with the rider's eyeline, so he's forced to navigate the manoeuvre while only able to see a few metres ahead.

The other curveball in this race is the disparity in skill levels of the riders. There is no qualifying cut-off time for Spa and that means race entrants include both seasoned pros and have-a-go amateurs who ride erratically and at a much slower pace. Mark is accustomed to racing against elite riders whose manoeuvres are easier to predict. In the dark, he narrowly avoids rear-ending one hapless rider.

'I was coming down the back straight, saw a tail light off in the distance, so put my head back down on the tank. Half a second later I was practically up the arse of his bike, he was going so slow. It's dangerous! Guys like that have no business being on the same track. It's like dodgems at 200 kilometres an hour.'

By now it's after 1.30 am and I gently persuade Mark to retire to the caravan to get some rest, even though I know that, following his latest near-death experience, his chances of sleeping are slim. Most riders don't sleep at all during these races, beyond maybe stealing a few minutes on the massage table. At the same time, Mark is so physically tired, I have to help him to peel off his sodden leathers.

In the meantime, I return to the team's mission control to have a tactical talk with the Yamaha boss and crew leaders. While I'm still a relative newbie to this sport, the management keeps asking me for my input as the de facto guardian of their star rider. Sitting down at the table, it's clear everyone is tiring, but the mood is still upbeat. Approaching the halfway point of the race, the team has consolidated its lead, although the chasing pack is still close behind.

We kick around ideas on how to extend our lead. Right now, the plan is centred on finding ways to conserve the riders' fading energy while sacrificing as little speed as possible. We try to identify the stretches of the track where we should go all out and where it's better to simply coast and mentally regroup. There's a lengthy discussion about the choice of tyres, but it's still pretty wet out there, with regular showers complicating the decision.

The main takeaway from the conversation is that while our progress remains steady, a lot of teams are struggling to adjust to riding through the darkness and their speeds have significantly dropped off.

'If we could get Mark to take on a couple of extra shifts, we can really pull ahead,' Christian, the Yamaha France head, says to me. 'Can you persuade him to get back on after Fabien?'

I think of how Mark crumpled into bed when I led him back to the caravan. How I had to make him force down a bowl of pasta to give his body the fuel to recover.

'Let me ask the question.'

It feels cruel to bang on Mark's caravan door and disturb his rest. But I justify it to myself with the knowledge that he's a professional sportsman to whom winning is everything. Initially, there's no answer, but when I knock again, Mark emerges blearily at the door. He looks pale and red-eyed.

'Sorry, mate, must have dozed off.'

I explain the plan. How as our star rider, we feel that harnessing his skills now, when most of the teams are fading in the darkness, could establish an unassailable lead.

'Thing is, mate, that means you'll have to head out again right now and then go for two hours instead of one. Reckon you can manage that?'

Mark absorbs the information in silence, his face pinched with fatigue. Standing there in his T-shirt and boxers, he looks like a little kid.

'Yeah alright,' he replies at last. 'I'll give it a go.'

I fetch his leathers from where we've attempted to dry them out, but they still feel clammy and cold. I help Mark haul them on – the fingers in one of his hands is cramping – and pass him a hot cup of coffee.

'Sorry to ask you to do this, Mark. I know you're tired. But you're the team's star rider and our secret weapon.'

'That's what I'm here for, isn't it? Besides, we've got a race to win.'

For all his bravado, Mark is clearly frazzled. He barely speaks as we prepare him for the changeover. The energy for small talk drained away long ago. As the rain starts bucketing down again, the team help him onto the bike and he accelerates off into the night. Watching his tail light disappear, I feel slightly emotional. He's putting in a brave effort here, but are we endangering his safety by not letting him rest?

This is the time of an endurance race when shit gets real. It's pitch black and cold, everyone is bone-tired and the excitement of competing has long since worn off. A couple of mechanics doze in camp chairs, but most have far too much to do. Keeping the bike running at these speeds for 24 hours when it's copping so much abuse is a non-stop maintenance job. At the end of the race, every component on the bike will require a complete overhaul. For now it's an ongoing patch-up job. There are 14 sets of tyres to swap between and a workshop full of spare parts to be used to try and keep the bike going.

The real concern now is with the riders, as this is the time when the potential for mistakes rises exponentially. When you're tired, a split-second loss of concentration can have fatal consequences, particularly in the wet. The number of teams who've retired from the race is now up to double figures. Some pit garages now stand silent, while smoke from the fans' bonfires continues to drift over the track like an evil dream.

I don't know how Mark is managing to keep racing. To keep pushing the bike at those wild speeds in the darkness as his strength wanes with every lap. But he battles on, doggedly picking up the apexes and chasing down the next tail light on the glistening track. There is something quietly heroic in his refusal to quit and his determination to keep riding through the driving rain.

As he goes by again, the French guy from Michelin walks over to watch the screen by my side. 'C'est incroyable,' he says. 'Je ne comprends pas.' He shows me a printout with Mark's lap times. At night, most of the riders are lapping at least 30 seconds slower than during the day. Mark is only dropping a couple of seconds. 'We double-checked, because it didn't make sense,' the man continues. 'Mais c'est vrai.'

By 11 am the next morning, the team's lead looks unassailable. Our tactics change accordingly and Christian briefs each of the riders in turn.

'We're in a great position,' he says. 'But ride defensively and don't do anything stupid. We've pushed the bike to its limit and you riders are tired too. Now is the time to stay vigilant. The last thing we need is a crash.'

Despite their visible exhaustion, the riders stick to the brief. In fact, we're in such a great position that some of the mechanics set up a roster that enables them to finally grab a quick power nap. God knows they deserve it. Our crew have been magnificent, handling everything from the routine pit stops to the emergency repair work with calm efficiency, allowing the riders to direct all their attention on the track.

In the last hour of the race, I'm called over by the head mechanic who's suddenly found himself short-staffed. Two of his guys haven't returned from their naps yet and Fabien needs a last-minute tyre change. 'Can you help us? You just need to follow my instructions.'

As the bike rolls in, one mechanic fills the tank with petrol while another hastily changes the tyres. Then someone yells my name and tosses me a discarded tyre to take inside. It's so hot that it burns my hands. Flakes of rubber are peeling off it due to the heat from the friction with the track. Like the team, it's given everything and is now on the brink of disintegration.

At 3 pm, the result is confirmed. With Mark spearheading the team's efforts, Yamaha Motor France have completed 473 laps of the circuit in horrible conditions. In the process, they've covered more than 3300 kilometres – a distance akin to driving from Melbourne to Perth. More importantly, they've finished four laps clear of the second-placed Suzuki GSX-R750. A 24-hour motorcycle race is invariably billed as the ultimate test of man and machine. Yamaha Motor France hasn't just survived it, we've beaten 62 teams to actually win.

Inside the team garage, there's much laughter, high-fiving and backslapping while plastic cups are filled with lukewarm champagne. Christian is dancing around, one arm draped around the shoulders of the Michelin chief. The three riders are so exhausted they can barely stand. Mark, in particular, looks buggered. His eyes are red, his cheeks smeared with grease, but there's a dazed grin plastered on his face. After so much disappointment over the last couple of years, this victory is particularly sweet.

I'm so bloody proud of him and indeed of all three of our riders. I'm in awe of the way they kept bravely fronting up to grind out lap after lap in the rain. I'm equally in awe of our crew of mechanics. They might not get the fanfare, but this win belongs to them as much as the riders. Over the course of the 24-hour race, the bike has spent a total of 20 minutes in the pits. Their no-nonsense efficiency and hard work gave the team the platform to thrive. Presided over by Christian's strong leadership, it's been a brilliant team effort that's combined shrewd tactics with remarkable grit.

Fair play to the crowd, too. Despite having spent the night in waterlogged tents, thousands have remained for the presentation ceremony, an endurance achievement in its own right. As the medals are handed out, Mark, Fabien and Jean-Marc stand in a three-way embrace on the top step of the podium, passing around a bottle of champagne in the rain. Standing next to me, one of the mechanics is silently weeping as his fatigue collides with delight.

Yet somehow it doesn't feel like I thought it would.

I've never been involved in a success like this before. It should be the professional highlight of my career. But while I'm thrilled for everyone in the team, I feel strangely hollow and detached. Around me it's all champagne-drenched exhilaration and whoops of hard-earned joy. Meanwhile I feel like I'm forcing my smiles.

What the hell is going on?

It must be tiredness. Like practically everyone else, I haven't slept a wink in 24 hours. It's hardly surprising I can't regulate my emotions when I'm physically spent. Every component on the bike needs to be repaired or replaced after a race like this. Mentally, I must be equally threadbare.

Or is it jealousy that I'm feeling? Deep down, do I really want to be up on that podium myself, basking in the praise and attention? Do I crave the press interviews and media fanfare? Is my issue here an egotistical thing?

Honestly though, I don't think that's what's going on. I'm well aware that I'm not a MotoGP rider. Frankly, I couldn't dream of doing what these guys do, whipping around corners at such breakneck speeds. Sure, I admire their ability, but not in an envious way. They occupy a different realm that's a world away from my competitive set.

What's going on, because shouldn't this be *it*? My job is to empower athletes with the mental tools to perform at their peak and win. Looking at this situation, it's a case of mission accomplished. The riders earned this win with a spectacular display of perseverance and courage. So why am I standing here, watching them cavort on the podium, feeling like a total fraud?

CHAPTER 6

Unfortunately, a good night's sleep doesn't cure my lingering sense of dissatisfaction. The strange emptiness continues when I return to France and refuses to go away over the following weeks. My reaction leaves me both confused and disgruntled. Right now, I should be revelling in the highlight of my professional career. Our team worked tirelessly to achieve an impressive goal, battling to see it through in the worst possible conditions. Yet instead of basking in the glow of satisfaction that comes from a job well done, the race has left me with a bitter aftertaste. How has the pinnacle of my career already curdled into such a downer? How have I managed to turn a genuine triumph into a source of unease? The questions rattle me because I honestly don't know.

As a psychologist, I'm familiar with the behavioural idea of 'the arrival fallacy'. The concept refers to the emotional dip that can follow the accomplishment of a hard-fought goal, where the champagne tastes unexpectedly flat. The explanation is that, in order to further the progress of our species, humans are hard-wired to strive for a specific goal with our efforts rewarded by hits of dopamine along the way. When these blasts of the happiness chemical dry up at the finish line, we can be left feeling deflated as the purpose that consumed our waking thoughts is suddenly replaced by a gaping hole. The resolution doesn't trigger the happiness and fulfilment that we'd imagined.

If a client presented to me with these symptoms, I know exactly what I'd prescribe. First, I'd get them to recalibrate their expectations and remind them how enjoying success in a specific field rarely triggers a transformation in the rest of your life. Winning a grand final, for example, won't cure a sick parent or fix a loveless marriage.

Next up, I'd urge the client to reframe their success in the form of a continuous journey rather than let it be defined by a single goal. Ideally, I'd encourage them to set multiple life targets that they can transition between in the years ahead. But what's going on in my head feels deeper and more tangled up with my broader sense of self.

What Mark Willis and his fellow riders achieved at Spa was one of the greatest displays of mental fortitude that I've ever witnessed. The way they soldiered on, pushing themselves through the darkness, exhaustion and driving rain to grind out 473 laps was truly exceptional. Ostensibly, I was the team sport psychologist, but I can't take much credit for their mindset. Sure, we went through a bunch of the standard tricks – the goal-setting, the positive self-talk, the visualisation. Yet I don't believe my words made much of an impact, just as I know that I brought very little to the tactical chats with the crew chief.

The bottom line is that I know virtually nothing about racing motorcycles and don't feel like I deserve any plaudits. What I actually feel like is an imposter who's opportunistically inserted himself into a winning set-up.

But the emotional hangover goes deeper than that. I've established myself professionally working with athletes who specialise in high-risk sports. I've counselled big-wave surfers and mountain climbers, cage fighters and cliff divers, ski jumpers and champion kickboxers. As with motorcycling, I'm not an expert in any of these sports. Yet I'm starting to realise that I also lack any understanding of the common theme uniting these pursuits. I've no experience of confronting physical danger in a competitive setting. Nor have I ever had to execute under pressure in a life-threatening situation. Staring down that fear is something I've never done.

That lack of expertise hasn't stopped me doling out advice like an armchair expert. I've happily lectured Mark on the mental causes of cognitive anxiety. Spouted off to a heavyweight boxer on the importance of staying loose and relaxed in the ring. But all these lessons have been lifted from textbooks and lectures. It's all theoretical guff that I can't verify through personal experience. I've never stood in the Octagon with a UFC fighter circling with murderous intent. I've never surfed the monstrous waves at Nazare, made a solo ascent of a cliff face or tried to land a 720° aerial on a halfpipe.

I may spruik my sport-psych principles with conviction but, truth be told, I don't know if the ideas really work in the line of fire. Effectively, I've been winging it and bluffing my way all along. The upshot, I realise, is that I can't honestly connect with these athletes or give them any authentic tips. It's all very well trying to tell a nervy bobsleigh racer that 'pressure is a privilege'. But when that's not informed by lived experience, the words lack real authenticity.

For a minute, I wonder if I'm being too hard on myself. After all, I don't believe that to be a clinical psychologist you have to have overcome personal trauma or mental illness. But the more I think about it, the more I fear that all I've done is to blindly accept the ideas of others without putting them to the test. That realisation scares me, because it's caused trouble for me in the past.

I grew up in suburban Auckland as the middle son of three boys – Michael was two years older than me, Stephen was three years younger. Roger, my father, was a textile agent who ran his own small business importing fabrics from China and India to sell to local fashion houses to make swimwear and dresses. My mum, Ondra, was a high-school teacher in German and French. But my parents' real vocations were religious.

Mum was the deacon of the local Baptist church in which my father served as an elder and occasionally played the organ. As regular churchgoers, they developed a passion for choral music and were determined to transfer this to their children. I started playing the piano at the age of four and was soon expected to bash out the tunes for my Sunday school singalongs. I quickly progressed, taking every piano grade exam available before branching out. By the age of 12, I was playing the tuba for the New Zealand youth orchestra. In short, I was a pretty strait-laced kid and meekly followed the path that my parents gently nudged me down.

Then I discovered surfing. My brother Michael had managed to salvage a surfboard from the local junkyard and the two of us, along with Dave Knight, a kid from church who lived nearby, used to plead with our parents to take us to the beach every weekend.

Surfing ticks a lot of boxes for teenage boys, with its heady mix of adrenaline and social connection. Progressing from a total kook into a vaguely competent surfer was a huge ego boost for an unathletic kid like me, whose parents had never encouraged any interest in sport.

The ocean was a vast, rule-free playground that provided a literal escape from the pressures of high school. Out on the waves, there were no teachers, parents or schedules. Just my brother and me whooping it up in a fizzing mess of whitewater. As a fairly reserved teenager used to toeing the line, the freedom of surfing delivered a life-affirming sense of liberation. It also gave me a brand-new identity. Soon my walls were plastered with posters of Mark Occhilupo zipping down a wall of electric-blue water, or Martin Potter pulling a huge aerial. Determined to buy my own board, I got a weekend job as a waiter at the local Chinese restaurant. For weeks, I saved my money until I could buy a Seasons surfboard made by a local Auckland shaper.

Surfing plunged me into a ready-made tribe and helped me to foster a new sense of belonging. My social circle broadened as I made friends with a bunch of wilder and more outgoing kids and threw myself into learning the science of the stoke. Until that point I'd always thought of myself as a risk-avoidant person who played it safe, followed the rules, and tried to be a good Christian. That was my identity. Surfing introduced me to an alternative way of life that was more exciting and adventurous. I still wasn't a particularly gutsy kid, but I was fascinated by the willingness of some of my fellow surfers to take mad risks and cheerfully hurl themselves into the path of huge waves without a second thought. They seemed to operate with a different form of mental hardware that allowed them to be bolder, more courageous and carefree.

Then my coming-of-age surfing narrative took an unlikely turn. When I was about 15, my brother introduced me to BJ, the local surfboard shaper in the Auckland suburb of Newmarket. This was the guy who'd actually made my very first board. Good shapers enjoy a special level of kudos in the surfing world. They are at once architects of performance, artisanal craftsmen and wellsprings of the local surf culture, with their intimate knowledge of the region's waves. BJ's vocation ensured he already commanded serious respect among wide-eyed grommets like me. It didn't hurt that he was also a decade older and infinitely more experienced, having travelled the world to surf in far-flung spots in Bali, Africa and Hawaii. To me, BJ was the epitome of laid-back cool, with his weathered poise and ability to nail a killer roundhouse cutback.

Subsequently, my friends and I started spending more time hanging around his surf shop. We'd chat and loiter while running our hands over the glass-smooth finishes of new boards, boasting about the waves we'd caught (or claimed to have caught) and watching surf videos playing on loop on the shop's TV.

Yet while the lives of most 20-something shapers revolved around waves, women and weed, BJ had an unexpected sideline. When he wasn't crafting rails in his workshop, he was the pastor of the Christian Revival Centre, a fundamentalist church that followed the teaching of the Bible with rigid intensity. It was a surprising denomination for a freewheeling surfer. Alcohol, swearing and sex before marriage were all banned.

For Michael and me, BJ's appeal was based more on his surfing wisdom than his theological ideas. But BJ used that access to preach to us about the Second Coming of the Lord (as well as the goofy-footed brilliance of Mark Occhilupo). Many of the born-again ideas he peddled were unapologetically hardline. The church taught that those who followed its teachings would enjoy the wonders of eternal life, while the rest of humanity, including other Christians, would burn in hell after the looming apocalypse.

These are not views typically embraced by teenage surf punks. But the compensating incentives were amazing. My brother and I suddenly found ourselves getting invited on surfing weekends to places like Taranaki or Gisborne, where we'd hang out with BJ's long-haired mates, who as accomplished surfers and grown men, seemed like rockstars to school kids like us. Before long, we were attending BJ's Bible classes on Wednesdays and Fridays, while Sundays involved trips to mass both morning and night.

My parents didn't really know quite what to make of all this. As regular worshippers themselves – albeit in a far more liberal form – they were initially pleased that Michael and I were undergoing our own journey of religious discovery. Yet they must also have harboured reservations about the church's dogmatic zeal, with its insistence on traditional gender roles, prayer taking precedence over medicine and the belief that same-sex relationships were the work of the devil.

I'm ashamed to admit that if I did harbour any questions or uncertainties, I quickly buried them. Adolescent boys are impressionable creatures governed by peer group pressure. BJ capitalised on our unalloyed admiration.

My adherence to BJ's church lasted several years and only began to unravel while I was studying at the University of Otago. I'd started off doing physical education before switching to the relatively new field of sport psychology. But I was still a regular churchgoer and one Sunday, I invited two Christian friends, Paul and Gemma, who lodged at the same hall of residence as me, to attend a sermon at the local branch of the Christian Revival Centre.

That morning's sermon was full-on. The pastor gripped the pulpit so tightly his knuckles turned white, his voice building to a thunderclap as he jabbed an accusing finger at the congregation while berating the shortcomings of our godless world. He warned how other Christians in mainstream churches were not true believers and besmirched the true doctrine with their pallid form of worship. Unless they saw the light and joined our church, he bellowed, they would all go straight to hell. Midway through this barrage of fire and brimstone, I noticed that Gemma was in tears.

In the carpark afterwards my friends rounded on me in bewilderment at the church I'd aligned myself with.

'That sermon was demented,' Paul said. 'The pastor seemed like an angry old man without a shred of compassion.'

'You're a good friend,' Gemma added. 'But we're never coming back to your church.'

At the time, I was dismayed and a little embarrassed. But my friends' words also resonated. After that evening, I belatedly started to question the blinkered teachings and mindset of the church. Nascent doubts that, until then, I'd suppressed finally began to germinate in my mind.

The real turning point came a few weeks later. My brother Michael was taking a year off after university and had saved up to travel around Australia on a surfing safari. A month into the trip, he was contacted by one of the church's senior pastors, who told him that he and his friends had been away too long and were neglecting their duties. Michael explained that they'd saved up for ages and were about to head to the world-famous Bells Beach. Unmoved, the pastor demanded they return.

The fact that they complied was testament to the strength of the church's growing hold over them. Yet by the time they got back to New Zealand they were already regretting their decision. The church's isolationist tactics had suddenly become clear and they now viewed the pastor's demands as a heavy-handed power play.

'They're trying to control our lives,' my brother warned me. 'How have we allowed this to happen?'

Given I was also chafing at the church's restrictions, Michael's words landed hard. We left the Christian Revival Centre and never returned. Somewhat belatedly, I realised that religion was not confined to the four walls of a church and that faith was a lived experience that can be found in all areas of life. From that moment, I lost my faith, not so much in God, but in established forms of religion.

Today, I don't beat myself up too much about how I drifted into the Christian Revival Centre. I was just an impressionable teenager whose obsession with surfing led me to get mixed up with the wrong crowd. But given some of the stories about the church that have subsequently emerged – tales of physical abuse and cult-like indoctrination – it's clear that Michael and I had a lucky escape.

What did bother me though was the ease with which I'd allowed myself to get sucked in. How I'd passively accepted all these extreme views that didn't align with my values. The reason why that happened was that I didn't properly question the ideas. By swallowing them whole, I let them take root without subjecting them to proper scrutiny.

Clearly, working as a sport psychologist is very different to accidentally joining a cult. But now, after the race in Spa, I'm struck by some uneasy similarities. All these psychological ideas that I've parroted to my clients I've just plucked from textbooks or lectures. While I've been happy to prescribe them, I've never personally tested them myself in a real-life scenario. Essentially, I've just bought into another second-hand ideology.

To be able to work as a sport psychologist with any meaningful authority, what I really need to do is independently road-test some of the ideas and practices that I coach.

Following my teenage experiences as a surfer, at university I became fascinated by the daredevil mindset that enables athletes to excel in dangerous sports (my master's thesis was on rapid decision-making in high-risk environments). Consequently, most of my clients were people who did sports where the physical risks are very real. To truly connect with these people and provide real insights, I need to stick my own body on the line and find a sport that tests my limits in a similar way. I need to stop being a spectator and put myself in the game. There's more at stake here than my professional career. I need to do this to restore my self-respect.

PART 2

CHAPTER 7

My new home of Le Lavandou is nestled on the Côte d'Azur between Toulon and Saint-Tropez, but the little seaside town offers a more relaxed vibe than its glitzy neighbours. Le Lavandou is based around a small but bustling port, with the surrounding coastline dotted with just enough beaches to be a low-key holiday option for those seeking a quiet stretch of sand.

The main reason I'm based here is because the Pulse boss, Dave Stewart – the guy who got me involved in running the team – is good friends with the former rider Hervé Poncharal, who lives in the town. Hervé recently founded a MotoGP team called Tech3, who race as a satellite Yamaha team. They did really well in last year's 250cc World Championship with their riders, Olivier Jacque and Shinya Nakano, placing first and second respectively. Due to his close relationship with Dave, Hervé is happy to share his advice and know-how, an invaluable resource for our rookie team as we work to establish a foothold in the sport.

While I appreciate Le Lavandou's Provençal charm, it's not the easiest place for a 29-year-old expat to meet like-minded folk, particularly given how bad my French is. My resulting lack of social life means that I have plenty of time to brood on my current pre-occupation: finding the right sport to throw myself into that delivers the necessary level of risk.

I reflect on Ernest Hemingway's line about how, in his view, there are only three true sports: bullfighting, motor racing and mountaineering. According to Hemingway, 'All the rest are merely games.' What he was getting at, I think, is that within those three sports, the stakes are always high. For participants, an unforced error doesn't just mean the loss of a point or a potential defeat; you risk being grievously hurt or worse. Facing that danger, I realise, is exactly the challenge I need. So could one of those sports provide the antidote for my woes?

Eyeing that list, I immediately rule out motor racing. The financial barrier to entry is too high and the reliance on a machine, for me, somehow takes away the purity of the endeavour. Mountaineering doesn't appeal either, as realistically my work doesn't give me the time to spend months travelling in Nepal.

Given that I'm currently living so close to Spain, I consider bullfighting for a while. The risk factor is certainly there, given how a brave matador constantly exposes himself to the threat of getting gored. The sport basically involves confronting a riled-up 600-kilogram beast charging at you at 50 kilometres per hour. No wonder more than 500 bullfighters have been killed in Spain since 1700.

Great matadors don't shy away from the danger – they dance with it as closely as they dare. The nearer he comes to the bull's horns, the better the matador's performance. He demonstrates his skill in the face of that risk.

What turns me off the idea is the inherent cruelty of the sport. The more I explore, the clearer it is that bullfighting is not a fair fight between man and beast, but a drawn-out and performative execution. I learn how each bull is carefully depleted of its strength before the event and then weakened in the ring by the barbed lances and wooden darts stabbed into its neck. I'm no vegetarian, but this seems less like a sport and more like a pageant of elaborate cruelty. Bullfighting, I decide, has far too many red flags.

The next sport I contemplate is something called wingsuit flying. On the plus side, I know it'll offer the necessary element of risk. It is, after all, the most dangerous extreme sport in the world.

Essentially, wingsuit flying is base jumping with a novel twist. You hurl yourself off something high like a mountain or bridge, but the wingsuit enables you to convert your freefall into horizontal flight before eventually using a parachute to land. Summoning the courage is just part of the challenge. Wingsuit flying also requires full-body control and balance as you rocket through the air at speeds of more than 300 kilometres per hour.

Mustering the courage to do that fills me with fear, but it also excites me. The problem is that it's a long road to reach the necessary level of proficiency to become a wingsuit flyer. The Australian Parachute Federation mandates a minimum of 500 freefall skydives, or 200 in 18 months, before you're ready to finally zip yourself into a wingsuit. Mastering those logistics seems impossible with a full-time job. Not only that, in a sport that dangerous, I don't want to cut corners. Small things become big things fast when you're whizzing through the air at breakneck speed. But I keep kicking the idea around and crunching the numbers. If I could scratch together the money to go skydiving every weekend, how many extra jumps could I pack in?

Given the broader Pulse team is mostly based in France, I've started taking French lessons in order to navigate the organisational elements that my role involves. My teacher, Julie, is gently encouraging, despite my Kiwi accent butchering her language's vowels. At the end of one lesson, she pulls out a DVD that she wants me to watch as part of my homework.

'C'est un classique qui s'appelle *Le Grand Bleu*,' she says.

I watch the film, whose name translates as *The Big Blue*, that very night. It opens with Enzo and Jacques, two plucky kids who grow up in the same tiny Greek fishing village, where they compete with each other diving for coins. The narrative then jumps forward into their adult lives when they have graduated to become professional 'freedivers' and are pushing each other to strive for greater depths.

I'm instantly spellbound. The cinematography is hypnotically beautiful and the film feels like a visual poem to the underwater world. Below the surface of the ocean, the footage exudes a powerful otherworldly quality as you watch the divers floating through the alien wonderland.

But that beauty is barbed with danger. Judging by the film's presentation, the physiological challenges of freediving are inherently risky when you're holding your breath at depths of 50 metres or more. Divers risk drowning, blackouts and respiratory trauma that can easily prove fatal. In *The Big Blue*, Enzo pushes himself too far and pays for his audacity with his life.

For most people, these sorts of dangers would be a dealbreaker. Yet for me, they provide just the level of risk that I've been looking for. Then it hits me: I live five minutes away from the ocean. Freediving could be *it*!

CHAPTER 8

The next day, I pop into my local café by the beach and order a ham and cheese omelette for lunch. It's an overcast weekday and the only other customer is an old man in a cloth cap who's muttering over his newspaper. On the table in front of him is a small glass of red wine. The café has become my daily haunt and I've got to know Christine, the proprietor, through our garbled conversations in franglais. When she asks what I've been up to, I mention how I've just watched *The Big Blue*. Immediately, her face lights up.

'C'est magnifique, non?' she says.

The film turns out to be one of Christine's all-time favourites. Some of it, she tells me, was shot in Hyères, a small town a half hour's drive from here, while the director, Luc Besson, apparently spent much of his childhood in the area. 'His parents were scuba-diving instructors,' Christine explains.

When I mention that I'm tempted to give freediving a go, she becomes even more animated. One of her good friends, Joel, apparently teaches freediving locally. 'Il est formidable,' she says. 'I make rendez-vous for you both.'

I murmur politely encouraging noises and return to my omelette.

Five minutes later, Christine returns with a grin. 'So I speak to Joel. He come and meet you here in one hour. Ça va?'

'What for?'

'So you can try la plongée en apnée.'

The offer takes me by surprise, but I feel obliged to go along with it. Hastily, I shovel down the remainder of my lunch and rush back to my apartment to get my wetsuit. It's early spring and the Mediterranean is still cold.

When I return to the café just before 2 pm, Joel is already on the terrace, sitting bare-chested in the afternoon sun. He's a lean 40-something, whose mahogany-coloured skin provides a canvas for the bold Polynesian tattoo that snakes around his upper body. He greets me with a smile and stands to shake my hand.

'On y va?' he says, nodding at his motorcycle while offering me a helmet.

On the way to the beach, riding one-handed while clutching his spear-fishing gear with the other, Joel tells me he lives 15 minutes away in Hyères. He seems to scratch out a living by renting out motorboats to tourists in the summer. Judging by the weathered state of his skin, he clearly spends most of his time in the water.

At the beach, he unmoors a modest boat and we jump onboard. Given Joel's non-existent English, small talk is limited. 'La bas,' he says, pointing to the horizon to show our destination: a patch of water that he tells me is about 10 metres deep.

We chug our way out in silence as I shoehorn myself into my wetsuit. With zero freediving experience, I have no idea what to expect. As a surfer, I'm pretty comfortable in the ocean. But all my watersports experience has taken place above the surface, not below it.

After about 15 minutes, Joel stops the boat in an apparently random spot before dropping the anchor line that I notice is punctuated with meaty knots spaced at regular intervals. He hands me a snorkel and dons a pair of fins before we slip into the water. Even in our wetsuits, beneath the gun-metal sky the water is cold. But as soon as he enters the ocean, Joel is clearly in his element, calmly navigating the choppy waves.

'Regardez-moi,' he says.

Joel executes a perfect duck dive, his fins momentarily flashing above the surface. Then he's descending headfirst in perfect vertical alignment, one hand by his side, the other holding his speargun. Through the snorkel mask, I watch as he propels himself unhurriedly further and further with smooth undulations of his fins. Joel keeps going until, on reaching the seabed, he turns his body to lie on the bottom with the relaxed poise of a man on a sun lounge.

From my position on the surface, his body looks tiny. I can't believe just how far down he is. How he glided to the seabed effortlessly, with the grace of a seal. I'm not wearing a watch, but I'm conscious of the passing time. Joel must have been underwater for at least three minutes, but he seems unfazed by the lack of oxygen. How is this humanly possible?

Eventually, he raises his speargun and takes a pop at a passing fish. He misses. Surely, he must have to come back up now? Instead he slowly retrieves the spear and reloads, pulling the rubber bow backwards while positioning the butt of the gun in his sternum, readying it for the next shot. It's only then that he finally turns upwards and starts casually wafting himself back to the surface.

'Okay,' he says to me in French. 'Now it's your turn.'

First Joel tells me how to equalise. It's not the easiest advice to decipher in French while bobbing around in the ocean, but what I understand is that, when you dive underwater, the water pressure rapidly increases in the first few metres. Any pockets of air in your body are squeezed as the air contracts under the pressure. That compression is particularly acute in your sinuses and ears, causing discomfort and pain.

To balance out this pressure, you need to push air back into your airspaces by 'equalising'. This offers relief to your middle ear channel, which is located behind your eardrum and connects to the back of your throat. The trick is to pinch your nose tight to ensure no air can escape and then simply blow as though you're trying to exhale through your nostrils. Get it right and you'll usually feel a 'pop' in your ears.

Joel then explains that the anchor rope is marked with knots at 3-metre intervals. My challenge is to swim down to the first knot and wait for him there. 'If you feel okay, then we'll go down to the next knot.'

Making it down to that first knot takes me 45 minutes. Freediving in *The Big Blue* looked peaceful and idyllic, but I don't find anything remotely natural or intuitive about trying to adapt to this underwater world.

My main problem is the equalising. Maybe I've mistranslated Joel's instructions, or maybe it's because I'm battling a cold and the accompanying sinus infection is causing some blockage in my ears. Either way, I'm struggling and getting increasingly frustrated. I only seem to be able to equalise one ear. Underwater, I feel like I'm trespassing in an inhospitable realm. As my hapless efforts to reach the 3-metre knot continue, I'm starting to feel embarrassed. My head is throbbing and my nose is streaming. Joel has brought me all the way out here, but I'm wasting the opportunity with my rookie display.

Finally, I find a workaround for the equalising. It needs to be done, I realise, almost every second in the early stages of the dive. At first, I'm tensing up my neck and body. But the real breakthrough comes after I clear my sinuses by snorting a bit of seawater out of my nose.

On my next attempt, the equalising starts to work and the pain in my ears subsides. I pull myself down the rope for half a metre, then pinch my nose to equalise, before grabbing the rope once again until I eventually make it to the 3-metre knot. I'm relieved that I've managed it and that my first attempt at freediving isn't a total flop. Suddenly Joel appears next to me, his scuba mask sucked tight against his face. He flashes the okay sign to me, which I return. Then he points downwards with his thumb. He wants me to try and go deeper.

I work my way down to the second knot at 6 metres. Rather than becoming exponentially harder, the equalising allows me to push through the pressure. At the second knot, Joel reappears. Again, we exchange the okay sign before venturing deeper once more.

At 9 metres, the surface colours have become darker blues. It feels ominously deep now, but somehow my ears seem to have acclimatised and I feel no pain. I'm aware of the lack of oxygen, but I can see the anchor on the bottom. I'm so close now – I have to have a crack.

I push myself down, fighting my way a little deeper, and manage to grab hold of the anchor. Then, for the first time in the dive, I stop focusing on my ears and look around. Above me is a blue fog of water the height of a three-storey building. Our little boat's bobbing silhouette seems like a galaxy away.

Joel arrives at my side. He nods excitedly and gives me a double thumbs up. His next gesture is less positive. He holds up one finger and then makes the upward signal with his thumb. He wants us to stay down here for another minute! My body answers the question for me as I'm suddenly overcome with a desperate urge to breathe and bolt for the surface. The next moment, I'm blinking in the sunlight and drawing in huge gulps of oxygen.

As soon as I get my breath back, I discover that I feel totally elated. I'm quietly delighted that I finally managed to work my way all the way down to the anchor. But I also enjoyed the sensory shift of entering the marine world with its immense calm and meditative hush. Beneath the waves, you're forced into a profound state, aware only of your immediate surroundings, your mind focused solely on the sensations of your body floating weightlessly in the big blue. Once my breathing has stabilised, I turn to Joel and ask if we can go again.

CHAPTER 9

Instantly, I'm hooked. I want to learn to go deeper, hold my breath for longer, dive with the same effortless grace as Joel. I love the minimalist elegance of a sport that allows you to explore the ocean powered simply by your own breath. Freediving, I now realise, could be the ideal vehicle to test my inner limits in a sporting context.

Happily, it turns out that Joel runs informal freediving coaching sessions every Wednesday afternoon. Soon I'm one of the regulars in the ragtag group. I get to know Alain (a quietly spoken mechanic), Jules (the local postman) and Arnaud (a chain-smoking waiter). Alain and Arnaud come along because they're keen spearfishermen trying to find ways to improve their breath-hold thresholds. In their game, the longer you can stay underwater, the more terrain you can explore, and the more fish you can skewer. Jules meanwhile loves the tranquillity and peace he finds beneath the waves.

'It's like being in a parallel universe,' he tells me. 'When I dive deep, I feel like I'm flying in outer space.'

Every Wednesday, over the following weeks and months, I learn about safety and how you should never, ever freedive alone. I witness exactly why after Alain pushes himself too hard in one session. Emerging from the water, he looks to be having a minor seizure and begins involuntarily shaking. Joel quickly swims over and holds

Alain's head above the surface of the water until the jerky movements gradually subside.

When a diver's brain is starved of oxygen, Joel explains afterwards, it triggers a reaction in the cerebral circuitry that can affect your motor control. Essentially, you lose control of your movements and start to shake. This oxygen-deprived state is named a 'samba' after the Brazilian dance. Without Joel's intervention, Alain's samba would have probably led to a blackout. And if no one was there to intervene, that's when drowning becomes a real possibility.

Luckily, 90 per cent of sambas and blackouts happen on the surface, while most of the others happen within 5 metres of it, where your dive partners should be on hand to assist you. Blackouts, it turns out, aren't regarded as such a big deal for freedivers; they're more of an occupational hazard.

The lesson that does most to speed up my progress is when Joel helps me to refine my equalising technique. He shows me how to exhale against my pinched nostrils or use my stomach muscles to push the air from my lungs up into my sinuses and nasal cavity. This results in an intense 'pop'.

It turns out to be a gamechanger.

Suddenly, I can go much deeper and my underwater world expands. After not being able to dive beyond 10 metres, now I'm reaching 20 metres with relative ease. More importantly, because I'm not fretting about the pain in my ears, I'm no longer fighting an endurance battle against the pressure. Instead, I'm enjoying the ride, revelling in the thrill of the descent, the darkening blues and passing flickers of silver fish. I love the sensation of weightlessness in this slow-motion world. Yet underpinning every dive is the physical challenge that ensures that each dip beneath the waves is spiked with adrenaline.

Pretty soon the session with Joel is the highlight of my week. Part of the pleasure lies in the fact that, as an expat living in France,

I'm still an outsider with few social ties. Now I've been accepted by a bunch of locals with whom I share a common passion. Often we'll sit around afterwards on the beach, talking shit and knocking back bottles of Kronenbourg as we swap stories about what we've just seen in the world's biggest aquarium. My freediving is slowly improving, and so is my French.

One summer evening, Joel invites me to join him for a drink at a local bar. We sit outside at a table on the pavement in the fading light, enjoying the warm air. The mild euphoria that often lingers after a good diving session combines with the cold beer to put me in an excellent mood.

Joel picks up on it and grins. 'So you like freediving, huh?'

'It doesn't come easy to me, but yes, I absolutely love it.'

'Bien sûr,' he smiles. 'Humans, all of us, are made to freedive and when you start going deeper that's when the real magic happens.'

Sipping his drink, he tells me about a phenomenon known as the 'mammalian dive reflex'. This physiological response is thought to be an evolutionary adaptation from billions of years ago, when all life on earth was aquatic.

In the 1960s, he says, marine biologists learned that the physiological adaptations they'd observed in seals and sea lions were also present in humans. As you dive deeper, to 50 metres and beyond, your lungs are compressed by the pressure, triggering an amphibious reaction in your brain. The blood vessels in your limbs constrict, pushing blood to your core that fills the space vacated by your lung shrinkage. Essentially, this hack stops your skeleton from buckling under the pressure of the water. By diverting blood from less important areas of the body towards your vital organs in a process called peripheral vasoconstriction, you keep your brain and heart oxygenated for longer. At the same time, your spleen also contracts, flooding the circulatory system with a fresh stock of red blood cells to keep the brain alert.

Meanwhile, in a bid to conserve oxygen, your heart rate decreases as soon as a splash of water touches your face. That's when your senses start to slow and you slip into a meditative state. 'A Swedish researcher called Scholander discovered all this,' Joel says taking a swig of his beer. 'He called it "the master switch of life".'

'So freediving is an innate skill?'

'Mais oui. Remember, once upon a time we all came from water.'

In the womb, he points out, babies float in amniotic fluid that's not unlike seawater. Before it starts to develop hands and feet, a month-old human embryo even grows fin-like protuberances that hark back to its evolutionary roots.

'A baby can comfortably hold its breath underwater for 40 seconds – just like the Nirvana cover,' he says, referring to the album *Nevermind*. 'Today, freediving is a forgotten practice but, in fact, it's the most natural thing in the world.'

One afternoon, Joel suggests we meet at a local open-air swimming pool so we can practise our static breath-holds. In the shallow end of the pool, we're assigned safety partners – I'm paired with Arnaud – and take it in turns to float face-down in the water. We start with a breath-hold of two minutes that I manage without too much strain. After a ten-minute recovery break, I nail the three-minute breath-hold, too. But the four-minute hold is a real battle.

Every 30 seconds, Arnaud taps me on the back to indicate the elapsed time. Just before the three-and-a-half minute mark, my body – presumably startled by the spiking levels of carbon dioxide – tries to trigger an intake of air by contracting the respiratory muscles and causing involuntary spasms in my chest and stomach. It feels horrible, but I try to ride it out. I distract myself by scanning my body from my head down to my toes, trying to ensure that every muscle is as relaxed as possible.

In an effort to dissociate from the urge to breathe, I push my attention towards the muffled sounds and echoes in the pool and try to switch off my brain. I drift into a weird, dreamlike state. Then Arnaud is tapping me repeatedly on the shoulder. I jerk my head up and exhale hard before taking in a huge gulp of fresh air. The world spins, my vision still fuzzy from the lack of oxygen, but gradually things settle down after I take a couple more breaths. I'm spaced out and a little high, but mostly I feel elated to have made it to four minutes.

'There was a new world record for the static hold this year,' Joel tells me as I towel off after climbing out of the pool. 'It was a Czech guy called Martin Štěpánek. He did eight minutes and six seconds.'

Eight minutes! That's double what I just managed and, given how tough a four-minute breath-hold felt, that seems like a staggering amount of time. But it also seems to prove what scientists have long suggested: what we perceive as our physical limits are often just cautionary signals telegraphed by the brain to ensure our survival. The result is that we tend to underestimate our abilities. Usually, our true potential is greater than we think. Freediving, it seems, invites you to explore that space in between. The sport tests your mental limits by depriving your body of its most urgent need and then seeing how long you can hang on. From that perspective, it's the perfect vehicle for me to trial my sport psychology ideas. All sports have a mental component, but in freediving it looms particularly large.

Increasingly, I'm also seduced by the experience itself, with its sensation of weightlessness and freedom. Part of the appeal, I realise, is that freediving offers a form of escapism from surface life. Right now, that's a welcome sanctuary, too, because things on dry land are not going well.

After barely a year, Pulse, the MotoGP team that I helped Dave to co-found, is on the brink of collapse. Severely underfunded from the outset and lacking a major sponsor, we've run out of money. While it was an achievement to get a new team off the ground and compete at the highest level, our results on track have been poor.

When we launched the team, Dave bought the Muz 500, a two-stroke V4 bike that was highly rated when it was introduced in the 500cc Championship a couple of years earlier. Since then, however, it's been technically unchanged while other teams have moved forwards. That's made it tough for our two riders, Mark and the Brit Jason Vincent. Both have been relegated to the back of the grid and we've only scored world championship points once, when Mark finished 13th at the 2001 Italian Grand Prix.

That lack of success has had a debilitating knock-on effect. Sponsors don't want to be associated with a losing team and TV coverage focuses elsewhere, denying you exposure. Cash flow is vital in any form of motor sport because running a team is incredibly expensive – you're forever haemorrhaging money on bike maintenance, specialist parts and riders' salaries. Our coffers are now empty and our backer is refusing to confirm whether he's willing to plough in extra funds, given we've already burned through a million dollars. One way or another, we need a resolution, but Dave can't get a straight answer, leaving us in a desperate state of limbo.

The upshot is that everything is crumbling. Our bike is patched together MacGyver-style because we can't afford to restock a few critical parts. Plans have been made to replace the original Mikuni carburettors with Keihins, but that still hasn't happened. Mark and Jason are demoralised and everyone in the team is aware that our bikes will soon exceed their typical life expectancy, after which they'll become dangerous to ride.

Given this hand-to-mouth existence, I fear that without some miraculous intervention, we'll soon have to pull out and disband. But that's not an easy decision, given we employ 20 people – many of them married men with families to support. They want clarity on their futures, but that's something Dave and I cannot provide.

We're not deliberately withholding info, we're trying to figure things out, but our silence has fostered an environment of mistrust and suspicion. Mark and Dave are no longer speaking and the close relationship I built up with our star rider is increasingly strained. The prospect of laying off our workers keeps me awake at night with anxiety. I'm wracking my brain for solutions, but the financial requirements seem impossible to meet.

Compared to the complexities of work, freediving is brutally simple. You strap on a mask and jump in the water. Then all you have to do is see how deep you can go on a single breath.

CHAPTER 10

Lodged between the Auckland suburbs of Takapuna and Milford, Lake Pupuke is a world away from the Mediterranean. The heart-shaped freshwater lake occupies two conjoining volcanic craters and reaches 57 metres at its deepest point.

I returned from France a couple of months ago and immediately realised how lucky I am to have a lake of this depth so close to my hometown. What I'm less thrilled about is the actual water. It's cold, murky and clogged with weeds, but the thing that really bothers me is the lake's growing population of eels. The big ones are as thick and muscular as your arm and writhe about in the blackness. There's something deeply unsettling about the snake-like way they twist through the darkness, their pink mouths agape. Eels really freak me out.

At we swim out, John Wright, my new freediving buddy, isn't doing much to ease my phobia. Instead, he's telling me about claimed sightings of an enormous eel affectionately called the 'Lake Pupuke Monster'. Allegedly, it's been known to pull birds under, attack dogs and even capsize kayaks.

''Course, it's not *really* a monster,' John says cheerfully, head bent low against the cold wind. 'Just a massive longfin eel – the old guy is probably 2 metres long.'

I've been hanging out with John on a weekly basis since moving back to New Zealand and signing up to the No Bubbles

Freediving Club that trains here on Lake Pupuke. As feared, Pulse ran out of money and the team was forced to withdraw from competition after just nine of the season's 16 races. Afterwards, I hung around in Europe for a while trying to get more work as a sport psychologist for one of the other MotoGP teams. When nothing materialised I was forced to come home. On the upside, Auckland has its own hardy band of freediving devotees.

The No Bubbles club was founded by John, who's the godfather of New Zealand's nascent freediving scene. A big, burly guy who played rugby league for the national team back in the 1970s, John opened a scuba-diving shop after he retired from professional sport. He subsequently discovered freediving and, as a former front-row forward, his natural reaction was to charge straight in. Soon he began trying to recruit others, running courses all over the country and designing training programs to help people improve.

'You got to remember this is still a pretty young sport,' he tells me. 'When I started, you couldn't even buy a long pair of fins in New Zealand and there's still a lack of info and resources. That means most people learn through trial and error. But what's good about that is there's a lot of "blue sky". We haven't scratched the surface of what people are going to achieve.'

John's guidance has already proved invaluable. As a former athlete, he believes that freedivers need to maintain a good level of base fitness that combines both strength and endurance. Freediving, he points out, involves a lot of kicking and you need the cardio capacity to reduce early-onset fatigue when pushing for the surface.

As well as sending me to the gym for regular sessions, John has also persuaded me to work on my flexibility, particularly around my diaphragm, chest and intercostal (that is, between the ribs) muscles. 'Flexibility helps you breathe more efficiently, and take deeper breaths,' he says.

There's no doubt that John's coaching has helped. He keeps challenging me to set myself new targets in order to progress. And things are slowly nudging in the right direction. My static breath-hold is now up to five minutes and I've refined my kicking technique to help me cut through the water with less exertion. But I'm still struggling to get as deep as I'd like.

Last week, I managed a new personal best when I reached 30 metres for the very first time. But it didn't feel like much of a success. I was nervous beforehand and, in retrospect, far too tense. As I descended, I wasn't ready for the mounting pressure that cranks tighter and tighter after 20 metres. The sensation was horrible. It was like my body was stuck in a vice. Focusing on my equalising, I forced myself deeper, trying to subdue the panic in my chest, the convulsions in my stomach, the overwhelming desire to breathe.

As soon as my alarm sounded to signal 30 metres, I scrambled for the surface, where I almost blacked out. The incident shook me up and, even after I surfaced, it took me some time to regain my composure.

John was philosophical about this negative experience. Praising my effort, he reminded me that it was just part of the learning curve.

'The pressure is intense, eh?' he said. 'Like you're being crushed in a massive bear hug. But your body just needs time to acclimatise and get used to that feeling. You need to come back next weekend, go down to 30 metres again, but this time you need to stay down there for a full minute.'

And so here I am today. Swimming out once again, trying to ignore the sense of impending doom building with grim momentum in my head. As we make our way out, John tells me that spending time in that discomfort at 30 metres will build my resilience and condition my body to withstand it more easily.

'There's always a sticking point for any diver,' he says. 'Practice is the only thing that'll help you push through.'

'How do you manage it, John?'

'With diving, mindset is more important than anything. When things get nasty and your body is pleading to quit, just remember that struggle is part of the process. You've got to hang out in that dark place and make yourself at home there. That's what will get you where you need to be.'

Having reached a sufficiently deep spot of the lake, John positions the device he's been using as a flotation aid during the swim. It's the inner tube of a tyre with a little wooden base attached to the bottom. That base has a hole through which he now feeds the rope that will measure how far we descend. With serious misgivings, I put on my mask. I then begin my breathe-up, keeping my inhalations and exhalations slow and long. After a minute, my breathing pattern changes. I start to take repeated sips of the air to pack my lungs as full as possible before propelling myself down into the lake.

I head down and down into the water, equalising at regular intervals. But I soon realise that John was right. Despite being mentally braced for the ordeal, the unpleasantness is impossible to avoid. As I swim past 20 metres, the pressure consumes me once again, a terrible weight crushing my abdomen and chest. Grimacing, I fight my way down to 30 metres. Now I somehow have to find a way to stay here for a minute. I press the timer on my wrist.

Come on, Ant. It's just 60 seconds.

I shut my eyes and clench them tight. Trying to ignore the pressure, to forget where I am.

Don't think about the time. It'll be over soon.

The convulsions in my chest begin again. It's a sickening feeling. I focus on trying to relax each muscle in turn. My feet, my calves, my hamstrings . . .

Holy shit, this is intense.

My glutes, my lower back, my stomach muscles . . .

Hang in there, mate. Stay strong.

My arms, my shoulders, my neck . . .

Fuck. Surely it must be 60 seconds by now?

I reach up and turn on the torch on my mask to look at my watch. And that's when I see it. Circling my legs is a giant white eel. Its sinuous form is sleek and fat as it twists and jackknifes in the black water, its eyes wide open . . .

For a split second I'm transfixed with horror. And then I'm pushing for the surface, kicking faster than I ever have before. Back on shore, John can see I'm still pretty shaken by my monstrous encounter and tries to calm me down as I sit miserably on the beach.

'Eels are nothing to worry about, but they're mysterious creatures for sure. You know they reckon they've been around for over 50 million years.'

'Yeah? Well I wish they'd piss off out of this lake.'

'You'll survive, mate – you did well today. And that's the thing about freediving in open water. It's different from breath-holds in the pool where everything is calm and stable. Out there, you have to deal with the pressure, deal with the currents, deal with the waves and, yeah, maybe the odd eel, too. You've got to deal with all that stuff and still keep focused enough to do your thing.'

Still thinking about the eel, I shudder and John gives me a consoling pat on the back.

'Come on, the main thing is you hung in there and did it. Didn't let that eel psych you out. Life is full of curveballs, mate, you just got to take them in your stride. And I should know, trust me. Don't forget, me and my missus have got bloody triplets.'

CHAPTER 11

'Anthony? *Anthony Williams?* Is that you?'

I'm walking down Ponsonby's main street when a female voice calls my name. Turning around I see a young woman eyeing me with an expectant smile from the doorway of the Vicki Taylor fashion boutique. It's Merryn Nicholson. I dated her in high school for three weeks when I was 14, before she brutally dumped me, telling me that I was 'too boring'.

She greets me with a hug and I catch a heart-stopping whiff of her perfume. Merryn was always cute but now she's blossomed into a real head-turner, a petite brunette with dark brown eyes and a vivacious charm. I haven't seen her for over a decade. We immediately start chatting, catching up on each other's news and the varied fates of some mutual friends. Suddenly, her boss is calling her from the boutique.

'I've got to go,' she says.

'Wait, can I get your number? Do you want to grab a drink later in the week?'

'Sure, I'd like that. Call me!'

'I will. Hopefully, I won't be "too boring" this time.'

Soon Merryn and I are dating and I'm spending as much time as I can with her, exploring the old bars and restaurants of my hometown. While France was an adventure, I'm quietly delighted to be back in Auckland. It's only now that I'm back in the social groove – hanging out with Merryn and catching up with mates for a surf or a beer – that I appreciate just how isolated I was in France. Beyond my freediving sessions with Joel, I never established any real connections, partly due to the limitations of my French and partly due to the constant travel on the MotoGP circuit, where I'd be in a different part of Europe every other week.

Work-wise, I'm still trying to land more gigs as a sport psychologist. I've sent my CV to various rally and motor-racing teams without much luck. Unfortunately, my chosen profession is still regarded with open suspicion in many sporting circles. If I'm going to avoid going back to pulling pints at the Chill Bar, I may need to consider branching out.

Being in a relationship fails to diminish my passion for freediving and, propelled by John's enthusiasm, I continue to progress. My breath-holds improve as I learn to become calmer and less bothered by the internal contractions. Equalising starts to become more natural, until it feels like changing gears on a car. Grudgingly, I even find that I can tolerate the Lake Pupuke eels. Yet while I'm definitely diving deeper, my efforts are capped. I'm struggling to go beyond 46 metres as I just can't withstand the pressure.

To try and find a solution, I delve into the science. Just 10 metres below the surface of the water, you're exposed to another whole atmosphere of pressure. For every 10 metres beyond that, you have to contend with yet *another* atmosphere of pressure. Beyond 40 metres that affects your physiology in far-reaching ways. Aside from the physical compression, the depth affects the gases in your blood and messes with your nervous system. To me, at least, it feels deeply unpleasant and very, very wrong. I assumed that regular exposure would make it easier to cope with. But even after weekly training and picking John's brains for tips, I still find it unbearable.

Then I find something that may help: an advanced freediving masterclass that's being run in Turkey. It's helmed by Rudi Castineyra, a veteran freediver and one of the most experienced instructors in the world.

Growing up in Cuba, Rudi started freediving at the age of four and as a teenager began teaching courses to local fishermen. What was different about Rudi's approach is that while many early practitioners viewed freediving as a quasi-spiritual pursuit, he viewed it more objectively through the prism of medicine and sports science. After immigrating to America, he researched biology and medicine in a bid to understand how our bodies react and adapt to greater depths underwater. In the process, he honed techniques that would take freediving to a whole new level.

In the mid-90s, Rudi worked with his Cuban compatriot Alejandro Ravelo, helping him break three world records. But what confirmed his expertise was when he started mentoring an inexperienced diver who'd only had a fleeting taste of the sport. Tanya Streeter began smashing freediving records almost immediately. Born in the Cayman Islands but schooled in England, in 1998 Tanya reached a depth of 113 metres to beat the women's 'No Limit' diving record, where you descend with a motorised sled and come up with an inflatable balloon. Then she started taking on the men. In 2002, Tanya broke the men's No Limit record by reaching a depth of 160 metres. In 2003, she also broke the men's world record in the variable weight discipline, where you descend with a sled and come up under your own steam, notching a staggering depth of 122 metres.

If anyone can help me to break the 50-metre barrier, it's Rudi Castineyra. So when I hear that he's teaching a master freediving course in Turkey, I have to do it.

Unfortunately, it's not as simple as just putting my name down. When I email Rudi, he stresses that the course is invitation-only, with positions allocated to elite freedivers with competitive experience. Over the next few weeks, I send multiple emails pleading with Rudi to let me sign up. I refer to my breath-hold times and experience as a sport psychologist but the knockbacks keep coming. Undaunted, I persevere with my pleas.

'Every week,' I write in yet another email, 'I practise in a cold, dark lake in Auckland that's writhing with eels. I hate and fear eels with a passion. But I force myself to put up with them because that's how much I want to improve as a freediver.'

Eventually, I wear Rudi down. He sends an email, outlining the details of the course that will take place in Bodrum, a Turkish port town on the Aegean Sea. Hopefully that's where I'm going to learn the secret of how to go deep.

Halfway through the course, I'm questioning my determination to force my way in. The schedule is intense, as we're out on the boat for at least five hours a day. It includes 90 minutes of diving, followed by individual debrief sessions where Rudi analyses computerised graphs of our dives and offers rigorous feedback. Every day revolves around freediving, which is, of course, why we've all come. But this sort of total immersion means I can't escape how limited my skills really are.

There are three other divers on the course, but they're all light years ahead of me. Bevan Dewar is a South African with a breath-hold of more than seven minutes and three national records to his name. A thoughtful red-headed guy, he takes a methodological approach to his training and swears by 'apnea walking' – a dry-land technique where you walk holding your breath – as having dramatically improved his tolerance to CO_2 buildup. After spending several days with Bevan, I still don't know anything about his life above the surface of the ocean because freediving is all he talks about. At every opportunity, Bevan peppers Rudi with questions about air-packing and monofin-kicking techniques. He's a nice enough guy, but utterly obsessed.

The second diver is Yev, a mysterious Russian whose muscle-bound frame coupled with his shaven head and gruff manner suggests to me a military background. At first, I assumed that Yev's aversion to small talk stemmed from his lack of English. But one night, after seeing him chatting up an American girl at a local bar, I realise that he just has no interest in talking to me. Yev doesn't compete as a freediver, but he's clearly done it for years. His technique is smooth and he seems totally unfazed by the pressure.

The final diver is an established name in the sport. Hailing from Finland, Topi Lintukangas is a former triathlete who set a world record last year in the unassisted constant ballast category by diving to 60 metres without fins or any type of propulsive aid. I'm longing to quiz him about his achievements, but Topi seems pathologically self-contained to the point where he barely speaks at all. As a sport that involves a fair amount of isolation, freediving seems to attract such introverted personalities. But even by those standards, Topi is remarkably withdrawn.

The lack of camaraderie is a shame, because right now I could use some moral support. My eagerness to clinch a spot on this course stemmed from the hope that Rudi might pass on the secret that would transform my diving. So far, that hasn't happened. We spend most of our time at a spot just off the northern Bodrum peninsula, where 20 minutes offshore, the water reaches 70 metres with good visibility, particularly in the early morning. Unfortunately, I have to take everyone else's word for that, having comprehensively failed to reach those depths myself.

I've hit a roadblock. I seem physically incapable of pushing beyond 46 metres. I've learned to endure the contractions in my diaphragm and neutralise the pain in my ears. But the pressure continues to defeat me – it feels like it's trying to mash my innards into soup.

I've used every mental trick in my repertoire to work around this. I've visualised a triumphant dive in technicolour detail and used dissociation tactics to halt my negative thoughts. But the skull-crushing intensity of the pressure is still too much.

Rudi offers a variety of tips to help me. We work on more efficient ways to equalise, slowing the speed of my descent and trying to focus more on the overall process than the specific depth. Yet nothing triggers the breakthrough I crave. Rudi views my plight with mild indifference and I can hardly blame him. He repeatedly warned me that this course was too advanced for me but I refused to listen. Understandably, he prefers to direct his expertise towards students with the technical proficiency to actually follow his instructions.

My frustration is undercut with embarrassment. I'm sure that Rudi believes I misled him by deliberately overstating my ability. Each day as we head out in the boat, I feel like an interloper who's holding the others back. Every dive only exposes my shortcomings and the daily humiliation chips away at my confidence. It feels like I'm only capable of paddling in the shallows, while my fellow divers explore the real depths.

On the final day of the course, Rudi has flagged that we're going to go as deep as we can. 'This will be your chance to put everything you've learned into practice,' he says. 'I want you to show me what you can do.'

The night before, we have to notify Rudi of our intended depths. When I tell him that I want to try and get past the 50-metre barrier, he looks at me questioningly. I'm not sure whether he doubts my ability to manage that depth or if he despairs at how little I've progressed.

'The base plate is around 65 metres,' Rudi says. 'Try and get as close to it as you can.'

Like it or not, I'm locked into the challenge now. This dive represents a chance at redemption. I've forked out $5000 to attend this course, and if I can just hit 50 metres, I can justify the expense and salvage a bit of pride. Yet, given my lack of progress so far, I'm struggling to rouse much self-belief.

The morning of our final day I wake at 5 am. In my small room in the guesthouse, I do my stretches and visualise myself emerging victorious after reaching 50 metres. I write down a list of reasons to be confident, reminding myself that I'm physically ready and mentally primed to deliver. Yet for all this cheerleading, I'm still too nervous to eat.

The boat chugs out towards the dive spot beneath an iron-grey sky. The air temperature is barely 14°C and the water is almost as cold with the wind ruffling up surface chop on the waves. They're hardly ideal diving conditions.

Don't use the weather as an excuse. You just have to get this done.

None of my fellow divers is chatty at the best of times, but today the atmosphere is even more solemn. Everyone, it seems, has retreated into their private worlds to mentally prepare. The silence only adds to my tension.

Trying to psych myself up, I think about the Natal Sharks rugby players in the dressing room before that semi-final against the Auckland Blues. How their game faces hardened and they began to rile themselves up with slaps and war cries, trying to muster the energy and aggression they'd need for the battle ahead. Mentally, I'm trying to do the same thing.

Push through the pain. Deal with the pressure. Stop being such a pussy.

At the diving spot, Yev and Bevan jump into the water to prepare for their dives and Rudi also hops in to administer a last-minute pep talk. I'm sitting at the bow of the boat, my fists balled at my side as if steeling myself for a fight. I turn around to see Topi in his wetsuit sitting on the boat's transom with his eyes closed. Inwardly, I groan as I realise that I'm going to have to sit next to him to put my fin on and enter the water. This is not a welcome prospect. So far, all of our encounters have been unfailingly awkward, due to Topi's highly reserved nature and preference for monosyllabic answers. It's like trying to engage with a statue.

Walking across the gently rocking boat, I take my seat next to him and he slowly opens his eyes. Predictably, Topi says nothing to acknowledge my presence. He just keeps staring out at the horizon with a blank expression on his face. After a couple of minutes, the silence is finally broken.

'Do you know what your problem is?' he asks in a matter-of-fact tone.

I'm blindsided by the question. It's practically the first time that Topi has spoken to me all week.

'No, mate,' I reply. 'I don't know what my problem is, but I sure wish I did.'

There's a long pause. The boat rocks while Topi toys with his mask. Eventually, he speaks again. 'I've been watching you dive. Your problem is that you just don't know how to let go. You don't know how to accept that, at a certain depth, it's going to get tough. You're going to be crushed by the pressure. You still don't understand that there is no way around it. That there is no escape.'

'So what am I meant to do, then?'

Topi looks me in the eye with his unflinching gaze. 'What you have to learn to do is accept that discomfort. It's part of the process, so allow it to happen. Allow it to wash over you. Get on with what you need to do. What you try and do instead is to fight and fight, trying to push through it. But you can never outmuscle that pressure. And you are never going to go deep until you learn how to let go.'

Topi pulls on his scuba mask. Without a backwards glance he slips into the water and swims off. Now I'm sitting alone, trying to process his cryptic advice, which has completely thrown my preparations.

It's so different to any advice I've ever had before. Whenever I played rugby as a kid or ran cross-country at school, whenever I confronted any challenge involving the possibility of pain, I always believed the best course of action involved toughing it out, pushing harder and being more physical. Topi is now telling me that approach is wrong. Instead, I'm being advised to do the opposite. Accept the pain, embrace my fate and trust my ability to survive it.

The advice feels counterintuitive. But as I stare into the grey sea, I realise that I've got nothing to lose. The irrefutable fact is that I'm about to head deep below the surface. After 30 metres, the pressure and discomfort will follow. This is inevitable. It's an inescapable part of the experience that I willingly undertake.

So just let it be tough. Let it be tough.

Rudi shouts that it's my turn to dive. Putting on my mask, I slip into the water. When I emerge I haven't reached my target depth of 50 metres.

I've nailed 66 metres instead.

CHAPTER 12

The journey from Turkey to New Zealand is not a well-oiled route. In order to get home, I first have to take a one-and-a-half hour domestic flight from Bodrum to Istanbul. From there, I fly for ten and a half hours to Hong Kong, where I have a two-hour layover before another ten-plus-hour flight to Auckland.

Luckily, I have something momentous to occupy my mind. I need to analyse exactly what took place in the Icarian Sea off Turkey's west coast. How did I just manage to smash my personal best dive by over 20 metres? How on earth did I go to 66 metres?

For almost six months, I'd been stuck at 46 metres. During that time, I'd done everything I physically could to push past it. I trained in the gym five days a week, grinding out pull-ups, deadlifts and squats in the hope that getting stronger would help me to maintain my form and move through the water with greater efficiency. I hammered my core with sit-ups, planks and leg raises to hold more streamlined positions, thereby reducing drag and conserving energy. Every night, I stretched religiously for 45 minutes in front of the TV, hoping that becoming more flexible in my chest and shoulders would enable me to take even fuller breaths. I also worked hard on my cardio fitness with 10-kilometre runs and interval training in the pool to give myself a solid endurance base. But none of this seemed to make much of a difference.

No matter how fit I was, I just couldn't overcome the 46-metre barrier.

Now I've taken a significant step forward. Yet there's been no dramatic change in my physiology. The real shift happened between my ears when I took Topi's advice to stop fighting the pressure. As a sport psychologist, I have to understand why mentally changing my approach had such an oversized effect and whether developing that mindset would unlock further success.

At Milas-Bodrum Airport, I buy a fistful of biros and a lined notebook. On the crowded plane, I take my window seat in economy and crack open the first page, trying to recap exactly what Topi said. The nub of his message, I realise, was an insistence on resigning myself to my fate and the reality that I was going to be crushed by the pressure.

'LETTING GO = ACCEPTANCE' I write on the opening page.

But why is acceptance such a power move? On reflection, it doesn't strike me as the promising foundation for a high-performance mentality. The concept actually strikes me as somewhat defeatist; a passive form of surrender. Beyond 40 metres, the physical sensation of the pressure is awful. The weight of the water feels like it's going to rupture your eardrums and make your vital organs implode. No wonder I fight against it. It's horrible.

Yet I'm also voluntarily subjecting myself to the ordeal. Making the decision to accept the reality of that discomfort, I realise, doesn't mean you have to pretend it's pleasurable. Of course, you want to try and refine your technique and make any possible tweaks to make that pressure easier to bear. But acceptance means that you simply acknowledge what's happening without letting your emotions cloud the picture and exacerbate the situation.

Why have I been so resistant to this concept? Previously, I think I viewed acceptance as somehow being submissive. Resigning yourself to a bad situation runs counter to the idea of self-improvement and shuns the possibility that you can positively change your reality. Viewed from some angles, it looks suspiciously like giving up.

What I'm now starting to realise is that acceptance can be active and intentional. Rather than denying or avoiding your situation, acceptance requires you to face up to your present situation. Instead of recoiling from the ugly details, you have to summon the courage to eyeball them straight up. It's only then, when you consider the full picture, that you can truly assess your next best move.

'Acceptance does not mean settling,' I write in my notebook.
'Acceptance is facing up to the here and now with total clarity.'

At Istanbul's Atatürk Airport, I grab a coffee and then pace the duty-free aisles, keen to stretch my legs before the long-haul flight ahead. Wandering through the perfume stands and rows of booze and cigarettes, I barely take anything in, my mind preoccupied with the idea that's percolating in my head.

On the next leg to Hong Kong, I ignore the in-flight movies and go back to my notebook. Jotting down ideas, I'm trying to tease out why acceptance could be a performance-enhancing mindset when it comes to freediving. I realise that when I'm trying to go deep, trying to resist the pressure is a waste of time. Ultimately, I can't outwit the laws of gravity. Hydrostatic pressure is the force exerted by a liquid on an object and the further down you go, the greater the pressure of the water upon you. For a freediver, that sensation is unavoidable.

Thus far, I've been doing everything I can to defy that pressure. I grit my teeth against the pain, attempting to distract myself and put my mind in a happier place. Yet however hard I fight, the pressure will always be there. This is one battle that I can never win.

And the effort of all that resistance comes at a price. It costs me mental energy and robs me of peace as I get increasingly wound up that, despite all my efforts, I'm still being overwhelmed. As Topi bluntly put it, 'You're going to be crushed by the pressure. There is no escape.'

The upside of accepting that pressure is that it could help me to reduce the all-consuming stress as I dive. This could free up my mind, allowing me to think with more clarity and strategic nous. Instead of wasting time agonising over something that I can never beat, I can use that headspace to focus on my equalisation and ensure every muscle in my body is relaxed and free from stress. I can concentrate on making myself as comfortable as possible, despite the reality of my situation.

'Pick your battles,' I underline in my notebook. *'Resistance is futile.'*

At Hong Kong International Airport, the departures board delivers bad news. My flight to Auckland has been delayed by four hours due to a technical issue. Bloody hell. If this wasn't a long enough trip already, I'm going to be a jet-lagged mess by the time I finally get home. But then my new philosophy intervenes.

This situation is completely out of your control.

What can you do to make the most of it?

If I was sticking by Bodrum's time zone, it would be 4 am right now and I haven't slept a wink so far. I find a quiet corner of the airport that has semi-reclinable chairs. I pull up my hoodie and stick on my eye mask and take the opportunity to grab a few hours of much-needed kip.

I wake up slightly refreshed and after an aimless wander around duty free, wind up in a newsagent/bookshop. I've still got heaps of time to kill and I find myself flicking through a new-age, self-help book that unpacks a number of Buddhist parables. The intro to one chapter piques my interest; in fact, it seems bizarrely relevant to my current predicament.

The author writes that suffering is actually a form of craving. So when, for example, I'm 60 metres underwater – and suffering big time – what I'm craving is respite from the pressure that's crushing my body. Suffering is inevitable and resistance to it is the true source of human pain.

To illustrate the point, the author relates the story of an old monk who's out walking one day with his student when they come across a giant boulder. The old monk asks his student whether the boulder is heavy.

'Of course it's heavy,' the student replies.

'Only if you pick it up,' the monk says.

That same logic can be applied to freediving. If I attach myself to the discomfort I feel underwater, I'm allowing it to invade my body and mind. Instead, I need to let it wash over me and not engage. Essentially, I need to learn how to uncouple myself from the pressure and pain.

Engrossed, I keep flicking through the book and come across another parable that feels even more relevant. It tells of a high-powered business executive who goes to a Buddhist retreat and asks the abbot how long it will it take for him to achieve enlightenment. The abbot explains that he's asking the wrong question, but the CEO keeps pestering him.

'Maybe ten years,' the abbot eventually concedes.

'But what if I really throw myself into it and try really, really hard?' the executive says. 'How long will it take me to achieve enlightenment then?'

'Twenty years,' the abbot replies.

Relating this analogy to freediving is instructive. Trying to fight through the pain is ultimately counterproductive. As Topi said, the mental trick I have to master is learning how to let go. I need to accept that while I will suffer, I will also find my way through.

CHAPTER 13

Back in New Zealand, my 'let it be tough' mantra soon begins to pay off. Four months after returning from Turkey, I manage a static breath-hold of six minutes and nine seconds at the Philips Aquatic Centre in Mount Albert. Not only is the time a personal best, it's a national record, beating the previous one by almost a minute.

Gratifyingly, *The New Zealand Herald* deems my effort worth covering and sends out a young journalist to interview me. 'I got a bit cold towards the end and shivering uses up oxygen unnecessarily, but I hung in there and it feels wonderful,' I tell him.

Intriguingly, this mindset of radical acceptance is also helping me on dry land. Exasperated by the lack of sport psychology work in New Zealand, I've taken the gamble of setting up my own training company. My courses leverage my sport psychology background to run team-building activities for corporate retreats. Most of the physical challenges are enlivened with some element of low-level risk and include anything from mountain biking to whitewater rafting.

It's the first time I've run a solo venture and the learning curve is steep. Securing my first clients is a struggle, but I keep Topi's advice front of mind. Of course, launching a start-up business is always going to be tough in the early stages. That's part of the process that you have to go through.

After a couple of weeks of speculative pitches, I finally land New Zealand Home Loans as one of my first clients. The response to the training is good, but I'm constantly on the lookout for new business and am speculatively touting my services wherever I can. My success rate for my sales pitches is about one in 30. When a proposal is rebuffed, rather than taking it personally and getting emotional, I'm surprised to discover that I can accept the decision without getting upset. Pitching for new business will always involve rejection, I tell myself. Rather than waste my energy getting distressed, I dissect my presentation for flaws and request feedback on what I'd need to do to offer a more compelling proposition. Similarly, when I lose an existing client, rather than rage at the decision, I find that I can regroup quickly and regain my focus. Instead of wasting time blaming the client, I turn inwards to look at what I could have done better.

Just as I'm now willing to get crushed by the pressure at depth, I'm also now more open to sit with the discomfort of rejection and try to learn from the experience in a more rational way. Topi's words have given me better control over my emotional thermostat as well as my freediving.

As far as that goes, I can now go deeper and hold my breath for times that would have been unimaginable when I first started out. John is delighted with my continuing improvement, which he sees as a validation of his coaching methods.

'Reckon you might be about ready for some proper competition,' he says at our weekly eel-wrangling session.

The comment solidifies an idea that I've been toying with for some time. There's no doubt that I'm becoming a more experienced freediver, but my underlying aim at the outset was always to test and refine my skills with a view towards helping athletes and professionals to perform better in high-stakes scenarios. I want to be able to pass on the skills to help them handle pressure, bounce back from setbacks and mentally prepare for competition. In order to do that with credibility I also need to compete.

Landing at Larnaca International Airport in Cyprus the temperatures are already in the high 20s, despite it just being early summer. Through the window of the taxi, the countryside looks dry and barren with citrus groves wilting in dusty fields and olive vendors sheltering from the sun in ramshackle stalls by the side of the road.

I've travelled to Cyprus to compete in the Bios Freeology Open Classic 2004, a competition that's hosting more than a hundred of the world's top divers. After my difficulty getting into Rudi's master course, I'd assumed that taking part in an international diving competition would be complicated, with qualification rounds and other criteria to navigate. It was only when I began to explore how to enter that I realised just what a niche sport freediving actually is. The email I sent asking for entry requirements was met with an open invitation simply to come along and take part.

Online details about the competition are scant, so I haven't built up a clear picture of what to expect. All I really know is there are men and women competing from all over the world and most of them are staying at the same hotel in Limassol on Cyprus's southern coast. Segregated to compete by gender, we'll participate in three disciplines. The competition is set to open with the 'Dynamic' freediving event, where you have to try and swim as far as possible in an Olympic-sized pool on a single breath. Next is the Constant Weight competition, where you try to reach the maximum depth in the sea propelled by a monofin. Finally, we return to the pool for the 'static breath-hold', where, as the name suggests, you just lie face-down in the water and don't move for as long as you can bear it. My plan is to use this trip as a glorified scouting mission into the competitive dive scene and collect as much intel as I can, with a view to having a serious crack further down the line.

The official enrolment for the competition happens at my hotel. I fill in a couple of forms that absolve the organisers of any liability in the event of my untimely death. In return, I'm given a Bios Freeology Open Classic T-shirt with 'ATHLETE' on the back, an idea that seems utterly ludicrous. I've never thought of myself in this way before and hardly feel like I deserve the title.

As I'm walking out, I hear an Australian accent and, aware that I don't know a soul in Cyprus, introduce myself to a tall, dark-haired guy called Bruce Mitchell. Bruce is a friendly engineer from Melbourne whose familiarity with the logistics of competitive freediving suggests he's pretty experienced.

'Got your nomination in for tomorrow yet?' he asks me.

'Nomination for what?'

'For the Dynamic comp. They need your nominated distance for the seeding.'

Bruce, it turns out, mostly trains in the Dynamic discipline as he struggles to find calm, flat waters to practise his depth diving back home. It's clear that he's looking forward to the first event, but nominating a distance poses a dilemma for a rookie like me.

'So how do you decide what to nominate?' I ask.

'Just go off your best swim and base it around that,' he says. 'Although don't forget most people tense up a bit in competition, so you're probably best to err on the safe side.'

After checking into my modest hotel room, I give my nomination some thought. One time in training back in Auckland I managed three lengths underwater at the Olympic pool. Admittedly, that was a freak result by my standards and I've never achieved that distance since. Then again, it's not as though I practise this discipline much either and my breath-hold has substantially increased since then.

Mulling it over, I wonder if it's better to be conservative to avoid embarrassing myself. Then again, I have flown halfway around the world to compete in an international comp, so surely this is the time for me to back myself and go big. The more I think about it, the more sense that idea makes. I go down to the hotel foyer and fill in the form. For my nominated distance, I put 150 metres, before carefully folding the paper and jamming it into the ballot slot.

The next morning when I head downstairs for breakfast, there's a hubbub in the foyer. A small mob of people are craning their necks to look at a noticeboard. Judging by their deep tans, sun-bleached hair and athletic physiques, they must be my fellow competitors.

Edging closer to find out what's going on, I peer over a shoulder to view the board. The focus of all the attention is a long sheet of paper entitled 'Bios Freeology Open Classic: Dynamic Nominations'. On it is a long list with each participant's goal distance printed next to their names. The list starts with some divers nominating a single length of the pool – a relatively modest distance, I feel, given the stage. Most of the entries sit between 75 and 120 metres before the number dramatically thins out. At the bottom of the list are three very familiar names.

The first is the Venezuelan Carlos Coste, the reigning world champion and one of the only professional freedivers around. Sponsors have flocked to support him ever since he broke the world record in the 'free immersion' discipline, where divers descend and ascend along a vertical line, pulling themselves up without the use of fins.

The penultimate name on the list is even more high profile. Herbert Nitsch is an Austrian pilot and the most famous freediver on the planet, with 12 world records to his name. Back in New Zealand, John told me a story that shows what a formidable competitor

Herbert is. In 2003, he was attempting a record while struggling with a sinus infection that made it difficult to equalise. During his descent, his ears suddenly blocked up. Rather than turn back, he pushed on, ignoring the pain of a ruptured eardrum to collect the tag and complete the dive. Bald-headed and physically imposing, Herbert is the closest freediving comes to a genuine superstar.

Finally, my eyes dart to the bottom of the list.

The final line reads 'Anthony Williams (NZ): 150 metres'.

As I stare at the noticeboard, the words fill me with panic. Carlos, Herbert and I have all nominated the exact same length, which means we'll be competing head to head.

What on earth have I done?

Suddenly, I feel sick. I've clearly misjudged things big time and now there's no way to back out. In the world of competitive free-diving, I'm a nobody. But I've accidentally thrown down the gauntlet to take on the best in the world and it's all going to play out on a very public stage.

I quickly head back to my room. I need to process all this and calm down. Right now, I feel like I've been thrust into a real-life anxiety dream.

Waiting for the lift, I bump into Bruce Mitchell. He shakes his head when he sees me and lets out an exasperated sigh. His friendly tone from yesterday is gone. In fact, he seems affronted by my very presence. 'Mate, what's your problem?' he says.

'Eh? What do you mean?'

'I saw your number on the nomination board. Are you just showing off or something?'

Luckily, the lift arrives at my floor, allowing me to make a hasty escape. I shut the door to my room and start pacing, trying to shake out the anxiety gripping my body. Things have taken a bad turn.

This trip was meant to be a reconnaissance mission that would allow me to quietly suss out how things were done. Instead, I've accidentally drawn attention to myself in the most brazen way possible. It's like a rookie club tennis player challenging Roger Federer and Rafa Nadal to a public match at Rod Laver Arena. Yes, it was a naïve mistake. But judging by Bruce's reaction, it's being read as a display of arrogance designed to hijack attention and announce myself on the scene. If I can't back it up – and frankly, I'm really not sure that I can – it'll be even worse. I'm going to look like a delusional try-hard with ideas way beyond my station.

There's a knock on the door. When I open it, there's a TV crew with two cameramen standing in the corridor. 'Can we get an interview?' one of the guys says. 'We saw you're taking on Herbert and Carlos tomorrow. Everyone wants to know more about this mystery competitor. Right now, it's the talk of the island.'

Waving the TV crew away, I lie down on the bed and try to stop hyperventilating. This is very, very bad.

Most forms of freediving don't work as a spectator sport because cameras struggle to track a diver's efforts as they go deep. Dynamic freediving is different. Taking place in a swimming pool, only a metre beneath the surface, it's easy for a spectator to watch a diver's progress and how far they can swim. For me, that audience scrutiny isn't welcome here. In fact, it feels like a recipe for public humiliation.

Okay, enough hysteria: it's time to get rational. Let's deal with the fear of embarrassment first.

Yes, it's an international competition that will probably attract a fair old crowd. But while things kick off at 9 am, my time to compete isn't until 4 o'clock in the afternoon. The weather is hot and I'm guessing there's minimal shade available at the outside pool. People are unlikely to hang around all day. The Dynamic might be the most viewer-friendly format, but there's still a limit to how much you can watch in the baking sun. Surely, the crowds will disperse as the comp goes on.

Next up, let's tackle the performance anxiety. You're stressing out because you've never competed in an event of this scale before and now you've put yourself in direct competition with the big guns.

Feeling a bit nervous about that is understandable, particularly when this whole scenario is so unfamiliar. But I didn't pluck that 150-metre figure out of the air. That distance was an honest reflection of my personal best. What other people choose to nominate is up to them.

Forget the other people, mate, focus on yourself.

At the same time, Bruce Mitchell's reaction to my proposed distance has turbo-charged my self-doubt. Frankly, I don't know why it riled him up so much. But I guess that if a total newbie strolls in and nominates a length that exceeds your own, then it does belittle your efforts.

Except you weren't trying to be cocky. You chose 150 metres purely based on Bruce's advice to use your personal best as a competitive yardstick.

The best response now is to go out there and nail it.

Can you really manage that, though?

I didn't achieve that distance in the heat of competition. Plus, there's no doubt that adrenaline does impact freediving by increasing your heart rate and accelerating oxygen depletion. Viewed from that angle, trying to replicate my PB in front of a crowd, coupled with the pressure of being up against the world's best, does make my 150-metre target seem ambitious. But that's the situation now. The question is how do I deal with it?

Let's start by thinking back to that PB in the Auckland pool. What were the circumstances that may've contributed to your performance?

Looking back, what I remember is that I'd had a big presentation for work the morning of that attempt. I'd been up half the night preparing for it and had only snatched about four hours' sleep before showing up to train with John. Maybe that fatigue actually helped me? When I'm really tired, everything slows down and I become more lethargic and withdrawn. Perhaps that exhausted mindset makes it easier to slip into the trance-like state I need to dissociate from the lack of oxygen in the pool. Either way, it's worth giving it a go. Tonight, I'll only sleep four hours max.

In the meantime, ignore the external noise. Don't let the likes of Bruce Mitchell psych you out and feed your doubt. Keep a low profile until the competition tomorrow. Concentrate on your preparation and zero in on the factors you can actually control.

The next day, I get to the pool an hour before my scheduled attempt – I don't want to leave too much time for my anxiety to fester. It's 30°C and the heat is bouncing off the concrete. Down one side of the pool there are shaded bleachers packed with far more spectators than I'd expected. There must be at least 150 people here.

I'm wearing sunglasses, a hat and headphones. Ostensibly, it's to blot out the distractions and allow myself to get in the zone. But it's also to deter people from approaching me. Yesterday's TV crew confirmed that I've attracted a disproportionate amount of attention. I don't want anyone else to come up and talk to me and tell me I'm a fucking idiot for attempting this distance. That much I already figured out myself.

On the microphone, an American MC is doing his best to whip up the crowd. 'Get ready, ladies and gents! In just 20 minutes, Herbert Nitsch – the world record holder in the Dynamic, with a distance of 183 metres – will be facing off against New Zealander Anthony Williams, who's shaping up to be a dark horse in the competition. They'll be in action very soon.'

I'm nervously fiddling about, double-checking my goggles, fins and nose clip. Then Herbert strolls past me as cool as a breeze. I've never seen him before in the flesh and my first impressions are not encouraging. Physically imposing, the Austrian is tall and muscular, parading alongside the pool, shirtless in a black pair of Speedos. His bald head somehow makes him look even more streamlined. His gear is intimidating, too. Under his arm, he's carrying a purpose-built monofin that looks like a cross between a piece of NASA equipment and the wing of a stealth fighter jet. Disconsolately, I look down at my own makeshift effort. It's been superglued together with foot pockets from some bi-fins and a monofin blade that a friend of a friend had fashioned himself. Herbert also has some weird black device hanging around his neck that I've never seen before.

'What is that thing?' I ask a nearby official.

'Herbert's personal invention. It's a tyre tube filled with 8 kilograms of lead shot.'

'What's the idea behind it?'

'It's to stop him from floating to the surface. When he inflates those massive lungs of his, he'll become really buoyant. The weight of that thing around his neck neutralises his body weight in the water so he can swim faster and more efficiently. It adds a bit of extra momentum, so every time he kicks, he glides a little bit further.'

'Pretty smart.'

'And you see that fin of his? He had it specially made in the Ukraine. Apparently it cost him $2500.'

For the contest, it's just Herbert and me in the pool. I'm in lane one, closest to the crowd. Herbert's at the other side of the pool in lane eight. We get into the water at the deep end, where a chair has been placed on the bottom to enable each of us to stand.

'Okay, everyone, quiet please for the last swim of the day,' calls the announcer. 'We'll start the two minute countdown now.'

I put on my goggles and nose clip. This ritualised action serves as my mental cue to get into character and become an athlete. It's the switch that tells my body it's time to perform. And suddenly

I do actually feel calmer and more capable. Packing air into my lungs, I just want to get started.

The siren goes and I push off into the lightly chlorinated water. I'm using this kick/glide technique that I haven't seen anyone else utilise, my monofin undulating like a dolphin's tail, my arms outstretched in front of me to keep a streamlined position. I'm happy with my initial progress and feeling good, but the discomfort starts to build around the 35- to 40-metre mark. That's a shock. Normally in training, I don't get that feeling until 60 metres at least.

Stay calm. That's just the pressure from competition. Relax.

The pep talk doesn't help. When I touch the end of the pool at 50 metres for my tumble turn, I'm not feeling good and the self-doubt builds. At 60 metres, I start getting involuntary contractions in my throat, my Adam's apple bucking downwards to try and bring in air. At 80 metres, my diaphragm starts quaking in a really powerful contraction. My brain thinks I'm in trouble.

Be cool – this is just the transition. Your blood is shifting, your spleen contracting, it's just the dive reflex kicking in. Keep going.

Approaching 100 metres, I feel like I've got an eternity still to go. This is really bad. But through my peripheral vision, I get the sense that Herbert is turning, too.

Hang in there, mate. Win or bin. You've got to make 150.

My throat is gyrating. Violent sensations wrench my chest.

Just tough it out. Accept the pain. Let go.

I must be near the home stretch now. I'm dimly aware of the cheering crowd. The end is in sight . . . I can see a blurred view of the wall. The lane ropes above.

Don't stop. Attack the wall!

I'm finally there. I can finally surface, but just then I make an impulsive decision to chuck in a turn. I touch the wall, kick off again and, despite my screaming lungs, it's like I'm propelled by a final burst of desperate effort. Then I crash through the surface into the noise of the crowd. Gasping for breath, I pass the safety protocol. The judge reads my distance: I've done 169 metres!

Over on the other side of the pool, Herbert has pipped me, but not by much – his final distance is 173 metres. But I don't care that I'm beaten. I'm overcome with delight that I haven't humiliated myself and proud that I dared to set myself a big goal and managed to chase it down. I've shown the naysayers that I'm not just some hairy-arsed chancer; I've come here to actually compete.

CHAPTER 14

The next morning when I wake up I'm still buzzing. To give the competitors a chance to regroup, there are no events scheduled today. It's the first time I've had to enjoy the island without the looming pressure of competition. At breakfast, I no longer feel like I have to keep an apologetically low profile and get chatting to a friendly bunch of Swedes, who invite me to come out with them to have a practice dive that afternoon.

Perfect weather only adds to my happy mood. Sunshine bounces off the turquoise water and there's a holiday vibe on the boat, with plenty of laughter and piss-taking. Tomorrow is the Constant Weight discipline where divers must descend and ascend using only a monofin. The consensus is we'll have a gentle practice session this afternoon along those lines.

I decide I'm just going to dive to 50 metres – a depth I've managed many times before. But I'm in such a relaxed state during the dive that I keep going, until my watch notifies me that I've made it to *68 metres*. It's a new PB and I've nailed it with relative ease. Privately, I'm delighted by the achievement. It's like the Mediterranean sun has somehow allowed me to raise my game.

On the way back to shore, I detach myself from the group, who are now playing a raucous game of cards while a CD player blares Europop anthems. I lie down at the back of the boat to soak up the sun, but beneath my sunglasses I'm trying to analyse why I'm now hitting this unusual run of form.

Relaxation, I decide, is everything in this sport. It directly influences your performance by having a positive impact on your breath-hold duration and overall safety. When your body doesn't have to fight tension it uses less oxygen, lowers your heart rate, and reduces that panicky mindset where you feel desperate to breathe. Mentally, it also frees you up, giving you more cerebral room to focus on equalising and taking care of business.

Back at the hotel, we have to nominate our proposed depth for the next day's competition. Given how the Dynamic played out and on the back of today's effort, once again I see no point in playing it safe and settle on a depth of 70 metres. It's by no means one of the most ambitious depths. The rumour that's circulating is that the top divers, Herbert, Carlos and Martin Štěpánek from Czechoslovakia, are all duking it out for the honour of becoming the first man in history to make it past 100 metres in the discipline.

Once again, some people are quick to criticise my decision to pitch for 70 metres. In the hotel foyer, after the nominations are revealed, people crowd around the noticeboard to scrutinise each diver's predictions. Afterwards, Bill Stromberg, a highly respected veteran from Sweden, introduces himself.

'Have you done this dive depth before?' he asks me in his stern Nordic accent.

'No, mate,' I grin. 'I absolutely haven't.'

'Well then, I have to say that I think this is just foolish behaviour. Not only are you are in danger of killing yourself, you could create all sorts of issues for the safety crew.'

'Okay, well thanks for your concern, I guess.' Bill walks off, shaking his head at my naïveté.

I'm mildly annoyed at all this interference and the way some people feel entitled to question my depth. Purportedly, their objection comes down to safety concerns, but I sense something else is going on. I suspect that my status as a newcomer is confronting to some of the more experienced divers. If a rookie beats them in his very first comp, that doesn't reflect well on their ability. My willingness to have a go and show a bit of ambition is a threat to their own self-regard.

Pondering this, I return to the noticeboard to check Bill's own nominated depth. Lo and behold, it turns out to be 10 metres less than my own.

For the Constant Weight discipline, the divers are competing over three days, with your allocation loosely based around your targeted depth. My nomination of 70 metres has me competing on the second day, giving me some time to rest and prepare. The final day is reserved for the three hotshots bidding to become the first divers to break the 100-metre barrier in Constant Weight. Herbert Nitsch and Carlos Coste are both gunning for 102 metres, while Martin Štěpánek is attempting to go one better with 103 metres.

Waking up on the day of my dive, I look out the window to see the weather has changed, with a brisk offshore wind ruffling the palm trees. I get myself down to the jetty, where a boat is transporting competitors out to an enormous barge platform. It's anchored about 2 kilometres off the coast, where the water suddenly deepens. Standing around, waiting for our ride, the mood is strained. Many freedivers like to retreat into their own mental zones prior to competing. As they wait around on the dock, most seem to be silently turning their gaze inwards while taking the occasional sidelong glance to size up the competition.

The tension mounts when we board the boat. On the water, the winds strengthen to stir up whitecaps on the choppy waves. Freediving in water like this is significantly more demanding, as it causes the guide rope to run at an angle, forcing a diver to swim further to make their distance. Significantly, this also makes your ascent tougher as you have to fight the current at a point when you're starved of oxygen and where any obstacle becomes disproportionately challenging.

Watching the other divers, I can see they're not happy about the conditions. But while they're far from ideal, I feel comparatively relaxed. While nearly all these divers are more accomplished than me, most live in Europe where they're used to diving in calm, warm waters. I've honed my skills in the chilly gloom of New Zealand. I've been on a few diving trips to the Poor Knights Islands off the Tutukaka Coast, where you always face plenty of swell, wind and rain. Lake Pupuke can also throw up its own challenges. Yes, the weather is a bit windy here, but at least there aren't any eels.

Walking around the boat, I spot Jean Huysmans, a veteran French freediver who's also nominated 70 metres today, the same distance as me. Jean's standing at the side of the boat looking out at the sea with a grim expression on his face. Figuring our common goal provides something of an ice-breaker, I wander over.

'G'day, Jean, I'm Ant Williams, I just wanted to say hello. I saw we're both pushing for 70 metres today. Good luck with your dive. How are you feeling?'

Jean practically winces and returns my gaze with palpable reluctance. He looks miserable. 'Look, man, nothing personal but the truth is I'm freaking out that you are here right now,' he says. 'As if there wasn't enough pressure. Now I've got a newcomer competing against me and going to the very same depth . . .' With an audible sigh, Jean turns to face the sea again.

I walk away feeling a little sheepish that my friendly approach backfired. This freediving lot can be a tough crowd. But the encounter has also buoyed my confidence. Some of these hardened veterans are clearly struggling to deal with the strain. Perversely, that makes me feel calmer and more in control.

By the time our boat arrives, the barge platform is lurching up and down on the waves. I'm keen to get into the water soon to stave off the possibility of getting seasick. All up, there are eight men competing in this session. Joseph Tufts, a photogenic American who's starring in a big freediving documentary next year, is aiming for 61 metres. Three of us are targeting 70 metres, while the remainder are attempting depths between 74 and 84 metres.

Maybe it's the trickiness of the conditions or the pressure of competition, but the overall success rate is low, with only three of the divers achieving their goals. Jean is one of the unlucky ones and blacks out. After he surfaces, safety divers crowd his limp body, blowing on his face and saying his name repeatedly until he coughs, splutters and jerks back to consciousness. Somehow, I still feel unusually calm.

You know what to expect, Ant. You know it's going to be brutal, you know that you're going to be crushed. Let go and accept it. Just get it done.

Four minutes later I surface with the 70-metre tag in my hand. Dazzled by the sunlight, I flash the okay sign and take a second to compose myself before offering the verbal confirmation the safety protocol requires. 'I'm okay,' I say a little breathlessly at last. But I'm way better than that. I've just pulled off the deepest dive of my life.

I sit with my legs dangling over the edge of the bobbing platform and watch my fellow competitors – hardened divers with track records that intimidated me three days ago – struggle to hold it together. Bruce Mitchell, the Aussie I chatted to at registration, blacks out attempting his 75-metre dive, while Ryuzo Shinomiya from Japan is disqualified after failing the safety protocol. By the end, of the eight divers competing today, only one posts a higher score than me – a Finn by the name of Timo Kinnunen who managed 80 metres.

On the boat on the way back to shore, many of the divers sit alone in silence. The atmosphere is glum, with some divers still feeling a bit fragile after their blackouts. Sitting in a corner, meanwhile, I'm in a private bubble of delight. I've nailed 70 metres, I've stepped up to the challenge, and this is just my first competition.

Timo Kinnunen sits down next to me and, mindful that most people don't have much to celebrate, we quietly congratulate each other and talk through our dives.

'After what you did in the Dynamic, you're in a good position, no?' he says. 'You do well in the static breath-hold, maybe a podium finish?'

'Don't know about that, but I'm pretty happy today.'

But as the boat chunters home, I realise that what Timo said is true. Even if all the top divers achieve their depths tomorrow, I'll still have done the fifth best dive in Constant Weight. Added to my second-placed finish in the Dynamic, my total points tally must put me among the front-runners. I don't expect to win, of course, but that's not the point. My trip to Cyprus was intended as a glorified scouting mission to see what I needed to do to become an elite freediver. But things have changed now and I have to recognise my opportunity. I'm not just here to make up the numbers, I'm now a genuine contender. This could be my big chance to announce my arrival on the freediving scene.

Two days later, I scuttle my chances.

I've told the judges I'm going to attempt to hold my breath for six minutes. It's an ambitious target to shoot for in competitive circumstances, with only two divers going for longer – Herbert Nitsch is targeting seven minutes, while Timo is pushing for 7 minutes 30 seconds. To put my nomination into context, Carlos Coste, who yesterday broke the world record for Constant Weight by reaching a phenomenal depth of 102 metres, is trying for 5 minutes 30 seconds. Nevertheless, I feel like it's worth going big. I've already placed second in the Dynamic and fifth in the Constant Weight. If I can manage six minutes in the static breath-hold, then I'm guaranteed a top three finish.

Unlike the last two events, I'm also not shooting to break new ground. I've done a static breath-hold of six minutes nine seconds before, when I clinched the New Zealand record. Since then, I've only become more experienced and further developed my lung capacity. On paper, I'm confident that I can pull this off.

The competition takes place at the hotel pool. Each diver will attempt their breath-hold one by one, accompanied by an official who stands by your side as a safety precaution. At some pre-agreed point – usually about two-thirds of the way through your designated time – the official will start tapping your shoulder every 15 seconds. You need to respond with a signal like a raised finger or an okay sign to demonstrate that you're still conscious and haven't blacked out. If you fail to reply, the official will tap again, but if that still fails to elicit a reaction, the official will roll you over and bring you up for air.

If that happens, you're automatically disqualified.

For a freediver, there are two stages to a static breath-hold attempt: the easy phase and the struggle phase. The first couple of minutes should be fairly straightforward, but, for me at least, things usually start becoming tough around the four-minute mark. That's when you're seized by a ferocious urge to breathe as the CO_2 buildup triggers your body's internal systems in a desperate attempt to try to bring in air. At this point, the involuntary contractions begin. After that, the breath-hold becomes a battle of endurance as you fight to hang on as long as you can.

I slide into the pool wearing boardshorts and a short-sleeved, thin wetsuit top. The weather is still warm, but I need to make sure that my body temperature doesn't drop too much as shivering uses up more oxygen. Pulling on my goggles and nose clip, I'm fixated on my time. Six minutes is just 360 seconds and I've proven I can manage that before. Now it's just a case of rinse and repeat.

During the countdown, I float on my back, staring at the white ceiling. The official, an avuncular American with a grey moustache,

Credit: supplied

Mark Willis in a MotoGP race in Europe, 2000.

Credit: supplied

The Spa-Francorchamps 24-hour endurance race in Belgium, racing with France Yamaha. Rider swap and refuelling with teammate Jean-Marc Delétang after midnight (2000).

Credit: Andy Ross (diving partner)

Pre-training swim with dolphins in Kona, Hawaii, the day before the USA Freediving Championship (2006).

In full control before surfacing after a competition dive to 95 metres (312 feet) in Dean's Blue Hole, Bahamas (2019).

Credit: supplied

Credit: supplied

Surface celebrations after a tough, deep and terrifying clean dive to 100 metres (330 feet) in Dean's Blue Hole, Bahamas (2019).

Credit: David Peart

Pool competition countdown. This is where I learned how to perform under pressure.

Credit: supplied

Meeting Hawaiian Laird Hamilton in New Zealand. A hero whose advice that day set me on a different trajectory in freediving – away from competition and towards ice diving.

First dive under ice to 10 metres (33 feet). I was suffering through the cold, dark, foreboding water in a rented scuba suit (2018).

Credit: Alex Voyer

Credit: Jonathan Sunnex (diving partner)

Acclimatising to the cold in the crystal-clear waters of Lake Sonnanen, Finland for the Kirkenes world record ice dive attempt (2019).

Credit: Yngve Gronkvik

Time minus three minutes before a world record attempt. It is a formidable mental challenge to stay calm, relaxed and focused before an ice-dive world record.

Credit: Jonathan Sunnex (diving partner)

Celebrating a successful world-record dive with ice-diving expert and freediving athlete Antero Joki.

Credit: Adam Stern (diving partner)

Diving in a Mount Gambier sinkhole in South Australia. It is a place to learn to settle, adapt and integrate into an alien environment.

Credit: Adam Stern (diving partner)

Another dive in a Mount Gambier sinkhole in South Australia. It is a place to explore without restraint, expectation or pressure.

Credit: supplied

On the way to a training dive with Danny Hurst in Torquay, Victoria. One of us is enjoying the ride. The other is quietly preparing for the dive.

yells, 'Time!' Then I roll over face-down in the water, my eyes closed, my body splayed like a dead man.

At first, I let myself simply adjust to the moment and focus on the sensory conditions of being underwater. The muffled quietness as the outside world fades into a soft, distant hum. There's the occasional echo as fragments of voices from the surface mutate and distort in the water. I savour the feeling of weightlessness. Notice the chlorine tang of the water and how its temperature is a little warmer than expected. Mostly though, I try to zone out and disengage from conscious thought.

I'm surprised when my stomach abruptly lurches into a convulsion. That's much earlier than expected and not a good sign. I'm pretty sure that I'm barely halfway through. What the hell? And all at once, the doubts begin to swarm in my head.

Something is wrong. You didn't take in enough air. The pool water is too warm. You can't have trained properly or you wouldn't be in this mess . . .

No! Don't catastrophise. Remember what a good performance looks like here. You need to stay calm and relaxed. The contractions are just part of the process. Your body is just switching gears, the discomfort is stimulating your mammalian dive reflex, it's part of the process.

But with the static breath-hold, unlike other disciplines, there's no activity to focus on to distract yourself from the discomfort. I can't stop thinking about the time and how disturbingly tough I'm finding it already.

Six minutes! You have to hang on for six minutes. But you haven't even had the four-minute shoulder tap yet. That means there's an age still to go . . .

I need to put my mind elsewhere, shift my concentration from the voice that's yelping in my head, pleading with me to give up and breathe. I try using the throb of my heartbeat as a metronome, counting very slowly up to ten, allocating five heartbeats per count.

At ten, I begin again and start the count. Finally, I get the tap on my shoulder, alerting me that four minutes have elapsed.

Thank God for that! Two minutes to go now, just 120 seconds . . .

Things are getting really gnarly now, the diaphragmatic spasms intensifying. Again, I try to dissociate, mentally tracking the sounds around me from the furthest away to the closest and then back again.

Another tap on my shoulder. That's four minutes, 15 seconds.

My mind is racing now, body on the edge of panic, imploring me to end this ordeal. To just turn to the surface and take a fucking breath.

Stay calm, get a grip. This is just a game. You'll be okay. You've done this before. Ride through the discomfort.

Four minutes, 30 seconds.

This is torture. I can feel a tightness in my chest, the gruesome squeeze in my lungs and blood vessels as they react to the lack of oxygen.

Hang in there, Ant. Submit to the pain, let it happen. Relax. You just need to tough it out for 90 seconds and a podium finish is yours.

Four minutes, 45 seconds.

I can feel a numbness in my fingers, a tingling in my face. That's hypoxia – or lack of oxygen – kicking in. Surely, we must've hit five minutes by now? This feels horrific.

Ignore it! Your body is just trying to psych you out. Your brain is the boss here, it controls what happens. Do not give up . . .

The final minute is a frantic blur of confusion and pain. My thoughts are foggy: how long do I have left again? Is my brain shutting down from lack of oxygen? The pressure in my head and neck is grotesque. Muscles in my upper body are cramping.

Five minutes, 15 seconds.

I'm not sure if I can hang on. I try to scan my body and relax each muscle, but I can't ignore the discomfort.

Six minutes. You've done it before. Dig in!

Five minutes, 30 seconds.

I'm at breaking point now, white-knuckling every second. My head throbs wildly, the contractions now berserk.

Five minutes, 45 seconds.

The reverberations of my heart pound through every inch of my body. My eyes are shut, but the darkness is now growing heavier, the noise of the pool becoming more distant. It's like a dimmer switch is being turned inside my head, fading everything to black.

There's a tap on my shoulder. I stand up and gasp in the bright light. I can't focus. The world is a fuzzy outline in black and white. I spin giddily, my balance has gone . . .

When I come back around, the official is cradling my head.

'Anthony? Breathe, Anthony. C'mon, man, breathe!'

'What happened?'

'Loss of motor control. You blacked out.'

'So does that mean . . .'

The American gives me a resigned smile. 'Yeah, a blackout means you're disqualified. Sorry, man. Just take it easy for a minute now. You're okay.'

A couple of minutes later, physically I'm fine, but mentally it's a whole other story. Disqualification means my podium hopes are over. I did all the hard stuff only to choke at the final hurdle.

The disappointment is gut-wrenching. That was my big moment and I simply couldn't handle the pressure. Getting out of the pool, I don't want to talk to anyone. I'm too full of rage and self-disgust at letting myself down and screwing up my opportunity. Hastily gathering my things I storm off, not yet ready to force a smile through the well-meaning commiserations that will surely follow.

CHAPTER 15

Back in my hotel room, I'm boiling with anger and self-loathing. My breath-hold attempt keeps replaying over and over on a torturous loop in my mind. I know it's a disproportionate reaction, but I can't seem to let it go.

I think of all the money I've spent to get here. The months of training. The opportunity I'd worked so hard to carve out. The reputation I'd started to build among my freediving peers. I've just ruined all of that, simply because I couldn't do the basics.

Lying on my bed, I try to distract myself from the gnawing disappointment that sits in my gut like a stone. Idly, I turn on the TV. Cyprus are playing in some international football match, but it's like it's being played on a different planet. I stare at the screen blankly without processing a single kick.

I feel humiliated by my blackout and it's severely dented my pride. Posting bold targets in the previous two disciplines clearly unnerved some of my rivals. They thought it was a cocky show of bravado that I couldn't hope to back up, that I was overestimating my ability in a dangerous way. I'd proved them wrong with my performances in the Dynamic and Constant Weight events. The satisfaction of those achievements was immense.

Now I've vindicated my critics' knee-jerk opinions and shown they were right all along. And the worst part is that my opponents didn't beat me today, I lost to myself. The static breath-hold is the discipline that revolves around mental fitness. I'm meant to be a sport psychologist, for God's sake, but I couldn't stop my mind from wrecking my efforts. That realisation is cruel and it hurts.

I'm not leaving Cyprus until tomorrow, but I decide to start packing all the same. I need some activity, any activity, to steer my thoughts away from my failure. I stuff my dirty laundry into a bag, sort my diving kit into another, but my mind keeps circling back to the pool. By the time my suitcase is half full I've started to calm down, my fury curdling into a state of bleak disappointment. There's no hiding away from this failure, so I might as well confront it head-on.

If I was working with a professional athlete in this scenario, I'd analyse everything that happened over these five days of competition and conduct a detailed post-mortem, breaking down the good, the bad and the ugly, while trying to ascertain the one percenters that separated them. I might as well get this over with. I sit down at the desk and take out my notebook.

Let's start with today's fiasco. Physically I was well prepared, but what happened, I now suspect, is that I became fixated on my six-minute target to an unhelpful degree.

What's tricky about the static breath-hold is that there's no activity to distract you from the discomfort. You can't focus on your swimming stroke or keeping your kick nice and fluid. That lack of diversion means you become painfully aware of the overwhelming urge to breathe that cranks up with every passing second.

The best tactic is to plug your mind into a meditative zone where you're not thinking about anything. You try not to engage with the flow of thoughts and ideas that gatecrash your brain. Instead you just stay present in the moment without judgement, experiencing and accepting the discomfort as part of the deal.

Today, I didn't do that. Obsessed with nailing six minutes, I was consciously monitoring the elapsing time, thereby reminding myself of my body's mounting state of oxygen starvation almost non-stop. That was a bad move that only made the time and discomfort feel longer than ever. While I pushed myself to the limit, I sabotaged my efforts by not focusing on the right things. I needed to concentrate on emptying my mind, not counting down the seconds.

On a brighter note, the highlight of the competition for me was the Constant Weight, where I nailed my 70-metre target in tricky conditions that caused far more seasoned divers to come unstuck. Mentally, what did I do right?

Looking back on it, the main thing was that I went into that dive feeling strangely relaxed. My confidence was high on the back of my performance in the Dynamic, but had been further bolstered by how I'd got on while practising with the Swedes the previous day. The upshot was that I felt happy, confident and backed myself to deliver. Self-belief is crucial to perform in any venture. The conviction that you will prevail feeds your internal narrative in a positive way. It makes it easier to persist through challenges by turning each obstacle into a manageable stepping stone that you skip along on the way to your goal.

That self-confidence was amplified by the jitters of my competitors on the boat. I watched far more experienced and accomplished divers than me get psyched out by the choppy conditions. Others were clearly bothered by my presence as a newbie and the fact that, given I was attempting similar depths to them, I could potentially show them up. Some of the divers were unable to handle that extra pressure and mentally defeated themselves before they even got in the water.

I start jotting down some notes.

When people struggle under pressure, it's rarely the actual situation that's to blame. Instead, it's what that moment represents to them. The reaction is shaped by an earlier experience or belief that is encoded in their mind at a deeper level.

In Jean's case, he understandably had a high opinion of himself as a freediver on the back of his years of experience. The possibility of being shown up by me, a rookie, preyed on his mind. It created a fatal distraction from what he set out do.

In high-pressure situations, most people think they're deciding their fate by what they do in the moment. But in truth, they've already made their move long before – by how they've rehearsed it, visualised it, or calibrated their mindset.

What all this means in terms of performance is that the 'moment of truth' is not actually what you think it is. In a penalty shootout, it's not the second that your foot connects with the ball. If you're giving a keynote speech, it's not when you open on your mouth while standing at the lectern.

Your success is effectively preordained by how you master the buildup to it.

More specifically, it's about knowing what things are likely to derail you when you have to act. Most people avoid thinking about those triggers. But if you can anticipate what those mental saboteurs might be and understand the negative responses they'll elicit, you can figure out ways to outwit and ultimately master them. The right preparation empowers you to replace that default reaction with a more effective response.

If Jean Huysmans had known in advance that he'd be fazed by the blustery weather, he could have taken measures to counter it. Perhaps he could have practised diving in rougher waters until it was no longer such an issue. If he'd known the presence of his competitors had the potential to unnerve him, he could have prepared for that eventuality by finding a quiet corner and putting on headphones to block out the external noise. Instead of being a victim to the circumstances, he could have found a way to work around them.

In my notebook, I try to wrestle these ideas into a more coherent form. Picking up my pen I write:

> *If the moment of peak pressure is Time (T), then T-1 refers to the moments directly before the action.*
>
> *This lead-up period is critical because that's when emotion takes over, stress narrows your thinking and unhelpful thought patterns ('I'm out of my depth!', 'I'm under-trained!') can cloud your judgement and eat away at your confidence.*
>
> *What you do in T-1 therefore ultimately determines your success in Time.*
>
> *During that prelude to the main event, you can default to a fear-based response, freak out and shrink away from the challenge. Or you can treat those final moments as the launchpad for your success by physically resetting, reframing your mindset, and switching into a performance-ready state.*
>
> *Mastering T-1 is therefore the key to building mental fitness. Refining the techniques of how to deal with this vital period can unlock your ability to stay grounded and calm under pressure, laying the foundations for you to excel.*
>
> *To become a better freediver, I shouldn't just focus on the dive. What I need to focus on are the moments* before *the dive.*

Reading back through my notes, I feel like there's the kernel of an idea here that could help me in the future – if I can get it right. Right now, though, it doesn't bring much comfort. I clap my notebook shut and sigh. This theorising is all very well, but I just wish I could've figured it out before I jumped in the pool for that breath-hold. Still, that's the problem with epiphanies – they don't have any respect for punctuality. (See page 288 for a QR code to find your mental fitness score.)

CHAPTER 16

Approaching my rented apartment in Manly in Sydney's north, I loosen my tie and sit down on a bench to take a moment to try to get my head straight. I let out a sigh that's a mix of tiredness and exasperation. It's been one hell of a day.

Merryn and I relocated to Sydney at the end of 2006 along with Luc, our one-year-old son. The move was intended to expand my career horizons. Back in New Zealand, my training company was going okay, but I felt like I'd hit a ceiling. While I'd received good feedback, I was increasingly being asked by clients to run corporate workshops. The demand was clearly there, but I knew that I lacked the experience in the business world to do it properly. In order to improve these skills, I made the decision to find work with the best corporate trainers around, with a view to applying them to my own business down the track. That led me to accept a managerial role at a large multinational consultancy firm, where I'm now responsible for designing and delivering internal training programs.

The logic behind the move was fairly sound, but now I feel like I've made a mistake. Walking into the office each day it's like I'm entering a high-stress world where I'm constantly on edge; a state of affairs that largely stems from my boss. Difficult and erratic, she delights at pouncing on the slightest error. Any encounter with her always simmers with the potential to erupt.

In response, I've become hypervigilant and find myself permanently monitoring my boss's mood swings, second-guessing everything from the wording of an email to the layout of a PowerPoint deck. Her feedback is wielded as a sharp weapon designed to keep me off-balance with knee-jerk criticisms that undermine my confidence. For the first time in my life, I'm being driven to keep a neurotic paper trail of emails and meeting notes, largely to protect my own sensc of reality.

Exacerbating all this is the fact that I've just moved my wife and infant son to a new country where we have no family support or social network to fall back on. Mercifully, Luc is a wonderful kid, but he's still a one year old who wakes constantly during the night and requires 24/7 care and attention.

I'm now mired in the situation that many new parents face: caught between work responsibilities and domestic duties. My boss scowls at me when I leave the office each day at 5.15 pm, which she considers to be indecently early and another sign of my lack of commitment. Yet I'm compelled to go, because I need to help Merryn after another non-stop day of toddler wrangling, plus I'm desperate to see Luc before he goes to bed. I feel like I'm in a lose/lose scenario: either I disappoint my boss or let down my wife.

Today did not go well. My boss marched me into her office for another dressing-down, where she berated me for 30 minutes because I'd sent an internal email that got the recipient's job title slightly wrong.

'How did this happen, Anthony? How is this even possible that you've made such a fundamental mistake? How did you not know?' she thundered. 'This is so embarrassing for the department and all the staff. You need to bring your team into line, sit them down and figure out how this blunder occurred. Report back to me on it immediately!'

Somehow I bit my tongue and managed to prevent it from escalating into a bigger showdown. But now I can feel the frustration and resentment smouldering inside of me. My left eye is twitching with stress and all I want to do is go and smash the shit out of a punchbag or neck half-a-dozen beers.

I'm aware that I need to stop this corrosive energy from the office infecting my home life. When I'm on edge it's all too easy to snap at Merryn or fail to be present with Luc because my head is still replaying my latest evisceration at work.

In an effort to stop this toxic transference, I've begun applying the T-1 principle at home. In order to show up and be a good father and husband, I have to find a way to park this negative spill-over and change my mindset from 'work mode' to 'dad mode'. I'm learning that what determines my behaviour at home is how I prepare and set my intentions before I walk in the door. To perform well as a freediver, I don't just concentrate on the dive itself; I focus on the moments *before* the dive. The same wisdom, I've decided, also applies at home.

That's why sitting on this bench, I now take a moment to change my breathing, slowing down the rate to four deep inhalations and exhalations every minute. Meanwhile I do a quick body scan from my head to my toes and focus on releasing the knots of tension bunched in my shoulders and neck. I unfurrow my crinkled brow and force myself to smile.

After a couple of minutes of this, I walk up the street to my apartment. Luc is standing on a chair waiting at the window and when he sees me his little face lights up. By the time I open the door he's almost shaking with delight as he charges into my arms smearing jam down the front of my shirt. He burrows his head in my neck for a sticky hug and I catch a faint waft of Play-Doh and warm milk. In my current state of fragility, it's the most wonderful smell in the world. (See page 288 for a QR code that will take you to a video on correct breathing techniques.)

Despite this frenetic juggling act, I'm still obsessed with freediving as is clear from the name of my son. His full moniker is Luc Enzo

Williams, the 'Luc' coming from Luc Besson, the director of *The Big Blue*, while 'Enzo' is the name of legendary Italian freediver Enzo Maiorca, who set 17 world records, and was fictionalised in Besson's cult film.

While finding the time to dive is now trickier, I'm lucky that Merryn knows how important it is to me and appreciates that free-diving has become my pressure-release valve from the strain of work. Ever since competing in Cyprus, I've become fixated on trying to break the world record in the Dynamic discipline, where you swim as far as you can on a single breath. The idea of clinching that record – which currently stands at 225 metres – isn't too far-fetched either and, just before we moved to Sydney, I came agonisingly close.

I'd trained hard for the attempt and organised for international judges to come to Auckland to verify my effort. At the West Wave pool, I felt like I was gliding through the water for the first 150 metres and still had something in the tank when I hit the wall to turn at 200 metres. At that point, I'd calculated that I only needed to complete seven good kicks to pass the world record distance. I thought I'd executed that plan flawlessly and came up to the surface to pass the safety protocol with minimal fuss, only to find the judges staring at me in utter bewilderment. Somehow I'd misjudged the distance, coming up *2 metres shy* of the world record.

Despite that disappointment, there's no doubt that my progress as a freediver has accelerated. I put that squarely down to two things: first, applying the T-1 principle to my preparation, and second, researching tactics to perfect my pre-dive routine. To master ways to physically reset ahead of a dive, I re-read *The Definitive Book of Body Language* by Allan and Barbara Pease. The book explains how non-verbal cues can push your mind into a better performative state. I also read multiple studies that pinpointed the differences between 'winning' and 'losing' body language. The research shows that when an athlete feels dominant, that mindset is usually accompanied by certain physical signs – the shoulders are pulled back, the chin is held up and the eyes look straight ahead. When athletes don't feel so good, they're more likely to slouch, look down and avoid eye contact.

Scrutinising footage of some of the best athletes in the world reinforces this idea. The All Blacks, for example, are one of the most successful sporting teams of all time, with a win rate of nearly 80 per cent. But they also have a secret weapon that enables them to collectively nail the T-1 moment ahead of the game: the Haka.

The Haka may honour New Zealand's Indigenous heritage, but it also gives the All Blacks a key psychological edge. With its chanting, stomping and powerful gestures, the Māori war dance is a body language masterclass that incorporates strong and expansive postures that are shown in studies to boost confidence. The dynamic actions serve to elevate the players' testosterone levels, while the rhythmic stomping and body shaking offers a cathartic release of tension. In addition, the full-on nature of the Haka means it's impossible to perform in a half-arsed way, while the concentration required makes it work as a form of anxiety circuit-breaker by providing a distraction from pre-match nerves. The fact that all 15 team members perform it in sync also fosters a potent sense of group unity and common purpose. Essentially, the Haka gives the All Blacks an unfair advantage right before every game. It's the ultimate T-1 preparation for a sport that requires physicality and aggression.

Given my sport requires a calmer state of mind, the Haka is probably not appropriate.

But I do start to search for related elements that I can incorporate in my own preparation.

Before each dive, I now make a concerted effort to adopt a more powerful stance. Opening up my chest and standing tall, I ensure my shoulders are aligned and pushed back. I place my feet wider apart to give myself a more secure foundation and, when speaking, throw in big, expressive hand gestures that research shows can make you feel more confident and in charge.

What I'm doing through this process is sending messages from my body to my brain and reassuring it that, on a physiological level, I'm in a happy place. I'm acting out the opposite of what happens to our bodies when we're in danger, when we instinctively cower to make ourselves a smaller physical target. Before I dive, I now concentrate on changing my body language to take up as much space as possible and creating a positive feedback loop between body and mind.

I've also settled on a specific ritual that serves as an ignition switch to click into high-performance mode. For me, that's the simple action of putting on my nose clip shortly before I dive. That is my personal statement of intent that triggers my transformation from a sleep-deprived dad into a competitive athlete.

That's all part of a larger pre-dive routine that I've plotted out in detail to ensure that my final two minutes before each dive are always exactly the same. I put on my goggles and nose clip in the same order each time. I do the same breathing exercises and go through the same visualisation process, where I imagine myself emerging successfully at the end of the dive.

To dissect what works best for me on a more granular level, I've also kept a detailed log of the lead-up to each dive in the last two years, in order to establish the precise factors that contribute to a good performance. I record everything from how many hours I've slept, to the food I ate for breakfast, how long I've stretched for and note if there's a perceptible effect on my dive.

Music has become another area that I've played around with to try to induce the right performance mindset. Hoping to establish a state of relaxation, the first music I experimented with was classical and the atmospheric soundtrack to *The Big Blue*. Neither of those turned out to improve my performance at all, so I then tried the opposite approach. I dabbled with Rage Against The Machine and AC/DC; I tried grungier options like Pearl Jam and Soundgarden. After one dive, I briefly thought I'd struck gold with the Foo Fighters, but subsequent listens failed to elicit the same positive effect.

Eventually, I find my musical sweet spot. I've never heard of reggae being touted as a high-performance tool, but for me it really works. Aside from the laid-back groove, reggae helps for three main reasons. First, the standard low-to-medium tempo is very close to my resting heart rate and naturally encourages my mind to synchronise with its calm, steady pace. Second, reggae basslines and melodies tend to be repetitive, with the predictable patterns inviting me to zone out into a more meditative state without having to process too many changes. Third, the one-drop rhythm of the reggae-style drumbeat places the emphasis on the third beat of the measure, creating a feeling of weightlessness and suspension, as if the rhythm is floating rather than aggressively driving forward.

Subsequently, I settle on a new pre-dive set of rituals. My personal breakfast of champions consists of a boiled egg and a banana, while the best tunes to prep my mind include ones by Steel Pulse, Katchafire and UB40. Taken in isolation, these details are comically trivial. Yet for me, they've become the one percenters in my T-1 routine that have taken my freediving to a whole new level.

Back at work, things are as grim as ever. As the months tick by, because of my inability to win over my boss, my job is becoming increasingly draining. The worst part is that I now fear that her frustrations with me may actually be legitimate. The no-nonsense style of management I learned from my time in MotoGP is clearly out of step with the more sophisticated approach of a large professional services firm. I need to change how I lead, how I follow, and how I fit into a very different culture.

The realisation that I'm ill-suited to my role does nothing to improve my self-confidence. The worst thing is I don't feel like I can quit because I've just transplanted my young family to Australia purely so I can pursue this career opportunity. Each day, I wake up feeling trapped and increasingly hopeless.

Desperate to find some way of coping better with the situation, I try to apply the T-1 protocol to my working day. I engineered it, after all, to help myself perform better under pressure.

I develop a pre-work routine that I stick to religiously. Each day, I take the Manly ferry over to Circular Quay to get to the office. That boat ride now becomes my time to mentally prepare for the day ahead. Every time I board, I sit in a similar area that's outside on the port side of the ferry. This allows me to admire the harbour and the greenery of the Botanical Gardens. At the same time, I do ten minutes of 'box breathing', a simple relaxation exercise where I inhale for a count of four, hold my breath for four, exhale for four, and then hold again for four, repeating the cycle to regulate my nervous system and achieve a sense of calm. Next up, I do a breath-hold of between three and five minutes, where I focus on emptying my mind and zoning out of conscious thought.

Just as the ferry passes the Opera House, I remove the tie from my jacket pocket and knot it around my neck. This is my 'switch' that signals my transformation into a corporate go-getter who's outwardly confident and professionally assured. Disembarking from the ferry, I plug in my headphones and listen to Bob Marley as I walk through the CBD towards the office, making a conscious effort to put a soft smile on my face.

I set this routine to try to bring a sense of familiarity and comfort, thereby establishing a positive foundation to start the day. And I stick with it, too, because it actually works. My boss is still as tricky as ever. But I find myself able to stay more relaxed and level-headed during her rants. Work remains a grind, but I'm handling it better and able to be more present at home.

Regaining that mental composure also brings greater clarity. I finally propose to Merryn and we get married in Fiji, surrounded by family and friends. It rains nearly the whole time we're on the island, but I'm so happy that I really don't care.

The brief trip away from Sydney also gives me some valuable perspective. While I'm navigating work more successfully, I realise that I'm not a good fit for this corporate role and, after discussing it at length with Merryn, I quit with no new job to go to. As soon I hand in my notice, I'm filled with relief. It's a decision that I should have made a long time ago.

The resignation is also a boon for my freediving. Shortly after quitting, I have another crack at the Dynamic world record that's now been extended to 248 metres by my Kiwi compatriot, Dave Mullins. At the Ian Thorpe Aquatic Centre in Ultimo I manage to swim a personal best of 240 metres, before a slight loss of motor control on surfacing prompts the judges to disqualify me. Personally, I feel like the decision is harsh, but take comfort from the fact that I'm continuing to progress.

Freediving is then forced to take a backseat to real life. Our second child, Chloe Belle Williams, is born in June 2009 and I fall in love with being a dad all over again. Suddenly, my hands are really full as I've just started a new job at Maximus International, a boutique consulting firm that specialises in leadership development and psychometric services.

Early on, my new boss gives me some feedback, telling me that he fears I'm 'over-resilient'. It's a back-handed compliment at best, but I choose to interpret it in a positive way. For me, it's validation of the mental fitness tactics I've developed. It also reassures me that the T-1 philosophy is just as effective on dry land as it is underwater.

CHAPTER 17

In 2012, I'm invited to Long Island in the Bahamas to compete in Vertical Blue. I'm surprised to be asked, given I've dived so little in recent years. It'll also be an expensive trip, so I'm thinking of saying no. But Merryn urges me to go. I've been working hard after being promoted at Maximus and we've relocated (again) to Melbourne, where I'm responsible for opening a new office for the business. 'You deserve a break,' Merryn says.

I book a ticket to the Bahamas before she can change her mind. Part of the reason I'm so eager to go is that I need some help. My freediving has improved a lot in recent years, but despite my efforts, I've hit a plateau and simply can't go any deeper than 82 metres. My problem, I believe, stems from my equalisation technique. Whatever I try, I'm unable to alleviate the pressure at serious depths and deal with the compression and shooting pain that plays havoc with my ears and sinuses. Psychological tricks don't cut it here; the barrier is physical not mental.

Luckily, the event in the Bahamas is attracting some of the world's greatest freedivers. Competitors include Will Trubridge, a Kiwi phenomenon who's hit 100 metres without fins; the impressive Spaniard Miguel Lozano; and Alexey Molchanov, the incredible Russian diver who's targeting a world record of 126 metres in the Constant Weight discipline. Like me, they all get to Long Island early in order to acclimatise and practise. At every opportunity, I'm interrogating them for tips on how to refine my technique.

They're unexpectedly obliging, largely I expect because they know I don't represent serious competition. Alexey offered suggestions about how to manipulate my glottis, the door at the back of your mouth that connects the oral cavity to the lungs. Will tries to coach me on how to control my soft palate more effectively to pack in a bit of extra air. I listen intently and take detailed notes. But when I attempt to put their tips into practice, I have the same problem. My personal best of 82 metres remains and I start to wonder if maybe I've just hit my personal limit.

The registration for Vertical Blue takes place at a ramshackle café on the beach where Johnny Cash provides a continuous soundtrack through the tinny speakers. Having completed the formalities, I'm drinking a coffee when a boyish American with a deep tan and an easy grin sits down at the next table.

'Hey man, Nick Mevoli, pleased to meet you,' he says.

I immediately recognise the name. Nick is a 31-year-old diver who's fairly new to the sport but has quickly established himself as a rising star, having clinched a US depth record of 91 metres in the Constant Weight. We quickly get chatting and I'm drawn to his energy and friendly charm.

Nick is disarmingly open, too. Within a few minutes he's told me his story. Raised mainly in Florida, but now living in Brooklyn, he was a keen BMX rider as a kid and was targeting a place in the X Games. But a nasty accident ended his career when he punctured a femoral artery in his leg. 'Almost lost an eye once, too,' he smiles.

From the age of nine, Nick helped his Uncle Paul dive for lobsters among the rocky crags of the Florida Keys. Like me, after seeing *The Big Blue*, he became fascinated by freediving and while still in his teens began going deeper and deeper. He turned out to have a natural aptitude for the sport and almost immediately was able to hold his breath for four minutes and dive to a depth of 30 metres.

He only started training properly last year after joining a free-diving club in New York. His first line dive was less than a year ago, but he's already going deeper than me.

'You make me sick,' I joke. 'I've been diving for a decade now and whatever I do I just can't seem to get past 82 metres.'

'Dude! I can teach you how to do that in two minutes. Seriously! What do you say?'

'I'd love that, of course, but I don't think you can. I've spoken to some of the best freedivers around. I just don't seem to be able equalise properly.'

'I got you, man,' Nick says. 'Here's what you do.'

The explanation is technically complicated, but Nick patiently talks me through it step by step. During my descent, he says, I need to slow down at 20 metres and do my normal 'charge', where you fill your mouth and throat by shifting the air from your lungs.

'Yeah, I already do that.'

'No, you've got to charge properly, man. And I mean *really* charge.'

Apparently, I have to bring all that air from my lungs up into my throat and mouth until my cheeks are puffed out as far as they can go and my head is arched back to create extra space in my throat. Next, I have to lock my glottis and bring my chin back down to the base of my throat. Nick says that should give me a strong enough buildup of air in my cheeks and throat to force the pressure back into the eustachian tubes in order to protect my ears and equalise. This air, he says, will be so compressed it'll barely form a pocket the size of a pea in my mouth.

'Once you get to 90 metres, use the back of your tongue to force that air back up into your ears and it'll replace enough pressure to get you deeper. It won't be a crisp equalisation, more a dull sensation, but it should be enough to see you home.'

I'm trying to absorb every detail, but inside I'm sceptical. Nick clearly means well, but he also seems a little naïve and gung-ho. He cheerfully admits to having turned up in the Bahamas with just one shirt and one pair of shorts. He's currently staying at the rectory of the Catholic church in nearby Clarence Town to save money.

'I couldn't hope for a better place to crash,' he says cheerfully. 'Father Doug is a great guy and is letting me stay for free in return for a bit of help repairing the church roof.'

That afternoon, I head out to Dean's Blue Hole for a practice dive. I'm still sceptical about Nick's advice, but I figure it's worth giving it a go, more in hope than expectation. But on my very first attempt using Nick's equalisation tips, I nail 85 metres, a personal best that I've strived to achieve for years.

Two days later, I manage 88 metres.

The day after that, I dive to 90 metres and it's still five days to the actual competition! I don't know if Nick is some sort of free-diving prodigy or aquatic savant, but his tips have proved a total gamechanger.

When the competition finally comes around, I decide to go for the milestone that I'd always dreamed of. It's momentous for lots of reasons, not least because I promised my wife that I'd retire from competitive freediving if I managed to make it to 100 metres.

In the end, Nick Mevoli's coaching hastens what I believe to be the premature end of my freediving career. On 20 November 2012, I become only the 23rd person in the world to reach 100 metres.

Afterwards, giddy with delight, I seek out Nick to thank him. He's somehow helped me to redefine my personal limits in a way that I didn't think was possible. I'm hoping to buy him dinner as a small token of thanks, but I can't seem to find him around the competition area or at the nearby café. Eventually, I run into Ted Harty, one of his American teammates, who explains that Nick has had to pull out. In a bid to protect his national record, he'd attempted 95 metres on his first dive of the competition, but struggled to equalise and wound up rupturing his eardrum. Now in excruciating pain, he's recovering back at the church and is keeping a low profile.

'He's an unbelievable talent,' Ted says. 'But he's pushing himself too far.'

Tragically, I never do get to thank Nick in person. A year later, he dies while competing at this very competition.

CHAPTER 18

I'm in the office in Melbourne when I get a call from Ryan, whom I've been working with for some time as a business coach. Ryan is the general manager of a luxury construction firm in New Zealand that builds high-end residential homes for the super-rich. Right now, he's got a problem that he wants to discuss.

Ryan's site manager is Tom, a solid bloke with plenty of experience whom he's worked alongside for several years. Tom's job is to oversee the construction process and make sure that everything stays on track in terms of time and budget. Many of the new builds are wildly ambitious and involve multiple tradies, designers and architects. But Tom's special power is coordinating all the moving parts to keep the projects on schedule. He smooths over supply chain delays when materials arrive late and tackles site problems, from wiring issues to plumbing hiccups.

'Tommy is always upbeat and gets on really well with all the tradies,' Ryan says.

What's less positive is that Tom isn't great on the finer details. That's not ideal, given the sky-high expectations of Ryan's wealthy clients. It turns out Tom's blind spot has now caused an issue. Last week, a new kitchen was installed in a waterfront home in Auckland, but Tom was too hasty in signing off on the benchtops. Made from Calacatta marble imported from Italy, the mineral vein lines of the stone were meant to line up seamlessly across the various cuts to create a continuous pattern, but they've accidentally been set in a disjointed way. Most people wouldn't notice. The client did. And they're not happy, given the price of the marble. They've demanded the slab be pulled off, reset and realigned, which will mean a two-day delay.

Ryan's headache is that those two extra days will add more labour and material costs that the client is unwilling to stomach, so they'll have to come from the project's dwindling profits. The bigger issue, though, is that Ryan will have to speak to Tom about adapting the way he operates and the need to be more vigilant when it comes to the details.

'You've had these concerns for a while?' I ask Ryan.

'Yeah, well, Tommy's always been a bit slapdash.'

'Have you discussed this with him before?'

'Not really, no.'

When pushed, Ryan admits that he's avoided the issue because the prospect of reprimanding Tom seemed too awkward. They're good mates, he explains. And Ryan values Tom's other strengths. 'I guess I didn't want to rock the boat,' he says.

I talk to Ryan about why it's so important to front up to these difficult conversations immediately. We discuss the sort of language he can use to get his point across in an effective way.

'Don't try to be a "nice guy" boss, who values harmony over performance,' I say. 'What you want to be is a boss who's developing a first-class team and getting the best out of each person in it by giving lots of rich feedback.'

It's not the first time I've given this sort of advice. In fact, I've come to believe that the most important work of any leader is usually done in these emotionally demanding spaces. Most people recoil from tough chats or confrontations, with many avoiding them entirely. Yet it's only by stepping up to confront those moments of discomfort that you can ever become a great boss.

The parallel with freediving leaps out to me here. After all, I was only able to start reaching serious depths when I accepted that discomfort was an unavoidable part of that process, a necessary paving stone on the road to success. The same willingness to face up to daunting moments is vital in leadership too.

This message seems to resonate with my clients. On the back of that interest, it forms the basis of a workshop I develop that soon becomes one of our most popular. People quickly accept that getting better at having difficult conversations is a key leadership skill and that unchecked problems tend to snowball with alarming speed. I've actually received so much positive feedback that I want to share the concept with a wider audience.

It's 2014 and TED Talks have exploded across the globe. They've become a cultural phenomenon, turning under-the-radar 'thought leaders' into bestselling authors and lecture circuit titans. The 12-minute format has found a sweet spot that leverages the power of big ideas and emotional storytelling with the pitiful length of modern attention spans. Since becoming freely available online, TED Talks' brand of mini-lectures spanning anything from creativity to conservation have been viewed more than a billion times. A TED Talk, I figure, could be the perfect vehicle to share my views – and get my message out to a bigger audience.

My idea is to repackage my T-1 principle. I'll argue that when you're tackling a tough challenge – whether it's at work, in sport, or in life in general – the *real* moment of truth is rarely what you think it is. Usually it's the moment directly *before* the climactic action – the moment when you're feeling really anxious, overwhelmed and desperately want to quit. How you manage that moment, I believe, determines how you ultimately fare. Handle it well and it'll be your springboard to success. Screw it up and it'll destroy your chances.

My TED Talk will explore this concept through the lens of my free-diving experiences, presenting the idea in a first-person story that's (hopefully) dramatic and engaging.

I submit my application and am delighted when I get a phone call from Jon Yeo, the head of curation for the Melbourne branch of TEDx. 'We're considering your application,' he says. 'But I'll need to have a series of conversations with you to really understand whether or not this is worthy of a TED Talk.'

So begins a lengthy back-and-forth process. After a couple of chats on the phone, Jon starts making encouraging noises and so we meet up in person in his Melbourne office. Following a coffee and a getting-to-know-you chat, he asks to see my TED Talk. It's still a work in progress at this stage and, feeling a little self-conscious, I present what I've been practising over the last few weeks. Jon watches me carefully and proceeds to deliver robust feedback on where I need to improve.

A TED Talk, he explains, follows a strict formula based on new research into the science of persuasion. 'The essence of a TED Talk is that you've got 12 minutes to tell us the story of your lived experience, explain why it's relevant to the audience, and then capture their hearts and minds. In addition, you've got to convey how your idea can be used by anyone listening to rethink the way they live their lives. You didn't do that today, Ant.'

'No,' I reply. 'I sure didn't.'

Jon offers me some pointers on where I'm going wrong. Apparently, I talk like a corporate presenter – understandable, given that's what I do – whereas I need to learn to connect with the audience on a more intimate level. My delivery has to feel natural, and the way to achieve this, Jon says, is by learning my script word for word and rehearsing it over and over again.

That's never been my approach to public speaking. I don't memorise a single sentence. Instead, I come up with a basic structure, plus the main points that I want to relate, then focus on delivering them with energy and enthusiasm.

But Jon reckons that won't cut it here. 'I don't want you doing that, because there's too high a risk you won't nail it on the day,' he says. 'I want you to be more prepared. Don't try to do what you've always done; if that's your schtick, you're the wrong person to do a TED Talk.'

I desperately want to be the *right* person to do a TED Talk, so I go along with what Jon has to say. Over the next few weeks I attend sessions on how to write a TED Talk following a set formula that consists of a clear intro, body and conclusion, with all the parts centred around a single bold idea. The introduction is designed to hook the audience, and the body presents evidence to build the case, while the conclusion summarises key points and delivers a strong 'call to action'. The ongoing refrain that's constantly repeated is that 'you must touch a person's heart before reaching their head'.

I rewrite my TED Talk and present it to Jon for feedback. Then I have to rewrite it several more times. I'm still refining it when there's an audition night. Ten other prospective TED speakers are trialling their talks. I'm dazzled by one woman whose presentation about bouncing back from rejection is so memorable and compelling that I collar her afterwards in the hope of getting some tips.

'That was amazing,' I say. 'How did you get your talk so crisp?'

'I've been practising that 12-minute spiel for over six months.'

Chastened, I knuckle down. I memorise my talk and rehearse it every day during my lunchbreak at work. I video myself doing the talk on my phone and critique my performance, agonising over every word and performative gesture.

Despite these efforts, I don't feel like I'm making much progress. I fear the strict 12-minute time limit is cramping my style and messing with my pacing. Parroting a script doesn't feel natural to me either and I feel like my words lack colour and verve.

The good news is that Jon confirms that I've clinched a spot at the TEDx night at the Melbourne Conference Centre in six weeks. This should be cause for celebration. Except when I watch my latest video, it becomes reason to panic instead. All I can see now are my blunders: the 'ums' that punctuate my sentences, the stuttered words, the awkward mannerisms. Has learning this new style of presenting extinguished my spark?

The irony isn't lost on me either. The underlying theme of my talk, after all, is 'how to perform under pressure'. But my delivery suggests I've got no bloody clue. The shakiness of my presentation undermines my whole argument. It's like writing a book on spelling that's riddled with typos.

My main source of anxiety is that the TED instructors keep stressing the fact that, although there'll be a crowd of more than a thousand people on the night, they're not the primary audience. The *real* viewing potential exists on YouTube, where people can watch the video forever more. Screw up, in other words, and your mistakes will be preserved for the hilarity of generations to come. The other thing that's freaking me out is that onstage, the house lights will be turned right up for the recording so I won't be able to see the audience. Normally, I like to feed off the crowd's energy. If I can't see them, I'll have no idea how they're responding.

Feeling slightly desperate and with time ticking away, I need to find some performance solutions. Instinctively, I fall back on my sport psychology background. In a bid to define my problem, I start by writing out my three biggest fears.

The main thing I'm worried about is the audience. The paying crowd in the auditorium, along with all the online viewers, could amount to a terrifying number of eyeballs. That's a *lot* of people expecting a life-changing epiphany in 12 minutes flat. Everyone will be judging me, critiquing every word, making snap decisions on whether or not I'm wasting their time. Fretting about all that is creating a debilitating level of pressure. What I need to do now is flip the script.

If I were experiencing this kind of anxiety before a freediving event, the first thing I'd do would be to reframe the situation in a less intimidating way. Downplay the importance of the outcome. I've learned the hard way that if I go into a competition thinking *I've got to crush this! I've got to win!*, I pile extra tension on myself that hinders my performance. A smarter play is to focus on trying to simply enjoy the dive as much as possible – I always do better when I'm relaxed and having fun.

Applying that know-how to this TED Talk, I realise I need to reframe my view of the audience. No one likes to see someone fail on stage, I remind myself. Nor does anyone want to watch a speaker who looks anxious and tense. *They all want you to succeed*, I tell myself. *Your audience wants you to appear calm, confident and relaxed. Nail that part and a good performance is more likely to follow.*

My second big fear is that I'm going to forget my lines. I've never rote learned anything before and it doesn't come naturally. One small verbal slip-up can totally derail me. If I momentarily forget a line or lose my flow, my brain starts frantically searching for the 'next sentence' and panic sets in. The upshot is that I feel like I'm not really communicating, but just trying to recall the correct sequence of words. There's no doubt my delivery is suffering as a result.

In freediving, my goal was always to try and stay present in the here and now. Easier said than done, because the more discomfort you experience, the more your mind braces against further discomfort, colouring your outlook with a negative filter.

To work around that, I learned to chunk each dive up into distinct sections and just focus on one at a time. Once I completed one chunk – say the first 60 metres of the descent – I would make a call on whether or not I was game to attempt the next one, and then the next. Not only did that tactic provide a mental escape clause, it also brought positive momentum and accomplishment as I ticked off each section. A 100-metre dive appears far less overwhelming when chopped into bite-sized pieces.

Using this principle with my TED Talk, I break it down into three main thematic areas that I memorise as individual blocks of text. When practising them, I move around the room, to occupy a specific area for each chunk, a small trick that I find aids my powers of recall. On the night of my talk, I won't be able to move around, as we have to stand on a small, fixed circle of red carpet for the lighting and cameras. I therefore adapt my strategy to use my line of vision as a similar form of cue. When I'm talking about things in the past, I look to my right. When discussing present events, I look straight ahead. For events in the future, I look to the left.

My final fear is the big one: how to survive the worst-case scenario. What do I do onstage if I suddenly freeze, forget my lines, or temporarily lose the power of speech?

Again, I cast my mind back to freediving and the countless mini-disasters I've experienced. One of the diciest happened in New Zealand's Lake Pupuke when I was experimenting with a new type of safety lanyard. I'd dived 60 metres to the bottom of the lake and was trying to make my way back up. With zero visibility, it took me a while to realise I wasn't making any progress. In fact, I was being pulled *backwards* and was eventually yanked right down into the mud.

Somehow I managed not to panic. Rather than thrash around and try to claw my way back to the surface, I had the presence of mind to stay cool. Something had gone wrong and I needed to find a solution. To pull that off I had to steady myself and act with methodical calm. Sixty metres underwater at the bottom of a pitch-black lake, with my oxygen levels fading, I couldn't afford to waste time. Every moment had to count.

The new lanyard was the likely culprit. It had probably got tangled in the base plate, thereby anchoring me to the bottom. Carefully, I removed my weight belt to detach myself. Did I now have enough air to get back to the surface? Or should I tug on the dive rope and signal for help? Reasoning I still had sufficient oxygen, I focused on propelling myself upwards with smooth, controlled kicks.

What freediving taught me is that when you're rattled and trying to move faster to escape a situation, it's often the wrong move. Counterintuitively, it can actually help to *slow down* to give yourself a better chance of making the right decision. Freaking out can lead to dumb moves and get you into real trouble.

If things do go wrong onstage during my TED Talk, I decide, I'm going to maintain a calm front. Standing purposefully, I'll take a deep breath and pause, maybe even smile at the audience. By holding the space with confidence and buying myself a moment to think, I'll boost my chances of remembering what comes next. If I do that, the audience may not even notice and still think that I'm in control. Projecting self-assurance onstage tends to cover the odd fluffed line. You'll pass the eye test that you're still worth listening to.

When the big night finally arrives, I'm still feeling unusually nervous. Backstage at the Convention Centre, my chest is tight and the red circle of carpet onstage looks like a spotlight waiting to expose my every flaw. The tension isn't helped when one of the speakers before me mangles his opening salvo. Maybe practice doesn't make perfect after all.

Years ago, while working with the Alpine ski team in New Zealand, one of the athletes shared his mindset at the top of each slalom run. 'I don't think of the whole slalom,' he said. 'I don't think of every gate. I just concentrate on the first two turns. Because if

I nail those two, I'll be in a state of flow and then everything will just happen automatically.'

That's the advice I use to snap into gear. For the next ten minutes backstage, I focus on breathing calmly while reciting the first few lines of my introduction over and over again in my head. Finally, my name is called. I take another deep breath and smile. Then I walk onstage into the blinding lights and do what I need to do.

PART 3

CHAPTER 19

Kala Alexander is sitting alone on the black sand of Piha Beach, west of Auckland. Hugging his knees, a grey hoodie pulled low over his shaven head, he looks deep in contemplation, a quietly dejected figure gazing out at the Tasman Sea.

This is not the mental image I had of the Hawaiian pro surfer and stuntman. The first time I heard about Kala was reading a profile of him in the surfing magazine *Stab*. The headline for the article grabbed my attention: 'THE TOUGHEST FUCKING MAN IN SURFING.'

Muscle-bound and heavily tattooed, Kala developed this reputation as the North Shore's most infamous enforcer. As the founder of Hawaiian surf gang, the Wolfpak (known in their Kauai neighbourhood simply as 'the Boys'), Kala took it upon himself to police the crowded waves of Oahu, taking punitive action against any non-locals who dropped in on others or failed to show the necessary respect. At Banzai Pipeline, the world-famous reef break, the Wolfpak effectively determines which waves go to whom. Those who breach their code are likely to cop a beating. If you're unlucky, this will include a brutal close-up of the word 'Wolfpak' that's inked across the knuckles of Kala's meaty fists.

Today, Kala doesn't look so fearsome. He's just been humbled in the longboard event of the 2016 Ultimate Waterman tournament. Turns out he's not the only top surfer brooding on his performance.

Twenty metres away, Mark Visser is looking equally forlorn as he stands on the beach in his wetsuit. The Australian surfer also has a crazy reputation, albeit one based on his big-wave exploits rather than his windmilling fists. He's best known for being the first person to surf Jaws, Maui's biggest surfing break, *at night*. Footage shows him descending the face of a 6-metre monster in the dark, the action illuminated by the infra-red lights he's wearing to enable cameramen on a hovering chopper to capture the madness.

But today, the two legends of the sport are disgruntled for good reason. Kala finished joint last in the longboard comp while Mark finished just one place above. Given they're both world-class surfers, their positions tell you all you need to know about the ferocity of this elite competition.

Now in its second year, the Ultimate Waterman is the brainchild of Greg Townsend, the chief executive of Surf New Zealand. The competition set out with the simple goal of finding the best all-round waterborne athlete on the planet. Eight sportsmen from a variety of aquatic disciplines were invited to New Zealand to battle it out in seven gruelling challenges ranging from a 16-kilometre outrigger canoe race to a 40-minute paddleboard contest through head-high surf.

The standard of athletes is frightening. Long-haired Brazilian Caio Vaz may look like a male model (largely because he is), but he's also the current Stand-up Paddleboarding (SUP) world champion. Connor Baxter, a skinny Hawaiian with unruly, sun-bleached hair, is widely considered the fastest SUP athlete on earth, having won the Maui 2 Molokai race seven times in a row, despite the fact he's only 19. Californian Danny Ching is a multiple outrigger canoe and SUP champion; Daniel Kereopa is New Zealand's top surfer; while Manoa Drollet is a Tahitian surf legend famed for conquering the biggest wave ever surfed at Teahupo'o, where fierce barrels detonate over a notoriously shallow reef.

After six rounds of competition, the current leader is Hawaiian young gun Zane Schweitzer. Aged just 20, he comes from a legendary seafaring family: his grandfather, Hoyle Schweitzer, invented the sport of windsurfing, while his dad, Matt, followed in his father's footsteps to become an 18-time world champion. The fact that Zane won today's longboard comp perhaps isn't entirely surprising. He entered his first surf competition when he was only three.

It's a formidable lineup of athletes who, to a man, have grown up with sea foam in their veins. But despite all their achievements, every one of these competitors is visibly star-struck by the big-name ambassador who's been drafted in as a commentator to add a touch of celebrity pizzaz. Even among these saltwater bad-asses, Laird Hamilton is on a whole other level.

'He's just the ultimate alpha male,' Mark Visser whispered to me earlier that morning as we observed Laird across the room. 'He's a super-approachable bloke, but the dominant presence in any room he walks into.'

Now, as the production crew pack up to prepare for the next event, Laird wanders over to Kala and sits down besides his countryman to console him. Laird has just turned 50, but even sitting next to Kala's conspicuous brawn, the older man's physical power is clear. Beneath his yellow-blond hair, Laird is square-jawed and ruggedly handsome, a bear of a man with a barrel-like chest and a self-assured air that you only get from conquering the meanest waves on the planet.

As always, I find myself watching him closely because, well, that's what all of us just do. We're in childlike awe of him. My fascination with Laird stems from a cover of *Surfer* magazine I must have seen about 20 years ago. He was surfing a mutant wave so big it made him look like a stick figure. The coverline simply read: 'Oh my God . . .'

So far, my interactions with Laird have only been fleeting as he's invariably been surrounded by a throng of wide-eyed admirers. So

I'm biding my time, waiting for the right moment to catch him and ask the questions I've already pre-planned in my head.

There's no shortage of material as Laird's story has been told many times in books, magazines and documentaries. Growing up in Hawaii, he was bullied at school by the locals due to the fact he was blond-haired and fair-skinned. Those scuffles may have forged his hard-knock resilience and willingness to put his body on the line. At 11, he leaped 60 feet off Waimea Falls on Oahu. By 14, he was cheerfully windsurfing the 70-mile distance from Oahu to Maui. Nor has middle-age blunted his edge. This year, video footage circulated of Laird shooting at high speed on his SUP through the heavy, wooden pillars on Malibu Pier, propelled by a fierce swell whipped up by Hurricane Marie.

Mostly though, Laird is lauded as an innovator. In the 1990s, he helped to popularise tow-in surfing, where a jet ski pulls a surfer into waves that are too large and too fast to paddle into. Tow-in surfing revolutionised the sport, opening up a brave new world of big-wave possibilities. Later on, Laird became one of the godfathers of the modern stand-up paddleboarding scene after he began messing around with an outrigger canoe paddle on a 12-foot surfboard. Want more? Laird also helped to develop the foilboard, a surfboard with a hydrofoil beneath, in order to maintain enough speed to zip down the face of a gigantic wave. In short, Laird Hamilton has done more than anyone to expand the frontiers of oceanic sports, enabling watermen to go bigger, further and faster.

Why am I here in such illustrious company? Obviously, I'm not competing. In fact, the reason I was invited is tenuous at best. As the show is being filmed in New Zealand, the producer decided a Kiwi co-commentator/ambassador was required, someone who could analyse the more niche events – particularly tonight's underwater challenge. Helpfully, I've developed a small local profile on the back of my freediving exploits and, perhaps more pertinently,

I've known Greg, the organiser, for more than a decade. When he asked me to get involved, I jumped at the chance.

Now I'm actually here, though, the reality is slightly awkward. There's not much for me to do, so I'm mainly standing about, trying not to get in the way. The tricky part is that I'm not exactly part of either crew. The production team bustle around with cameras, rigging up lighting and mics. The athletes meanwhile are focused on their preparation ahead of each event. That's left me in a weird state of limbo.

To be fair, it's how I increasingly feel in my personal life. I'm no longer freediving competitively and don't train with any purpose or intensity, only heading out for the odd recreational dive every now and then. Part of the reason is that real life has caught up with me.

Professionally, I'm busier than ever. I've just started my own consultancy business called Modus that applies the principles of performance psychology to the corporate world. The overlaps between sport psychology and business turn out to be surprisingly profound. Techniques that athletes use for goal setting, visualisation, stress management and teamwork also work for business leaders and can help them create more resilient and motivated teams. My experience as a freediver plays well in this environment and gives me a unique point of difference. As the main breadwinner with a young family, starting out on my own is a gamble, but I have to give it a go.

Speaking of family, I've also got my hands full with two kids aged five and eight. Understandably, given my domestic responsibilities, Merryn doesn't want me to dive any deeper. She's been spooked by a series of freediving tragedies and, to be honest, I've been rocked by them, too.

Just last year, Nick Mevoli, the happy-go-lucky American who helped me refine my equalisation at depth, died at Dean's Blue Hole – the same 'portal to hell' where I nailed my 100-metre dive. Attempting a 72-metre descent, it's thought he ran into problems while equalising. After surfacing, he blacked out and began to bleed from the mouth. Attempts to revive him failed and he died of a pulmonary haemorrhage. He was only 32 years old. It was the first recorded death in a freediving competition and Nick had touched so many people with his charismatic energy that it took a heavy toll on the community. We all struggled to process how this could have happened in a well-supervised event.

Sadly, Nick isn't the only recent freediving victim. Carlos Coste, whom I competed against at Vertical Blue, suffered a stroke caused by an air embolism while training for a No Limits dive in 2006. And in 2012, Herbert Nitsch, the Austrian who beat me in the Dynamic discipline in Cyprus, suffered multiple strokes that forced him to relearn how to walk, talk and move around after a record-breaking dive to 253.2 metres.

I still believe that freediving is reasonably safe – as long as you're sensible and aware of your true capabilities – but I no longer have the same appetite to try to go deeper. I can't risk my wife having to raise our two children alone.

At the same time, I miss having a physical goal to strive for and a target to base my training around. Most of all I miss the sheer challenge of the sport and the impetus to push myself further. I worked so hard to get to the point where I could think of myself as a legitimate athlete. Now that part of my life is gone and privately I mourn the loss. While I love being a dad, that responsibility has overwhelmed the other facets of my identity. To be honest, I feel a bit lost in this mid-life psychodrama. Letting go of the thing that came to define me is hard.

That night, the Ultimate Waterman production heads back into Auckland for the event that's most relevant to my personal experience. Held at the National Aquatic Centre, the Underwater Strength Run and Swim is a brand-new event for the competition. Each contestant must dive into the 25-metre pool and hold their breath for

30 seconds, before running along the bottom carrying a 25-kilogram dumbbell in each hand. Then, after dropping the weights on a mat, they must shoot to the surface and sprint swim as fast as they can back to the start. Each athlete will have two attempts, with their best time deciding their final result.

On paper, it sounds like an event designed for big-wave surfers who have to condition themselves to withstand long hold-downs when they wipe out in heavy waves. The static breath-hold is meant to measure your ability to relax and stay calm without oxygen – an essential skill when you're getting hammered by big surf. The 25-metre underwater run is to test the power you need to fight your way back to the surface. Finally, the sprint swim measures your paddle strength, which is necessary to generate the necessary board speed to catch a wave.

Ahead of the contest, I'm interviewed alongside Mark Visser by the Red Bull TV crew. I know Mark well, having helped him with his breath-hold technique ahead of his night surfing at Jaws. What I most like about Mark is his honesty. Despite all his crazy feats, he's not one for empty bravado and speaks openly about how scared he gets ahead of his wilder stunts.

Conducted on the bleachers by the side of the pool, it's a soft interview, with the producer clearly just looking for a couple of soundbites to overlay on the footage. But when Mark is asked about what he learned from training with me, his response surprises me.

'Ant, when you first started putting me through the underwater breath-hold training, my mind just couldn't comprehend what you were telling me to do. The barriers that you have to break down in your head are the hardest things about breath-holds. You're physically thinking that you're going to die. Your body is going through these convulsions, but it's actually just an internal shift as the blood is pulled from your limbs to your heart. Having to sit through that with you telling me, "C'mon, Mark, just stay calm" – that was a tough one, for sure. But you've got to let go of that fear. In our game, you're always going to be fearful of something, whether it's drowning, being crushed by a huge wave, or reaching a depth that you may not come back from. What Ant taught me to do is to overcome that obstacle.'

I'm touched by Mark's testimony. I'll never master the waves he's ridden (even in daylight), but it's nice to know I've got something to offer a top surfer like him. The fact that my credentials are still valued and relevant in these elite circles fills me with a surprising amount of pride. I hadn't realised how much I still crave that sporting validation.

When the underwater competition finally gets underway it doesn't play out as you'd expect. You'd think the big-wave surfers would have an unfair advantage, but it turns out to be more of a crapshoot. Scuttling along the pool floor carrying the heavy weights is a real leveller. Gaining traction on the tiled bottom is hard and makes it impossible to build up any speed, so everyone's times for that section of the race are almost identical. That means it all comes down to who is the fastest sprint swimmer. Danny Ching is a former college swimmer and has the explosive power to blitz the freestyle swim and edge past Mark and Manoa Drollet. If it was a 50-metre pool, it would pose far more of a breath-hold challenge but blackouts, I guess, don't make for great TV.

The next day, the production crew and athletes all meet at Viaduct Basin, a former commercial harbour on the Auckland waterfront that's been transformed into a buzzy precinct of restaurants and apartments. From here, a boat is scheduled to pick us up and take us up the coast for the 16-kilometre Stand-up Paddleboard Race. It's a bright spring morning and most of the athletes are fussing about with their kit bags, double-checking their equipment. I'm sitting on the wharf, legs dangling above the water, when I notice that Laird

Hamilton is standing a few metres away chatting on his phone. When his call ends, I seize the moment.

'G'day, Laird, I'm Ant Williams. We met briefly on the first day.'

'Sure man, yeah, I remember. I've been looking forward to having a chance to chat.'

Dressed in a fleece, board shorts and thongs, up close Laird looks part surfer dude, part Viking warrior. He must be 6′3″ at least and beneath his broad shoulders and freckly tan, his physique feels like a middle finger to the ageing process. Knowing that I'm a freediver, Laird immediately starts to quiz me about breath-hold tactics and how to relax when getting smashed by big surf. 'Lately,' he says, 'I've started to close my eyes when I practise that stuff. Seeing, I find, only disorients me and makes me use more oxygen.'

While I'm chuffed that Laird is taking an interest in me, I'm aware that I've got a slim window of time here. I don't want to talk about myself because I'm overflowing with questions. As soon as there's a pause in the conversation, I pounce.

'Mate, do you mind if I ask you something?'

'Fire away.'

'As a freediver, a lot of people look at what I do and assume that I'm an adrenaline junkie, that I take unnecessary risks. To be honest, I don't agree with that at all. But I was interested to know about you. Do you see yourself as a thrillseeker and, if so, how do you feel about that tag?'

'It's funny, you know,' Laird chuckles. 'Over the years, I must've had more than a thousand stitches. I've cracked my ribs, chipped elbows, crushed vertebrae. I've broken my ankles maybe six times. One time I got a surfboard tip through my cheek – *that* was gnarly. But do I see myself as a "thrillseeker"? Categorically not.'

'And why do you reject that label?'

'For me, a thrillseeker is someone who's usually inexperienced. They're just going along for the ride, doing stuff that's stupid and that's probably going to wind up with them getting hurt. They're putting themselves in dangerous situations just for a buzz. Now don't get me wrong. Riding a wave that's seven storeys high – yes, it's the ultimate sensation, man. But do I see myself as a thrillseeker? No way.'

'So what do you see yourself as, then?'

'What am I? I'm a calculated risk taker. Are there dangers to what I do? For sure! But I've been doing this stuff all my life. I've been surfing since I was three years old. Even today, I still train hard, my skill set is advanced and my experience level is very high. Yes, I do things that push my limits. But I always know what my limits are.'

'Is that something you've learned the hard way?'

'I was a wild kid, I guess, but I always knew the line. Back in the day when we started doing tow-in surfing, it might've looked crazy from the outside but, believe it or not, we always operated conservatively within that environment. "Ride to ride another day" was our motto. We might have gone after some heavy waves, but we tackled them in a way that would allow us to do it all over again tomorrow.'

'I love that you say that and I totally get it. That's how I feel, too.'

'Right? Because in those kinds of scenarios, you can only really get to appreciate them with repetition. The first time you ride a 50-foot wave, it's like the first time you go more than 100 miles an hour on a motorbike. All your senses are so in the moment, you can't remember what was going past or even if there were any other cars on the road. But after you've hit that speed 20 times, that's when you start being able to look around and enjoy the ride.'

Laird sits down on the pontoon and gestures for me to join him. I hastily comply. The boat is now approaching and I'm keen to squeeze out some more of his saltwater wisdom.

'There's one other thing I've been wondering. As you say, you've been doing all this for a long, long time, but you're still at the cutting edge. You're an ambassador for this show, I just watched some wild video of you on YouTube surfing under the pier at Huntington, you're always in my Instagram feed. How do you stay so relevant?'

Laird stops and thinks for a while, rubbing his preposterously square jaw. 'Y'know, I think part of it comes down to the fact that, as a surfer, I never took part in competitions. I hated being judged – that was just never my thing. I don't like man-against-man competitions, I'm more into man against the elements. Not being part of that structure meant I didn't get eclipsed by the younger guys coming up and I wasn't limited by having to tour and be a part of a season. It meant I was free to try out new things.'

'Like the tow-in surfing. Or the hydrofoil stuff.'

'Exactly. I like trying new things. When we first decided to try to ride Jaws, no one had ever ridden waves that big. Period. We didn't know if we were going to disappear into a black hole never to be seen again. But when you're doing things on waves that you have never done and no one else has either – that's pretty spectacular.'

'But does that mean you have to keep chasing bigger and bigger waves? Or, in my case as a freediver, keep trying to go deeper and deeper?'

'It doesn't have to escalate that way, y'know. Personally, what stimulates me is to go out to the edge of my sport. I like to seek out that edge, and then I like to play there and explore. Yes, that could be chasing big waves. But it could also be anything that's going to challenge me, anything where I've got to work out what new equipment I need to achieve it, where I've got to discover new approaches to overcome whatever hurdles are in my way. That's where I learn new things about myself and, for me, that's where all the growth, all the learning, all the exciting stuff happens. The way you change a sport is by playing about on those outer edges.'

'So it's about refusing to get stuck in a rut?'

'Kinda. But it's more like how when you're little and you ride a one-footer, then a two. Then a ten. It keeps evolving. For me chasing that progression in some shape or form is how I retain my passion. What can I say, man. It works for me.'

CHAPTER 20

Two weeks later, it's a Wednesday night and I'm back home. The kids are finally asleep and I'm mindlessly flicking through the TV channels before landing on the sports news, where I'm delighted to see the Parramatta Eels have lost in the NRL. Ever since my days on Lake Pupuke, I've despised eels in all their slippery forms. Then the sports presenter says something that grabs my attention.

'A Russian freediver has just become the deepest man under the ice, reaching a depth of 65 metres on a single breath. At the North Pole, Konstantin Novikov set a new world record. His 65-metre dive took two minutes and 12 seconds to complete and smashed the decade-long record held by Croatian athlete Kristijan Curavic, who achieved a depth of 51 metres in 2005 . . .'

It's a brief clip less than a minute long, but I'm immediately fascinated. Freediving under the ice sounds like total madness. Imagine the sense of entrapment you'd feel entombed in freezing water beneath a ceiling of ice. Would I be able to handle it?

The more I think about it, the scarier it gets. Ice diving combines a number of deep primal fears – suffocation, darkness, claustrophobia. These fears are hardly irrational either. They're a logical response to an utterly terrifying situation.

But ice diving is also *exactly* the sort of venture that Laird Hamilton was talking about. It would take me in a new direction, forcing me to explore the outer edges of my sport and build on my existing skill set to learn different techniques and strategies. I've been searching for another physical challenge; could ice diving be it?

There's something else that excites me about the idea. This Russian freediver may have broken a ten-year world record, but he clinched it with a dive of 65 metres. I've proven that I can nail a 100-metre dive in normal temperatures. Surely, water is just water? Sixty-five metres is two-thirds of my PB. So what's stopping me from having a crack at the world record?

I'm certainly not a fan of cold water. But when I used to run cross-country back in New Zealand, I clocked my best times in winter when the weather was hovering close to zero. Back then, I always claimed that I 'went better in the cold'. Maybe the same will be true for ice diving?

I do have one issue that's potentially a much bigger challenge to overcome than sub-zero Arctic temperatures. After breaking the 100-metre barrier I promised my wife that I'd no longer compete as a freediver. Merryn has always been supportive of my strange hobby. When we got together, she was aware of what I did – I was already developing a bit of a profile in New Zealand as a freediver and even getting the odd speaking gig where I'd share some of my strategies about how to perform under pressure. But after Dean's Blue Hole, I vowed I was no longer going to push my limits in the water.

'Hon,' I say gently that night in bed. 'I've had this crazy idea . . .'

I outline my plan of trying to break the world record for diving beneath the ice. Unsurprisingly, Merryn is not thrilled.

'Swimming under the ice sounds a lot more scary than going deep,' she frowns. 'It sounds so claustrophobic. So dangerous. What about polar bears?'

I explain that it's actually not as mad as she thinks and that polar bears won't be an issue. I've done some tactical prep for this conversation, taking the T-1 approach. On my laptop, I show her pictures that I've found from an ice-diving event in Finland at which people from all over Europe compete.

'Most of them aren't even elite freedivers,' I explain.

'But what if you swim up and bang your head on the ice and knock yourself out?'

'That's a possibility,' I acknowledge, 'albeit an outside one. But that's exactly why they have teams of safety divers and paramedics on standby. The good thing about ice diving is that you don't go that deep, so you're always close to the surface. If something goes wrong, it's much easier to rescue you.'

'I still don't like it, Anthony.'

We talk it over some more. I reiterate how the 65-metre depth I'd have to reach to break the record is a fraction of my personal best. We consider how my freediving has given me a point of difference professionally. How a world record could open the door to a range of speaking opportunities and deliver national publicity for our business. We crunch the numbers to see if the trip is financially viable and figure we can make it work.

'You know I'll accept your decision either way,' I say. 'But I'd love to have a crack at this.'

Merryn sighs with resignation and I can tell she's still not enthused. My wife, by her own admission, is a worrier. She never wanted to accompany me back when I was actively competing, for fear that her anxiety would distract me from the task at hand. After every dive, I had to call her immediately, no matter the time zone, to reassure her that I'd got through unscathed. Merryn would sleep with her mobile phone next to the pillow waiting for the call.

'I never want to hold you back,' she says. 'Still, I suppose there are worse kinds of mid-life crises.'

I know my wife well enough to realise she's just given me a tacit 'yes'.

The next morning, before either of us can have second thoughts, I take to social media to declare my intentions to the world and make myself publicly accountable. 'Just found my next big challenge,' I write. 'I'm going to break the world record to become the deepest man ever to dive under the ice.'

Six months later, I'm landing in Helsinki for my first proper taste of ice diving. It's the tail end of the Nordic winter and beneath a low-hanging sun, the city is covered in snow. I'm travelling with my friend Brendon, who's not much of a freediver but is a true outdoors man with years of experience in the Canadian Rockies, where he worked as a mountain guide. Our plan is to spend two weeks in Finland on an exploratory mission to see what freediving is really like in sub-zero conditions. Our visit is timed to coincide with a non-competitive diving event at Lake Päijänne in the Finnish resort town of Lehmonkärki. I want to experience ice diving myself to see if I'm really cut out for it and discover what I need to do to break the record.

We're picked up at the airport by the event's organiser, Antero Joki, in his ute. I became friendly with Antero when we met at my first freediving comp back in Cyprus. Antero was a welcoming presence eager to pass on his tips, and we've stayed in touch ever since.

Heavily built with a ponytail, Antero doesn't look like your typical freediver, but he's one of the most experienced ice divers in the world, not to mention a 100-metre competition freediver, too. Now an instructor and international judge, he currently serves as technical officer for AIDA, the sport's international governing body.

We drive for a couple of hours over icy roads through thick forests. From behind the wheel, Antero gives us the lowdown on what it's like to dive in freezing water. 'Of course, the cold is another obstacle, because you are not so relaxed,' he says. 'But maybe there's an advantage too because of how strong the dive response is.'

Exposure to really cold water, he explains, triggers the heart rate to slow and the blood vessels in your extremities to constrict to conserve oxygen and prioritise blood flow to vital organs. Those physiological responses are central to the mammalian dive reflex that allows divers to stay underwater for longer.

'The downside,' Antero chuckles, 'is that it's very, very cold!'

I find out just how cold the following morning. Antero's event doesn't start for another week but Brendon and I want to acclimatise and give ice diving a try. We decide to head out to the nearby lake for our first attempt.

My cold weather equipment is limited but I've got gloves and two brand-new wetsuits from my sponsors made of 5-millimetre-thick neoprene. On my feet I wear a pair of Crocs, a form of footwear that Antero reckons are the best possible options on a frozen lake. 'They offer incredible grip,' he told me via email.

Outside, the sun is barely cresting the horizon, casting long, blue shadows onto the snow. The temperature is –2°C. It's a short walk down to the lake, whose surface is frozen solid, with the ice thick enough to support a truck. It no longer resembles a body of water but a vast plain of white covered with a heavy crust of snow. Stepping onto it is a weird sensation, knowing that underfoot you're standing on water not land.

A sauna is positioned near the man-made hole where we're planning our first immersion, but I've barely set foot on the ice when Brendon points to my wetsuit. One of the panels of neoprene is flapping loose after somehow coming unstuck down the side. Then I notice the same thing is happening on the left leg. The cold is so intense that the glue that binds the wetsuit together is disintegrating. Figuring I must have got a dodgy sample, I head back to the log cabin where we're staying and get into my spare wetsuit, which is also brand-new.

Back outside, the same thing happens again. It's a pointed reminder that I'm facing a new form of extreme cold whose force shouldn't be underestimated by wetsuit manufacturers.

In the small town of Lehmonkärki there's only one dive shop and, not surprisingly, it's not well stocked with high-performance, freediving wetsuits. The best I can manage to hire is an old scuba suit. Heavy and cumbersome, it's got a big zip up the front and offers minimal flexibility. Meanwhile the shop owner gets on the phone to order me an upgrade from Helsinki, although the best he can source is a spear-fishing suit.

'Diving isn't so popular here,' he says with a shrug. 'It's too cold.'

An hour later, I'm finally standing by the ice hole in my rented scuba suit. It's now started to lightly snow and I'm already shivering. The ice hole is a window with no view. All it reveals is water so black that it feels like I'm looking into an oil well. Warily I sit on the edge of the hole and dip my feet into the water. The cold is lacerating. If I'm going to do this, I need to move fast before I can talk myself out of it.

Sliding my upright body into the icy lake, my scuba suit immediately flushes with freezing water. There's an explosion of stinging pain as my goosebumps turn into tiny needles. Instinctively I gasp, my heart pounding like a wild animal. All composure shatters into a million hairline cracks. Every sense goes into fight-or-flight mode. Whoa!

This is the opposite state I need before a dive where relaxation is key. I take a few seconds to try in vain to regulate my breathing, then I duck dive beneath the ice.

In the blackness, the cold is electrifying and my hands and feet immediately start to throb. My face is numb, my muscles tense, while my eyes feel like they might freeze in their sockets. I force myself down about 10 metres before aborting, praying I can find the hole in the ice. By the time I resurface, I'm shaking with cold as I rush to the sauna to heat up. Sitting on a wooden bench, skin tingling, head buzzing with endorphins, I find myself laughing at the intensity of the experience.

After I've warmed up a bit, I'm back outside to watch over Brendon as he undergoes his own baptism of ice. He's done enough cold plunges over the years to know that a slow descent only prolongs the agony. Instead he enters the ice hole in a single, decisive action. A weird guttural yelp escapes his lips as if the cold has punched the breath from his body. His eyes widen in astonishment like he's been jolted with an electric shock and I find my own teeth clenching in sympathy. He manages to last 60 seconds before scrambling out, shivering hard with steam rising from his body. He looks both triumphant and slightly mad.

'Holy fuck, that's cold,' he stammers.

We return to the ice hole the next day and the next, but progress is painfully slow. In the first five days, I can't get down past 30 metres. It's like my body is unable to process the ferocity of the cold. After my initial wetsuit problems, I'm still not sure I can fully trust my equipment in the freezing conditions and I proceed with caution. It feels like I'm dealing with a completely new element.

When the spear-fishing suit arrives from Helsinki, things improve slightly in terms of my ability to handle the temperature. Mentally though, freediving in the ice is a different game because you're not only having to grapple with the lack of oxygen but the shock of the cold.

Managing that stimulus puts my body on red alert. The hyper-vigilant voice in the back of my head takes on a different tone in the freezing water. It becomes shriller and more alarmist. That makes it hard to relax which, in turn, plays havoc with your breath.

The darkness is a further obstacle as the visibility deep beneath the ice is almost nil. This disorienting effect is exacerbated by the fact that I also seem to feel the woozy onset of narcosis earlier in these freezing conditions, which saps my energy and affects my decision-making. That's a worry when you're sealed beneath a thick layer of ice with only a solitary exit hole to aim for. With ice diving, there is zero margin for error.

The only way to get used to these factors, I realise, is repeat exposure. I have to practise and practise until my mind stops lurching into panic mode and finally allows me to relax. Rather than fighting the sensations, I have to embrace them. I have to accept that the water will be skull-thuddingly cold. Accept that the darkness will overwhelm my senses and that the experience will be an ordeal. All these mind games are necessary to convince myself that I'm capable of thriving under the ice.

A man in the cold, I remind myself, is not necessarily a cold man. I just need to pre-heat beforehand in the sauna, then stay as warm as possible under the ice by getting some decent gloves and a proper wetsuit that doesn't leak. Most importantly, I need to minimise how long I spend in the freezing water.

Over the course of the week, I slowly begin to acclimatise. The cold becomes less of a visceral shock, until, by day five, I'm almost enjoying it. Diving beneath the ice is like venturing into some magical cocoon. Within that dark void, there are no colours and no sounds. The solitude is both peaceful and terrible.

When Antero's event finally begins, it's not what I'd expected. All the freediving events I've previously been to have been competitive, and that format inevitably sets the tone. Participants tend to be focused and earnest, targeting specific depths and distances that they've spent months training for. Päijänne on the Rocks, on the other hand, is designed for hobbyists and enthusiasts. One hundred people have travelled here from all over Europe and the mood is friendly and fun. Coming from Australia, Brendon and I are exotic curiosities and people seek us out to chat about our motivation and why I'm determined to try and go so deep.

Antero has organised things to allow people to try multiple forms of ice diving and I take full advantage. One dip is organised for divers without wetsuits. There's a night dive that exposes me to an inky level of pure darkness that's beyond anything I'd ever imagined. Trying the various events broadens my understanding of what ice diving truly requires. I discover, for example, that you have to work harder to manage your buoyancy to avoid floating up accidentally to clatter the ice.

As one of the more experienced freedivers, on the penultimate day, Antero approaches me and asks for some help to set up a 20-metre swim between two ice holes.

'The swimmers need to follow a rope to make sure they don't veer off course,' he says. 'Can you swim between the two holes with the rope so we can feed it through the second to create a guide line?'

'But it's so dark. How will I not get lost?'

'I'll be at the other hole and I'll put my arm down with a torch that I'll wave around. When you get a bit closer, you'll be able to see it.'

Instinctively, I agree but once I'm in my wetsuit, I soon begin to question my decision. What I'm volunteering for is the stuff of nightmares. If I lose my sense of direction and drift away from the holes, I'll be stuck under the ice, running out of oxygen in freezing water. But Antero has already thought of a safety precaution to eliminate the risk. 'We'll tie a rope around your waist,' he says. 'That way if you get lost, we'll be able to pull you back.'

I get into the icy water gingerly and submerge. Instantly, my visibility is reduced to almost nothing. Mired in darkness, I swim along in what I hope is the right direction, but my anxiety has stopped me going deep enough and I keep bouncing off the underside of the ice. Each bump disorientates me, but I push on.

I can't see the torch. Am I going in the right direction? This is getting scary now, should I turn back? My head bangs into the ice again and suddenly, I'm seized with a desperate urge to breathe.

Keep swimming – you've done ten times this distance before. Where is that bloody torch?

Finally I see a glimmer of the beam and I strike out for it at full pace. Emerging from the ice hole, the relief is overwhelming and my breath is so ragged with fear that I feel too dizzy to stand. Once I'm eventually back on my feet, I can see the passage I've just covered above the ground. In reality, the distance is pitifully short, but under the water, it felt like an unbridgeable chasm. That brief swim under the ice was the most terrifying thing I've ever done.

CHAPTER 21

The trip to Finland only hardens my resolve to become the world's deepest ice diver. I give myself one year to train for the challenge that I vow to attempt in the next Scandinavian winter. Grudgingly, Merryn agrees to support me. Although she does make me double-check my life insurance.

Her main concern is that I'm going to push myself too far. She mentions a middle-aged Australian, Francesco Enrico Marchetti, who's just died of suspected altitude sickness while trying to summit Mount Everest. She even brings up Steve Irwin, who kept deliberately thrusting himself into high-risk situations with dangerous creatures.

'Just don't be that guy who doesn't know when to stop.'

'I promise you right now, I'll dive within my limits. I won't take any unnecessary risks.'

While I accept I've still got much to learn about ice diving, I'm hopeful that in 12 months' time, I'll be ready. I'm convinced the reason why the world record is a relatively modest 65 metres stems as much from the logistical challenge as the difficulty of the task itself. Most freedivers simply don't have ready access to an icy lake in which to train. Even if they do, most lakes aren't deep enough to enable the world record to be broken.

These sort of practical realities narrow the field and make ice diving a sub-genre in an already niche sport. If you want to become a record-breaking ice diver, you have to get yourself somewhere with sub-zero conditions, before spending enough time there to acclimatise to the cold. Sourcing the gear, building your backup team and dealing with all the travel expenses means that ice diving quickly becomes an expensive business, unless you happen to be a Scandinavian, an Inuit or a polar bear.

There's no doubt the expense will sting – I estimate the trip will wind up costing about $40,000. But the organisational side doesn't faze me after my brief and ill-fated stint running a MotoGP team. The most crucial part, I believe, will be assembling a support crew of experts with the right blend of specialist skills. I need a team that I can trust with my life.

First up, I need someone with an encyclopaedic knowledge of ice diving who can act as my consultant and Scandinavian fixer. Immediately, I think of Antero Joki, the mastermind behind the Päijänne on the Rocks event. His experience of diving in sub-zero conditions is second to none. Antero will be a pragmatic advisor and ice coach. Most importantly, we get on really well.

I also need some form of medical support in case anything goes wrong. Fortuitously, Antero's partner, Maria, is not only a free-diver, she's also a trained paramedic and qualified surgeon. When I approach the pair about helping me out for a small fee, they're delighted to get involved.

Another vital addition is a safety diver who can fish me out of the water if I black out. The first person I think of is Jonathan Sunnex, a fellow Kiwi who's become a good mate and leads safety teams at freediving events all over the world. Johnny was a friend of Nick Mevoli, the American who taught me how to refine my equalisation technique in the Bahamas, just a year before he died. After Nick's death, Johnny quit competitive freediving and made it his mission to try to make our sport safer. Subsequently, he's supervised the safety procedures at numerous international competitions and is now the safety officer for AIDA, the sport's governing body. When Johnny agrees to help me, it's another massive win.

Given their collective know-how, I couldn't have picked a more accomplished crew. Knowing they'll be with me every step of the way is reassuring, but I still need a couple more recruits. While I'm determined to break the world record, I also know that when the atmosphere around me is too earnest, I don't perform as well. It rubs off on me and I get unhelpfully tense. With the final crew selections, I'm therefore keen to introduce people who'll bring a bit of fun and excitement as well as some form of practical skill.

What I found so thrilling about freediving right from the beginning was the personal challenge and excitement. Now in my late forties, I'm aware that opportunities for adventure are increasingly scarce in a stage of life when most people are trying to juggle work, family and mortgages. Part of my motivation for this record attempt is the desire to rekindle that initial sense of wonder. And while I definitely need some hardened professionals by my side, I'd also like to have some people with a fresher perspective who'll bring some wide-eyed enthusiasm and fun.

Listing the various requirements for the challenge, I'm aware that I'm going to have a load of diving equipment and related kit that needs to be prepped, organised and monitored. It's not a highly technical role, but it's still important. The more of these responsibilities I can delegate, the freer I'll be to concentrate on my job as an athlete.

The person I think of for this 'kitman' role is Andrew Kelly, a middle-aged industrial designer whom I met at a freediving competition in Brisbane. Andrew is relatively new to the sport and still in the honeymoon period where he can't get enough of it. The idea of tapping into that enthusiasm appeals.

Andrew and I got to know each other after I saw him black out in a static breath-hold event. I shared a few tips about how I'd dealt with similar issues and we've kept in touch ever since. While his familiarity with freediving is helpful, the real clincher for why I'm asking him along is more romantic. Despite being in his late forties, Andrew has never seen snow in his life. An Arctic adventure like this will be a mind-blowing experience for him.

The final crewmember I need is a multipurpose problem-solver. After watching my wetsuit disintegrate from the cold in Finland, I know that unexpected obstacles are bound to pop up in extreme conditions. Will my homemade monofin work okay in the icy water? Will the carabiner I use to attach myself to the line still open if it's frozen solid and subjected to seven bars of pressure in icy conditions?

I'm kicking these questions around one night when I get a call from Simon Gordon, an old mate from New Zealand. Charismatic and full of energy, right now Simon is going through a difficult patch: his wife and mother of his six children recently left him for another man. Not surprisingly, Simon is heartbroken. I'm listening to his woes over the phone, gently trying to console him as he reveals his devastation. Simon is a strong and level-headed character, but it's clear that he's not doing well.

Then it hits me. Simon would be a great addition to my ice-diving crew. As a professional engineer, he'd bring some hands-on skills to the team, while his can-do attitude means he's unlikely to be fazed by any sub-zero curveballs. At the same time, I reckon a bit of respite from his current predicament might be exactly what he needs. When he agrees, my team is complete.

There are still months to go before we're due to head over to Norway, where Antero has already scouted a lake for the attempt. In the meantime, I practise getting myself match-fit. As part of a relocation for work, I've moved with my family to Torquay in Victoria, not far from the famous Bells Beach. Every weekend, I head out into the ocean with a couple of freediving buddies to condition myself to going deep once again. It's six years since I made it to 100 metres in the Bahamas and I need to reacquaint my body with the pressure that real depths bring. In Torquay, it's hard to find accessible diving spots deeper than 70 metres, but I soon find that I'm managing that depth with ease.

In fact, there's nowhere in Victoria where I can find cold enough water in which to practise. Instead, I head over to New Zealand with Andrew and Simon to dive in Lake Taupo, the large crater lake on the North Island. With a water temperature of about 12°C, it hardly matches the 2–4°C you'd find in a Scandinavian lake, but Lake Taupo at least offers the necessary depth. I'm soon getting down to 85 metres on a consistent basis. In Norway, I only need to hit 70 metres, albeit in far less hospitable conditions. Gradually my confidence is growing. If I can just learn to manage the icy temperatures, then a world record attempt feels like a distinct possibility.

Knowing that a solid period of acclimatisation is crucial, we set off for the attempt in March 2019. The team meets in Helsinki in order to use Antero's annual ice-diving event as a form of training camp designed to familiarise everyone with the practical realities and safety precautions. My idea is that Päijänne on the Rocks will give everyone the chance to learn their individual responsibilities in a setting that's supervised but also good fun.

Throwing together a disparate collection of people is always a slight gamble, but I'm delighted with how everyone seems to bond. Once again, the event at Lake Päijänne is a lively affair punctuated by big group dinners and parties for divers from all over the world. Predictably, Andrew is thrilled by his first attempt at ice diving, with the warm-blooded Queenslander equally delighted by the novelty of snow. Simon is a big personality, but his outgoing nature is a hit, helping to bring different groups of people and nationalities together.

Given his recent dramas back home, he's clearly up for a good time and revels in the social side, hanging out and drinking with all these ice-diving Europeans.

One afternoon, Simon, Andrew, Johnny and I ditch the event to do a snowmobile driving course. It proves to be hilarious as driving these vehicles, it turns out, is far more complicated than it looks. The throttle of a snowmobile is highly sensitive. Tug it too hard and the sled rockets forward, as I discover to much laughter when I lose control and almost flip the machine. Reading the terrain is also challenging. What looks like a pristine blanket of snow can conceal rocks and logs – as Andrew discovers when he's knocked into a spin by a hidden tree stump. It turns into a day of endless laughter and piss-taking. As a team-bonding experience, snowmobile driving has much to offer.

Back in Lahti, there's a big farewell dinner at a wood-panelled restaurant to mark the end of the event. I'm not drinking in a bid to stay sharp ahead of my dive, but I'm very much in the minority. There's a party mood, with lots of people necking shots of Kossu, a clear Finnish spirit with a lethal kick judging by all the smiles and flushed faces. I quietly slip away from the festivities as I'm mindful I have to fine-tune the arrangements and accommodation for the next leg of the trip. Tomorrow we're off to Kirkenes, the remote location in northern Norway where my dive is due to take place. I might have come here to break a record but in the meantime I'm also the tour organiser and logistics coordinator.

The next day, I wake up feeling knackered, but I organise the crew into two hire cars, ahead of the two-day drive to Kirkenes. Driving that far in icy conditions is a taxing effort, but the mood in the team is buoyant. Amid all the chat and laughter, I feel like a teacher on a high-school excursion.

I've made a late decision to break up the trip with an overnight stop near Rovaniemi, a Finnish town on the edge of the Arctic Circle that bills itself as the 'Official Hometown of Santa Claus'. After being bombed in World War II, the Finnish architect Alvar Aalto redesigned the place in the shape of a reindeer head with the outer roads shooting out like antlers. Despite the fact that it's now March, the festive spirit continues. In Rovaniemi, it seems, it's Christmas every day.

Entering the town, it's clear that Rovaniemi has leveraged its quirky layout to become an unlikely tourist hotspot. There are adverts for dog-sledding excursions and igloo-building classes, while Antero points out a nearby hotel that apparently has an entire bar made of ice. On every street there are souvenir shops, many of which are run by 'elves' in pointy red hats peddling an extraordinary selection of Yuletide tat. After finding our accommodation, we walk through the snow to explore the town, which is still lit up with fairy lights. Yes, it's a cheesy concept, but somehow it reels us all in. We end up in a shop buying up all sorts of festive oddities, from Santa socks to canned reindeer meat. I snap up a cheese slicer made from reindeer antlers for Merryn, while Simon buys a jumbo bottle of Finnish vodka.

Walking out of the shop, someone calls my name. Turning my head, I cop a snowball from Simon full in the face. The next second, everyone is involved in a full-scale battle. I catch Andrew with a lucky shot to the back of his neck, then get pelted by Antero. The cold air is filled with the *whizz-thud* of exploding snowballs. We're carrying on like children and I'm laughing so hard I can hardly breathe. Privately, I congratulate myself on my masterful recruitment strategy. I feel like I've assembled the perfect team.

CHAPTER 22

When we get to Kirkenes the following afternoon, the temperature is –36.5°C. The cold is now a hostile force. Even in the brief time it takes to unload the cars, I watch the vapour in my breath freeze into a cloud of ice. Miniature icicles soon form on my eyebrows. The air bites with a metallic sharpness and any patch of exposed skin becomes numb within seconds.

I've rented a huge log cabin with seven bedrooms to accommodate the team and I'm struck as I walk around its perimeter by how the thick snow deadens all sound. This is no winter wonderland but an unforgiving environment that feels inimical to all forms of life.

Almost immediately Antero gets to work. In the back of his car, he's brought three wooden stumps that he connects together into a sort of three-legged stool. This will provide the platform for a pulley that my dive rope will run through before it's fed into the icy water with a weight attached to the bottom. I'll follow that rope down, hopefully to a world-record depth of 70 metres and then back up again. The reason for Antero's contraption is that it's not safe to run the rope straight off the ice; you need some elevation to help you pull it up quickly in case of an emergency. The contraption also gives me something to cling onto when I surface from the ice hole.

While Antero soldiers away in the freezing conditions, Simon is watching him intently out the window while sipping his vodka.

Soon he starts muttering out loud. 'Oh no, what the hell is that thing? What is this guy even trying to do?'

Chucking on his snow jacket and hat, he goes outside to speak to Antero. The next thing I can hear raised voices. An argument has flared up. Looking out the window, Antero is standing there with his arms folded, a livid scowl on his face, while Simon is jabbing his finger at the legs of the wooden structure. There's a bit more shouting and a few seconds later, Antero storms in and slams the door shut before disappearing to his room.

'What's going on?' I ask Simon when he walks in.

'Well, I went to ask Antero what he's trying to do with that piece of shit,' he says. 'He explained how it was meant to hold the rope and could yank you out of the water if you black out. But I'm not comfortable with that set-up at all and just pointed out some problems. Those wooden legs will collapse under your weight and the whole thing will fall down the hole, never to be seen again.'

'Did things get a bit heated?'

'Not really. Well, he's a stubborn fella. But I'm an engineer, remember? That's why you brought me along. And I'm telling you this pulley design is terrible, it doesn't have self-reinforcing sides, there's nothing bracing it. Mate, it's a bloody disaster waiting to happen. This guy has no idea.'

Inwardly, I groan. Antero is a great bloke, but like many Finnish men I've met he's also wilful and proud. As a freediving expert, he won't have taken kindly to some newbie rubbishing his handiwork. Figuring it's best to tackle the issue before it escalates, I go see him. When he opens his bedroom door, he's still furious.

'Anthony, I've been using my invention for ten years in ice diving without incident. I've done many record attempts, many events, many training sessions. I have been using it for ten years! Now this New Zealand man, who does not even know how to freedive, is criticising my work? Saying it is useless? Who the hell is he to tell me that? I'm sorry, Anthony, I cannot work with this idiot.'

The mood is now strained. Simon and Antero aren't speaking and there's no respite, given that we're all stuck in a log cabin deep in the Arctic.

I'm hoping tonight's feast will lighten things up a bit. I've roasted some root vegetables to accompany a huge side of smoked salmon and some giant king crabs that we caught underneath the jetty near the lake. Despite the crab being the most divine seafood I've ever tasted in my life, the conversation remains stilted and the atmosphere as frosty as the weather outside.

Afterwards, I retire to my room for an early night, but 20 minutes later, Andrew knocks on my door. When I open it, the expression on his face is grave.

'Can I have a word, mate?'

'Of course, come in.'

Andrew sits down looking shell-shocked. It takes a moment for him to compose himself to speak. 'Just got off the phone with my wife. She got some results back from her doctor. She's got cancer, Ant. Kylie has cancer.'

It's crushing news and Andrew is understandably blindsided. I let him talk and talk, not knowing exactly what to say. His wife is due to undergo further tests in the coming days, but right now there's no clear prognosis. Inevitably though, Andrew's mind is already jumping to scary conclusions.

'Mate, I think you should go home as soon as possible. You need to be there for Kylie. I'll pay for a new flight if necessary. We just have to get you back. I can drive you to the airport tomorrow.'

Still in a state of shocked disbelief, Andrew nods and goes off to call his wife again. When he returns, I ask how Kylie is getting on.

'She's hanging in there, poor girl. One thing she's adamant about, though, is that there's no point in me coming back now. She pointed out there's nothing I can do and it'll take several days to get back to Brisbane anyway. By then, she'll already be out of hospital and we'll have more info on what's going on. She just wants me to hold tight.'

'How do you feel about that?'

'I don't know, mate. I want to be with her, but I can see her point, too.'

We talk it over, flipping the issue this way and that. I'm still encouraging Andrew to go home and reassure him that we'll be able to manage without him. But after a further conversation with his wife, he decides to stay.

That night, I find it hard to sleep. I feel horrible for Andrew and don't know how to support him in this nightmare predicament. Not only has he just discovered that his wife has cancer, but he's stuck in a remote destination that could hardly be further away. The poor guy is in an impossible situation.

From the back of my mind, another thought slowly emerges. Andrew is, of course, now preoccupied with his wife's condition as any right-minded person would be. Given all that mental noise, will he still be able to focus on his fairly involved role, prepping, maintaining and double-checking all my equipment? It may not sound like a major issue, but small things quickly become big things when you're fully submerged in freezing water at depth.

The next morning at breakfast, Andrew is subdued. But Simon is his usual bouncy self, chatting away to everyone apart from Antero – that relationship seems irrevocably screwed. I wonder if Simon's cheery mood has anything to do with the nips of vodka he's chasing his coffee with.

Today, we've got to go and cut the ice hole. To reach a deep enough spot for my attempt we have to drive for more than an hour across the frozen lake on our five rented snowmobiles. Antero has drummed it into me how often snowmobile mishaps occur and we've established certain safety guidelines that I reiterate to the team. Everyone is to ride in single file, maintaining a conservative speed and leaving a safe braking distance between each vehicle. Each driver must stick to the centre of the ice and always stay well within eyeshot of the rest of the party.

We've only been riding for about 15 minutes before Simon gets bored and shoots off into the distance, hooning around at high speed and letting out the occasional whoop. I appreciate that he's had a tough year and is here to blow off some steam, but his disregard for the instructions is vexing.

The ice is a metre and a half thick and cutting a hole through it proves heavy going. First we have to shovel away a thick layer of snow to give us a clear surface to access the ice. Antero then outlines the ice hole in the form of a 2-metre triangle, a shape chosen because it requires fewer cuts than a square. The triangle is then subdivided into multiple smaller sections to ensure the hunks of ice that we'll eventually pull out aren't too heavy. Using a powerful chainsaw with a nice, long bar, Antero starts to go around the perimeter of the triangle making shallow perforations at regular intervals. Then, applying steady pressure, he slowly rocks the saw downward, allowing the chain to bite into the ice.

It's a long and arduous process. Simon gets bored after a couple of hours and heads back, saying he'll drive into town to get supplies. I suggest he takes Andrew with him. The poor bloke has looked withdrawn and miserable all day.

The ice is so thick that it takes us eight back-breaking hours to carve out the hole. Then there are more than 20 giant ice cubes to remove in a painstaking process that takes yet another hour. Antero drills a hole in each ice cube and then drops a rope through with a metal bar at the end, allowing us to yank them out one by one. Some of the cubes are so big they require six of us to lift them.

When Antero finally removes the last cube with a special pair of tongs, I let out a cheer that's swallowed by the knifing wind.

Back in the log cabin, shivering from the cold and exhausted from all the shivering, I discover that Simon has crashed the hire car on the way into town after skidding on some ice.

'A farmer had to help me get it out of a bank with a snowplough,' he says cheerfully.

The following day I'm due to try a practice dive ahead of the world record attempt. There have been so many distractions that I've barely thought about what we've come here to do. Finally I can concentrate on the task at hand.

Physically, I'm shattered. Yesterday, I felt obliged to help cut the hole in the ice, but the effort has taken a lot out of me, coming as it did on the back of jet lag and a jam-packed few days. Keeping track of all the organisational requirements as team leader while trying to ease the interpersonal friction has proved more taxing than I expected.

I put on my wetsuit, then layer up for the journey to the lake in my Arctic expedition gear. I'd planned this hour-long snowmobile ride over to the ice hole as my chance to mentally rehearse each step of the dive. That plan is quickly scuppered when Simon manages to crash his snowmobile into a 3-metre bank of snow. He's not hurt, but it takes us two hours to extricate the vehicle and the incident does nothing to improve relations between him and Antero.

By the time we eventually get out to the lake, Antero has already been there for some time. He's been using the chainsaw to redefine the ice hole that's already slightly frozen over. Keen to avoid getting cold, I get into the sauna to warm up. Inside the tiny pine box, the temperature is only 4°C, but it's still better than outside and I take advantage of the relative warmth to do some preliminary breathing exercises. I need to get myself into the zone.

Somehow a few hardy locals have heard about my attempt and there are several people standing about in thick snow jackets including a local reporter and photographer.

'As there's some media, maybe you should wear the white mask instead of the black one,' Andrew suggests. 'It goes much better with your wetsuit.'

'Why not,' I agree. 'And mate, where's my monofin got to?'

'I left it outside by the hole.'

'You left it on the ice? You better quickly grab it then, it'll be frozen solid.'

'Oh shit!'

The monofin, it turns out, has been sitting on the bare ice for two hours. Its black carbon fibre blade is now encrusted with snow and the foot pockets, which are made of high density rubber, are banked up with ice crystals. It's viciously cold when I insert my feet, to the point where it's actually painful. Aside from the discomfort, I'm also worried about whether the cold may have compromised the structural integrity of the fin. Could it snap in this brittle state?

Andrew is mortified by his mistake. I don't want to berate him, given everything that he's got going on, plus I haven't got much choice but to press on. I put on the white mask, hoping that taking his advice will make Andrew feel a bit better. Then Johnny Sunnex and Antero carry me from the sauna to the hole because I can't walk in my monofin.

Sitting on the edge of the ice hole with my feet in the water, it doesn't feel any colder than my frozen fin. My feet are already throbbing painfully.

'Anthony, you need to start the dive as soon as possible,' Antero urges. 'The longer you wait, the more dangerous it'll be.'

Feeling a little rushed, I start my final breathing preparation, packing the cold air into my lungs and trying to ignore the fact that my feet are completely numb. Then I slip into the freezing water and start my descent.

Once again, I'm amazed by the density of the blackness. But I'm also startled by just how fast I'm hurtling downwards. What's going on? Then I realise we haven't adjusted my weight belt since Finland. I'm now carrying way more weight than I normally would for a dive of this depth. That's unsettling as it'll make it harder to swim back up.

After about a minute, I've reached a depth of 50 metres and I still feel like I've got plenty of air. But then I'm aware of a plinking sound and a tiny explosion in my mask. A gush of freezing water sloshes over my face. The lenses on the white mask must've imploded due to the pressure. What the hell? The icy water stings my face, but I know that if I open my eyes now, my retinas will freeze and I'll need surgery.

Keep going, Ant. You keep your eyes shut anyway, remember. It's a curveball sure, but nothing serious. Just hang onto the line.

I pusher deeper but I'm really stressing out now and after a few more kicks I decide to abort. Fighting my way back to the surface is hard work. I'm battling those extra kilos on my weight belt and it takes real effort to claw my way up.

Just get to the surface and regroup.

Back in the sauna, I'm not happy. I'm shivering and exhausted while my feet are pulsating in agony. Admittedly I made it to 67 metres, but between worrying about my mask, my fin and the weight belt, it turned into a grim ordeal. Johnny Sunnex comes in for a debrief and I explain what happened.

He shakes his head at the lack of professionalism. 'That could've got hairy,' he says. 'In these conditions, you can't mess about.'

'Mate, let's face it: that was a total fiasco. In fact, I'm genuinely concerned now. Do you think I should continue with this attempt?'

'I reckon everyone just needs a bit of a talking to,' Johnny says. 'You've got to make sure they understand the risks. Everyone needs to grasp that we can't afford to make mistakes like that.'

On the way back to the cabin, Simon manages to crash another snowmobile.

After dinner, I call everyone together for a team talk. I've planned what I'm going to say quite carefully and want it to be constructive and encouraging. But I also need to be firm and direct. It has to be a serious meeting because what we're about to undertake is a serious business.

'Tomorrow I'm going to attempt to descend to a depth of 70 metres. While mistakes can always happen, we need to collectively try to eliminate them, as each one could have potentially serious consequences. Focus is critical now and everyone needs to be totally aligned and clear about their roles and responsibilities.'

I speak to the group for about 20 minutes, outlining the next day's itinerary and recapping each person's duties and the specific things they need to watch out for. I spell out the responsibilities for each step of dive in detail: who'll be manning the rope, who'll be timing my dive underwater, the safety plan if anything goes wrong. There's a lot to remember and, as I run through the list, I'm probably more concerned with covering all the bases than I am with dancing around sensitivities and egos.

During the talk, everyone listens and seems gratifyingly engaged. But at the end of the meeting, almost everyone gets up and slopes off to their rooms. Perhaps I came across a little sterner than I intended?

When no one re-emerges, I begin to think that maybe I've misjudged my tone. I know that Johnny and Antero will be fine. They understand the severity of the consequences. Andrew, I reckon, should also be okay. He knows that he screwed up with my equipment today and will surely recognise that he needs to be more alert tomorrow. Simon is the one I'm most worried about. He can be an emotional character and I fear I may have rubbed him up the wrong way. Rather than fretting about that possibility in silence, I decide to check in on him.

'Can we have a chat?' I say at his doorway.

'Of course, mate, come in.'

I perch on the end of his bed, while Simon sits at the desk. It strikes me that I must've known this guy for about 15 years now. We've been fixtures in each other's lives through a big transitional period that's evolved from bachelor days to family life. That bond means a lot to me. And while I'm frustrated by Simon's snowmobile driving, his drinking and his unnecessary spat with Antero, he's still one of my oldest mates. Surely I can be honest with him now?

'Simon, I just wanted to check in with you, mate. I know we might have slightly different motivations on this trip. I know how you desperately needed a break because of all the craziness back home. I know that I sold it to you as a big adventure. But tomorrow is where everything gets very real for me. That means we've all got to align and focus on this common goal of nailing this record. Do you feel ready to do that? Can you focus on this thing for me tomorrow, so we can all come together as a team?'

'Yeah, of course, whatever you need.'

I go over his responsibilities for the next day once again. I plead with him to be more careful on the snowmobile. I reiterate how important his role is, not just from a practical perspective but also in terms of team morale.

'Can you maybe lay off the booze tomorrow, too? If I get the record, we'll celebrate properly, I promise.'

Simon challenges me on a number of points. He argues that Antero is obstructive and refuses to entertain his point of view. He insists that he was driving the hire car safely and blames the crash on a treacherous patch of ice.

I leave his room reasonably happy with how it's all gone. It was a slightly tricky conversation, but I haven't ducked it and I feel like

I've made my point clearly while keeping it within the realms of a friendly chat.

Back in the living room, Antero and Maria are playing cards in front of the fire. Outside, the snow is falling once again. I sit down and read a few pages of my book to try to take my mind off tomorrow. But after an hour or so, I realise that Simon hasn't reappeared. After a while, this begins to prey on my mind. Did my conversation with him go as well as I thought it did? Or have I accidentally upset him?

For peace of mind, I go and knock on his door. There's no answer. I check to see if he's slipped back into the living room, but there's no sign of him. Returning to his room, I knock again before poking my head around the door. He's not there. Then I realise his expedition gear is no longer hanging on the back of the chair. Seriously? Has Simon gone outside? Looking out the window it's completely dark. The temperature is about –30°C. What on earth is he up to?

By this stage, it's after 9 pm and most people have gone to bed. I go around and knock on their doors to ask if anyone has seen Simon. No one has seen him since dinner.

I sit down in my armchair again and try to read my book. But I can't concentrate; my eyes keep darting to the clock. Soon I'm getting worried. The conditions outside are dark and freezing. We're in an incredibly remote location where there's certainly no street lighting. Simon's absence could actually be quite serious. We don't know where he is and he doesn't have a phone on him. What do we do? By 10 pm, there's still no sign of him and I decide I need to speak to Antero.

'We have to make a search party,' he says gravely. 'No one should be out in this cold.'

Most people are now ready for bed, but instead we go through the tiresome rigmarole of putting on our cold-weather layers, snow jackets and boots. Then we form pairs and head out on foot into the freezing darkness with torches. I'm genuinely worried now. Simon is impulsive and hardly in the best emotional space, given his domestic troubles. Surely he hasn't done something silly?

Outside the darkness is immense, the only sounds are the constant whistle of the wind and the heave of your breath as you battle through the snow. The world shrinks to the small pool of illumination from the torch lights. I'm walking with Andrew, but, given the limited visibility, our search feels ineffectual as we try to follow the blurred remnants of tracks in the snow. After 30 minutes of aimless wandering, the chill is kicking in and we're forced to head back to the cabin.

Inside, Simon is sitting by the fire. Antero found him walking down the road and brought him back. I'm filled with relief that he's okay. But I'm also pissed off.

'What the hell were you doing? Everyone was out looking for you!'

'Oh, I just needed some space. You've heard of cabin fever, right? I had to get some air and fancied a stroll.'

'You didn't think to tell anyone?'

'Mate, I didn't realise I needed permission.'

I'm angry and confused. I can't fathom how anyone could be so irresponsible. What was he thinking? Did Simon want his disappearance to be discovered, maybe taking some perverse satisfaction in making everyone go out and look for him? I honestly don't know and I don't want to ask him either.

CHAPTER 23

I wake up at 5 am, but I'm too aggravated by last night's events to go back to sleep. I have to park that now. I can't spare the mental resources to try to understand what Simon was thinking. This is the day of my world record attempt. I've got to focus.

What's stopping me from doing that, of course, are the growing concerns about my support crew. Andrew's mind is understandably elsewhere, given his wife's cancer diagnosis. And I no longer feel like I can count on Simon, given his reckless behaviour. I should be concentrating on myself and my preparations. Instead I'm fretting about whether it's safe to put my life in the hands of these people. Can I honestly afford to risk it?

Rather than catastrophising, I make a conscious decision to defuse my anxiety by regaining control over my immediate surroundings. I make my bed perfectly. I unpack my suitcase and repack it with military precision. I go through my run sheet for the day that lists everything that needs to happen. Establishing this order brings a sense of calm. I will not allow external factors to unsettle me.

I head into the kitchen to grab some breakfast. Johnny is already sitting at the table with a coffee before him, scratching his black beard. I join him. I've always got on well with Johnny, but he's a quiet and reserved figure who doesn't volunteer much information unless you ask him directly. I trust his judgement implicitly. The reason why he's such a respected safety diver is that he's a perfectionist with sky-high standards. I know he'll give me a straight answer.

'Johnny, after everything that happened yesterday, I'm having some serious reservations, and it's not just pre-match nerves. You know I value your opinion. Do you honestly think we should go ahead with today's attempt? Do you think our team is up to the job?'

He looks at me hard and takes a sip of his coffee. 'Ant, you've brought these guys out here and some of them, let's face it, are not helping your cause, or they're making it more difficult than it needs to be. We need to discard them or at least limit their involvement.'

'But do you think that's problematic?'

'Mate, think about it for a second. All you really need to make this dive happen is Antero and me. Right?'

'Yeah, I guess so.'

'So if you're comfortable with that, I reckon we're still good.'

'On that basis then, I guess we go ahead. But I might need you to take on a bit more responsibility.'

'Whatever you need.'

'I need you to be my coach. I need you to be my sport psychologist. I need you to be my driver. I don't want to talk to these guys while we're doing this record attempt, I can't afford to lose my focus. I need to rely on you.'

'Yeah, no worries, I got your back. Just make sure you're fully prepared.'

After a while, people start trickling in for breakfast. Maria cooks up some eggs. Simon is the last person to surface. If he senses any ill will towards him after last night's outing, he ignores it. We have an amicable if strained conversation and then I return to my room for some last-minute preparation.

Unexpectedly, that brief encounter with Simon has rattled me. It's clear that I haven't yet managed to let go of my resentment from last night's fiasco. Once again, I try to figure out what prompted his disappearance. Have I neglected his needs? Upset him in some way? His whole trip – which I've paid for – was always building up to today. So why would he disrupt things at such a critical juncture? There are two possibilities here and neither is great.

I should be doing my visualisation exercises now but instead I'm second-guessing myself all over again. Johnny is right. I should be okay to just rely on him and Antero. But it's hardly the ideal scenario. Should I postpone the attempt? Come back next year with a more professional team? It's a tempting idea, but I'm not sure I can afford a rerun. I've already paid for everyone's flights, accommodation and car and snowmobile hire. It's a substantial investment that I agonised over. I can't go home to Merryn empty-handed. Yet at the same time, this isn't just a financial decision. The events of the last few days have left me increasingly frazzled and strung-out. My head isn't in the right space for something like this.

There's a knock on the door and Antero looks in. 'There a snowstorm forecast later this afternoon,' he says. 'If we're going to do this, we need to do it now.'

An hour later, our convoy of snowmobiles is skittering towards the ice hole. The cold has a real edge today – it's –10°C and windy – and when we get to the hole I jump straight into the sauna to stretch and warm up my muscles. The heat in the poky, cedar-scented box has been cranked right up, but such is the weather that the inside temperature is barely 3°C. I do a two-minute breath-hold to prime my lungs, but I feel jittery and lacking confidence. All these months of planning and now everything is turning to shit.

Worry about that later. You're here now. You've got Antero and Johnny in your corner. It's business time.

When I step outside, the cold is like a slap to the face. The heat radiating from my skin creates a cloud of mist. Everything is white. Am I ready for this? Can I really do it?

Johnny approaches me and claps me on the back. 'Here we are, bro,' he says. 'This is who we are and this is what we do. Now let's get it done.'

His words trigger a shift in my mind. I stop thinking about all the recent stuff-ups. Johnny is right. I'm an accomplished freediver, I've trained well, I'm in great shape and I'm backed by an amazing ice diver and the best safety diver in the world. It's time to deliver.

I put on the monofin that thankfully isn't encrusted with ice this time and Johnny and Antero carry me over to the edge of the ice hole. Antero urges me to get in the water as quickly as possible. 'You have to start your dive within three minutes. Otherwise you'll get too cold.'

I put on my goggles and nose clip and slip into the hole. The water is electrifyingly cold and provokes an instinctive shudder of mild panic. I feel hyper-alive. Johnny gives me a thumbs up and then I plunge into the freezing blackness.

My world is now silent except for the beat of my heart in my ears. The cold is a purifying force, stripping away my thoughts to leave only an awareness of my body and the freezing embrace of the water. My face is so numb that, as I descend, it's hard to control my lips to keep the air in. I have to put one hand to my mouth to ensure that it's clamped shut.

This body position slows my progress but I continue to go deeper and deeper. I'm equalising well, the desire to breathe not yet too intense. I zone out for a second in the blackness. And then the 70-metre tag is in front of me. I manage to wrestle it free with my frozen fingers. Immediately I turn back. The wetsuit feels heavy and the monofin stiff and unresponsive, forcing me to kick harder. The urge to breathe is fierce now and the upward swim is a slog. My mind is wandering with narcosis, I'm starting to feel dizzy, but the hole is just metres away.

I break the surface and make the okay sign with trembling fingers and blue lips. I feel close to blackout, but I suddenly don't care. I've just completed the deepest ever dive under the ice. Despite all the obstacles, I've done it.

CHAPTER 24

Back in Australia, Merryn throws a big party to celebrate my world record. She fills our house with 'welcome home' balloons, organises a team of caterers and invites about 50 of our friends over. By end of the evening, I'm sore from all the backslapping.

I smile and drink in the plaudits and, to be fair, have a pretty great time. Yet when it comes to the achievement itself, I'm conflicted. There's no denying the pride I feel at having achieved the world record in circumstances that were hardly ideal. But when I reflect on the experience it increasingly feels like a Pyrrhic victory that's been achieved at a personal cost. I may have broken the world record but to make it happen I've left behind a wake of misgivings.

Simon is one of my oldest friends and, frankly, I don't know if our relationship will ever be the same again. That bothers me. You can always make new friends, but you can't make new old friends. Andrew has also become increasingly distant ever since that night in the log cabin when I bluntly outlined the reality of our situation and demanded that the team raise their game. I still check in with him about his wife, whose cancer is now thankfully in remission, but the friendship was strained for a few years.

My pride in the world record is tempered by all this collateral damage. But what's worse, the more I think about it, the more I realise that it was also my fault. The team that I'd hand-picked didn't function properly and underperformed in a dangerous way. Careless mistakes were made and the collective morale broke down.

Ultimately, though, I was the leader, so all those problems were my responsibility to solve. But I failed to do that. Despite having created a successful business in which I literally coach leaders for a living, I was unable to bring the team back into line. Realising how badly I fluffed that role hurts. Rather than forget what happened, I need to pinpoint what went wrong and learn from the experience.

With the benefit of hindsight, I now recognise that my biggest mistake was spreading myself way too thin. I was both the athlete at the heart of the challenge and the leader of the attempt. Trying to do both things at once was simply too much of a burden. It's like trying to be the director of a film as well as the star of the show.

Take, for example, the job of cutting the ice hole that took us nine hours in freezing conditions. As the leader of the group, I felt duty-bound to muck in and help. But it was hard, labour-intensive work that was too physically taxing for me at a point when I was about to put my body on the line. I should have delegated far more responsibility. The effort of wearing two hats left me unable to summon the mental energy to serve as an effective leader.

On paper, I still believe that I assembled a great team of amazing individuals. I had an ice-diving expert in Antero and an underwater safety guru in Johnny in whom I had absolute faith. Maria was a surgeon and paramedic, making her an ideal one-woman medical team. Simon had an engineering background, while Andrew had enough freediving experience to oversee all my equipment.

But teamwork always beats talent. Recruiting a group of accomplished individuals doesn't automatically translate to good performances in the field or, in my case, out on the ice. You've still got to manage your personnel and lead your team effectively. You've got to set a clear goal and get every person excited about achieving it as well as understanding how they can contribute. Politics are inevitable in any group of people. As a leader, you have to manage the various personalities and get them cooperating to overcome their differences and work collectively to achieve the common goal. Aligning the team around that vision is critical.

Unfortunately, I was negligent in this regard. I failed to provide regular feedback and only really stepped in when drastic intervention was needed after the disastrous practice dive. My frustration led to me calling that team meeting to try to rally them, but I then proceeded to make another blunder.

Given the dangers of the challenge and the proximity of the record attempt, I adopted a 'command' style of leadership that was autocratic and direct. Essentially, I told the team they needed to buck up and perform with greater diligence and care. Command leadership uses explicit directives and a forceful tone, which is why it tends to be deployed in crises where clarity of the message is key. In retrospect, it was the wrong leadership style for this scenario. The team clearly found it jarring when I swung from being a hands-off leader to a stern taskmaster.

What I didn't appreciate was that most of my team was operating in a completely alien environment. With the exception of Antero and Maria, no one had much experience of managing sub-zero conditions, let alone carrying out their technical roles amid the ice and snow. They needed more guidance and coaching about how to perform their duties. I failed to provide that and then proceeded to come down on them hard.

Instead, I should have adopted a more 'visionary' style of leadership. At that team meeting, I should have spoken about the common goal we were trying to achieve. I should have communicated how excited I was to have them there and what valuable roles they were playing. In terms of all the practice dive mishaps, I should have engaged with them in a more positive way and asked for their insights on how we could operate better as a team. Involving them more would have aligned them better and got them working together to build a game plan for the attempt.

I did the opposite of that. While I tried to be diplomatic, essentially my speech was one long rebuke. Instead of bringing the group together, it pushed them further apart.

My failure to deliver timely feedback proved a particular issue with Simon. He was drinking vodka and behaving irresponsibly. The guy crashed his snowmobile three times, as well as the hire car! But I didn't tackle the issue early on and, by letting it go without comment, it was like I was tacitly endorsing it.

Part of the reason for my reluctance to confront Simon was that he was an old mate. Our history made it more awkward to assume a hierarchical position. But as a leader you have to choose discomfort over resentment. You have to front up to have those tough conversations. The ability to sit with that discomfort is where the magic happens. By the time I tried to do that, it was too late.

When I did eventually speak with Simon I cocked that up as well and only wound up pushing him further away. In retrospect, I should have used the same approach that I constantly advise managers to use when it comes to sensitive conversations. The fact that I didn't implement it myself is as disappointing as it is baffling.

First up, I should have set up the conversation better. By telling him I wanted to give him some feedback, I instantly put him on the defensive. To stop things from escalating, I should have framed the chat in a more positive way.

'Simon,' I should have said. 'I'd love to catch up to talk about how today went because you have such a critical role, but a couple of things didn't go entirely to plan. It'd be great to get your thoughts on how we can do things differently for the actual record attempt and work through a couple of things that I observed to make sure that we nail it tomorrow.'

Then I would have moved onto the 'Triple E system' in which the first E stands for 'explain'. I'd explain what I'd witnessed during the day and the direct consequences of that action. The impact of him crashing the snowmobile en route to the ice hole, for example, delayed all the preparations as we had to dig the machine out of the snow. That meant we had people waiting out on the ice for two hours, I had to restart my preparations, and it proved a major disruption and all-round ball-ache. I'd have kept this part of the conversation as brief and factual as possible, using it primarily to establish the context for this situation.

The second part is to 'explore' the issue by involving the other party. I'd have got Simon to tell me what happened with the snowmobile, giving him the chance to share his perspective. Maybe he crashed after swerving to avoid an obstacle. Maybe there was a fault with the vehicle. This part of the conversation is designed to be a dialogue rather than a foregone conclusion or a scolding.

The third part of the system is designed to 'empower' the individual by encouraging them to come up with solutions rather than simply laying down the law. In this case, I should have asked Simon what steps we could implement for the team to maintain better safety when driving the snowmobiles. Eliciting his suggestions would hopefully lead to greater buy-in and result in some form of commitment for which he'd be accountable.

I might have clinched a new world record, but it was in spite of my leadership not because of it. And in a sport where the smallest mistake can be fatal, I'm under no illusions that I was bloody lucky to get away with it.

CHAPTER 25

It's January 2024 and I've just returned from an early morning surf at Winkipop, the right-hand break just around from Bells Beach. When I get home, the kids are still asleep and I take the opportunity to quickly check my emails. In my inbox, there's a message from someone at a British TV production company. Apparently, a client has commissioned them to make an 'immersive film' about ice diving using some new form of whiz-bang camera technology. They want to line up a Zoom call with me to discuss my potential involvement.

I close my laptop and go and make myself a long black. I'm in no hurry to reply. In my experience, TV production companies are notorious time-wasters. They come to you bearing grand plans and lots of flattery, preying on your vanity while dangling the promise of some life-changing project. Naturally, you get all excited and start imagining your name up in lights, only for the conversations to drag on (and on) before eventually fizzling out. Most of the time, nothing ends up happening, and you're left feeling like a sucker for getting your hopes up.

I went through this rigmarole just last year. Another production company approached me about the prospect of teaching the American magician David Blaine how to swim under the ice. The opportunity intrigued me, given Blaine's previous stunts, like balancing on a tiny platform for 35 hours and being buried alive in a transparent coffin for a week. I sat through countless meetings and interviews until the producer finally delivered a last-minute knockback. They'd decided to film in the northern hemisphere, he explained, and reasoned that it would be cheaper to go with European ice divers instead. The experience was both time-consuming and deflating and I'm in no rush to put myself through that again.

The other reason for my lack of enthusiasm is that I've basically retired from freediving. I'm 53 and consider myself extremely fortunate that I got to travel the world and achieve most of my goals. Sure, I was never a world champion, but I did break a world record and had a pretty good run.

A few days later, the British TV production company send me a follow-up email. I'm about to politely decline but then figure there's probably no harm in having a chat. An invitation for a Zoom meeting duly follows, but I keep my expectations low.

When I sit down to take the call, I'm already regretting my decision. The meeting is scheduled for 8 pm to fit in with the UK. I'm hoping we can keep it short and that I don't have to endure too much bluster and bullshit. My approach, I decide, is to be transparent and direct.

There are two people on the call from Atlantic Productions; a young male producer and the director, Charlotte Mikkelborg, a polished, middle-aged woman who used to be the BBC's Shanghai correspondent. Charlotte does most of the talking and it's immediately clear she's very switched on. After a bit of preamble, the conversation shifts to ice diving.

'What if you had the opportunity to go to Iceland and do another dive?' Charlotte says. 'What would you want to do there?'

I answer without giving the question too much thought. 'Well, I guess I'd try and get my world record back, because Alexey Molchanov, the Russian world champion, broke it in 2021. If you're willing to pay, then I'd love to have a crack at going a little bit deeper. Alexey did 81 metres, I think, so I could maybe try for 85 metres.'

Charlotte smiles tightly. 'The thing is, we've got these special cameras and, given how dark it gets at those depths, they simply won't work. Is there anything else you'd like to do?'

I feel like she's trying to lead the conversation in a specific direction, but I don't know where that is. I'm started to get a bit frustrated. There's clearly an agenda at play. Why dance around the issue?

'Look, maybe just tell me what you want me to do? It's not like I'm the only ice diver around. You've seen that Netflix doco on Johanna Nordblad, the Finnish lady? All she does is ice dive. Are you speaking with her?'

'Yes, we're speaking with Johanna.'

'Great. Then there's Arthur Guérin-Boëri, the French guy who's got a bunch of world records. Are you speaking with him?'

'Yes, we're speaking with Arthur.'

'Well then, why are we having this conversation, guys? I live on the opposite side of the world to all the best ice-diving spots. I haven't done a lot of it, apart from that one world-record attempt which, to be totally honest, was a bit of a fluke. I'm 53 and retired from the sport. This conversation doesn't seem to be going anywhere.'

'I understand where you're coming from,' Charlotte says. 'The reason we've contacted you is that we're making this film for a big client, who I can't reveal just yet. We're backed with proper funding and some amazing equipment that will show freediving in a whole new light. As I mentioned, a deep dive won't work. But please can you have a think if there's any other challenge that you'd like to do and maybe we can talk again.'

I end the call feeling slightly relieved that's probably the last I'll ever hear from them. Except Charlotte turns out to be surprisingly persistent. Another call is arranged and this time, she's more forthcoming.

'Would you consider swimming from one point to another under the ice?'

I think about it for a second. The only time I've ever tried to swim any meaningful distance under the ice was on my first trip to Finland, when I helped Antero feed the rope between two ice holes. They were only 20 metres apart but that was one of the scariest experiences of my life. On a normal dive, your escape route is always directly above you. Under the ice, it's sealed shut by a ceiling a metre thick. During that 20-metre swim, I vividly recall my panicky feeling of disorientation as I realised how uniformly dark and featureless the ice sheet looks from below. Until you're right under it, the exit hole is practically invisible.

'You want me to swim from one hole to another under the ice? Honestly, I don't really know how to do that. I've only ever swum 20 metres under the ice before, and it sounds like you're asking me to go much further than that.'

'How far do you think you could go?'

'I really don't know, because I've never tried it. Back in the day, I did a fair bit of Dynamic freediving, but that was in normal water. Diving under the ice is different. It's much harder.'

'Do you think you could do 100 metres?'

Okay, at least we're getting into some specifics now. Could I manage 100 metres under the ice? Frankly, I'm not sure, but given I've managed 240 metres in normal water, I guess it's theoretically possible with training and practice.

'I reckon 100 metres is potentially doable. But I'm not promising anything.'

Charlotte shoots an excited glance at her producer. 'Wow, so you could possibly do 100 metres. Do you think there's any chance that you could go *past* a hundred?'

'Look, what do you want me to say here? How far do you need me to go for this to be story-worthy?'

'Anthony, that is totally up to you. We don't want to pressure you.'

'Come on, let's cut to the chase. You're busy, I'm busy. Let's not waste any more time. You're obviously fishing for something, so what do you want me to say? Do you need me to try for the world record?'

'Well, of course, that would be amazing if we could go back and tell our client you'd be willing to try for that. But is that realistic?'

'I really don't know is the honest answer. How long is the world distance record under the ice?'

'It's 181 metres,' Charlotte says. 'Just have a think about it, okay?'

And I do go away and have think about it. In fact, I go away and think about it a lot.

I look into the recent history of the challenge. The previous world record was 175 metres and was set in 2017 by Arthur Guérin-Boëri. The Frenchman is a freediving phenomenon who specialises in Dynamic Apnea and has won five world titles. His six world records include becoming the first person in history to swim 300 metres underwater, the equivalent of six lengths of an Olympic-sized pool. Arthur's nickname is 'Aqua Man' for good reason.

His record was unofficially broken by the man who's universally considered the best male freediver of all time. Alexey Molchanov swam 181 metres under the ice in 2020. Over the years, the Russian has broken a staggering 35 world records in a variety of freediving disciplines. Imagine a cross between Michael Phelps and Novak Djokovic who can hold their breath with the ease of a dolphin and you'll get some idea of Alexey's natural talent.

This is all a bit dispiriting. I'd always believed that lack of access to Arctic conditions and the sheer expense were the main obstacles to ice diving. But the pedigree of Arthur and Alexey is impossible to match. Not only that, they're both professional freedivers who dedicate their lives to training and competing full-time – Arthur reportedly practised for several months in ice water before clinching his 175-metre distance record. In comparison, I run a busy consulting business and haven't freedived in earnest for some time.

Logically, those reasons should put an end to our conversation. Yet I can't quite shake the idea. While I know I'm not a diver of the same calibre as Arthur or Alexey, I have managed over 200 metres in normal water and, given my adventure in Norway, I've got some hard-won experience. Iceland in winter will be brutally cold, with temperatures around −30°C. But I've faced similar conditions before and come out unscathed. If I get a decent length of time to train hard and practise, then I'm fairly confident that I can manage 150 metres. After that, well, who knows?

Deep down, there's another reason why I keep circling the possibility and finding reasons not to give it up. Now in my fifties, I'm painfully aware that my physical peak is well behind me. But I'm not ready to surrender to a life of golf, gardening and trousers with elasticated waist-bands just yet. There's a reason why so many middle-aged men sign up for an Ironman or ultramarathon, wrestling their guts into Lycra when they hit a certain age. What they want to prove is that they're still athletically capable and game for adventure. Apparently I share that same desperate urge.

There's a mental dimension to all this, too, in that I don't want to lose my nerve. For a variety of reasons, most of us become less physically brave as we get older. We develop a heightened awareness of risks and their negative consequences, while our susceptibility to peer-group pressure wanes. Already, I can feel this happening to me, too. I notice when I'm surfing I've become more cautious and reluctant to take on really big waves. Yet I also hold that while bravery depends on belief, you also need to maintain it with practice. It's a question of 'use it or lose it' and I'm not ready for the latter just yet. Viewed from that perspective, I feel this isn't a challenge that I can turn down.

Weirdly, Merryn is relatively amenable to the idea this time around. It possibly helps that the impetus for the challenge hasn't come from me for once, and that all my expenses will be covered. The fact that a big production company is involved also makes it seem more legit. I'm at pains to emphasise that I won't even be diving for depth, but a distance that should be theoretically doable.

'To break the record I have to swim 181 metres. That's almost an Olympic-sized swimming pool *less* than my longest underwater swim.'

'I'll agree with one condition,' Merryn says eventually. 'Ant, this is your last hurrah.'

During our next Zoom call, Charlotte asks me the question point-blank. 'So Anthony, have you had a good think about this? Do you want us to tell our client that you're happy to go for the world record?'

'Okay, I'm going to lay my cards on the table. Yes, I'm happy to announce that I'm going for the world record—'

'Oh my God, that great! The client's going to be over the moon!'

'The thing is, though, that after looking into it, I put my chances of beating 181 metres at about 5 per cent. So your client needs to entertain the reality that the most likely scenario is that this film will end with me blacking out under the ice and having to be rescued by the safety divers. I'm not the sort of a diver who's going to pull up early and abort. This film will end one of two ways: either I achieve a new world record or I black out. How do you feel about that?'

There's a long pause before Charlotte answers. 'Well, we'd have to take this back to our client and see what they think. But you know, in principle, I'm actually okay with it. Your safety is, of course, paramount and we'll make sure we have every precaution in place and that there's a team of highly trained safety divers on hand to fish you out if there's a problem. But not every story has to end with a happy ending. Even if you don't succeed, it'd still be a riveting adventure about grit and resilience. About mustering the willingness to back yourself in later life and have a go. On that basis, I'm personally fine with it.'

'Okay. Speak to your client and see what they think. If we do get the green light, how long will I have to train? The truth is that I haven't held my breath in two years.'

Charlotte frowns slightly before answering. 'The turnaround is actually quite tight,' she says. 'You'll need to do a recce trip to Iceland in the next couple of weeks.' Then she delivers the killer blow. 'The real ice dive will be seven weeks from now.'

CHAPTER 26

Seven weeks is what I have to play with. That equates to 49 days or 1176 hours to prime my body and hone my mind. Whichever way you slice it, it's not a lot of time and how I spend it will be critical to how I fare beneath the thick ice of an Icelandic lake. The countdown has begun and I can't afford to waste a single day.

Having retired from competitive freediving two years ago, there's no denying that I'm seriously undercooked. To get myself up to speed, I need to train twice a day, six days a week. But I've also got to be prudent and listen to my 53-year-old body. Using my Apple watch, I'll track physical metrics including my heart rate variability, resting heart rate and oxygen saturation. If I start getting really fatigued and my energy levels drop, I'll ease off and take a break. Until that point, I'm going to push as hard as I can.

Under my new training regimen, I wake each morning at 6 am. After necking a long black and a protein shake, I head to my local CrossFit box: a no-frills, warehouse space that reeks of chalk dust and sweat. Amid the clang of barbells and thudding medicine balls, I grind my way through my first workout of the day. This generally involves some ugly combo of Olympic lifts, chin-ups and interval sprints out the front of the gym.

This ordeal is necessary to build up my strength as well as my aerobic and anaerobic capacity. To freedive competitively, good cardio fitness is a non-negotiable. When you're fit, you have a lower resting heart rate, so you burn through your fuel tank of oxygen more slowly, while cardio work increases the number of capillaries in your muscles, creating a more efficient network for delivering oxygen and removing waste products like carbon dioxide. The latter is significant because when you're underwater the urge to breathe is not triggered by the lack of oxygen but the buildup of CO_2 in your blood. High-intensity training enables your body to tolerate higher CO_2 levels.

Coming home drenched in sweat, I shovel down some breakfast and shower before switching into dad mode, helping the kids finish any last minute homework and helping Merryn make their lunches, before bundling them off to school. Then I start my working day at Modus. One benefit of being the boss is that I can adjust my hours to accommodate my training. At 4 pm, I leave the office and head straight to the pool. Most days, I'm accompanied by my son, Luc, who supervises my laps and monitors my safety.

Initially, I'm just focused on refining my swimming technique with the monofin to ensure I can glide through the water with maximum speed and efficiency. The faster I can swim, the quicker I'll be able to escape the icy water. Some days, I just swim lengths for 90 minutes with my fin and snorkel, trying to get my legs accustomed to the lactic acid buildup. Other days, I practise underwater swims, but nothing more than 50 metres, concentrating on speed and power. At the end of each length, I take a 30-second breather and then go again.

Before designing my training plan, I studied my career results and the events where I performed especially well. One competition stands out. In 2015 at the Pan Pacific Championships in Brisbane I managed 223 metres in the Dynamic discipline. Up against the world's elite, I finished second to Alexey Molchanov and achieved my best result in competition. But when I look back at my training logs, one of the reasons I excelled was because I took a different approach. In the lead-up, I didn't attempt any maximal work and capped my underwater swims at 100 metres.

On that basis, I've decided to take a gamble by *not* practising any maximal dives or swims this time round. My personal bests now include a static breath-hold of eight minutes, while my Dynamic record – albeit in non-freezing water – is 240 metres. But I'm not going to go anywhere near those PBs in training.

Part of the logic behind this is to alleviate some of the pressure. In the past, I'd often try to push close to my PB on a weekly or fortnightly basis in order to measure my progress. But such efforts would take a lot out of me both physically and mentally.

The night before attempting a PB in training, I'd struggle to sleep. Pushing your body to the limit involves real discomfort and that prospect filled me with dread. After a night of tossing and turning, I'd agonise all day about the max effort that I was going to put in and whether I was going to black out or not. After the session, I'd feel relieved that I didn't have to do it again for another week. But the knowledge that I would have to repeat the ordeal in seven days' time was still unnerving and remained a source of low-level stress.

All that may have been unnecessary. When I examine my results, I now believe that pushing myself to the brink on a regular basis wasn't just unpleasant, it was counterproductive. The effort required was so demanding that I often underperformed in the actual competition due to the mental fatigue. Elite sport is about peaking at precisely the right time. A serious weightlifter, for example, wouldn't try to lift their one-rep max each time he or she went to the gym. It's just too demanding, and an inefficient way to train. The juice ain't worth the squeeze.

I'm reminded of Eddie Hall, the British strongman, who in 2016 became the first person in history to deadlift 500 kilograms. Hall achieved the Herculean feat but estimates the strain took ten years off his life. The effort was so extreme that he had blood leaking out of his ears, went temporarily blind, and suffered concussion from the sheer force generated inside his own skull. The next day he was still so mentally frazzled that he couldn't even recognise his own brother.

Clearly, I'm putting myself through a very different sort of physiological challenge. But the same logic applies. If you're training consistently, you don't want to push yourself to the point of failure. Physically, the recovery time is too long while mentally, it's simply too draining. Max efforts are not an efficient way to train.

Another contentious move is that I've decided that I'm not going to worry too much about the cold. You'd expect that I'd be enduring daily ice baths to get used to the Arctic water. But I've opted against that. Obviously, I've heard all the ice-bath zealots raving about the mind/body benefits of cold water, but the truth is that I really don't like it. I've already proven that I can perform in the cold in Finland and Norway, and I'll have a few days to acclimatise to it in Iceland. My training is already full-on, so removing one pain point from the equation makes sense.

After three weeks, I feel like I'm hitting my groove. I feel strong and sharp, which bolsters my self-belief that I can have a genuine crack at this. Given that I'm finding my rhythm, it's a bit annoying that I have to break my routine and fly around the world to spend two days in Iceland for a recce of the production set-up. I voice my frustration about this in a phone call with Charlotte, hoping that I might be able to avoid the around-the-world trip.

'Ant, you remember the client I said we were making this film for?' she says.

'You mean the mysterious entity whose identity you can't reveal?'

'Yes. Well, now we're all locked in, I can share that with you. Anthony, the client is Apple.'

Charlotte explains that Apple has developed a new form of spatial computing that blends augmented and virtual reality. Placed over your eyes like a sort of high-tech mask, the Apple Vision Pro delivers 7K resolution for each eye to create an immersive viewing experience. It's set to be the best on the market and purportedly the next big thing in home entertainment technology. Due to Apple's involvement, this is going to be a big-budget production and everything needs to be done properly. All of which, apparently, necessitates me flying around the world to spend two days in Iceland.

On the one hand, the news that Apple is driving this film is exciting. This is a company, after all, that's redefined entire industries by embedding its products into the fabric of modern life. It's not just a tech company, but a cultural and economic force. Now I'm on their team, and that means I'll be backed with serious resources. In addition, the personal exposure I could get from all this could be incredible.

What I'm less sure about is the fact that the film Charlotte is making will *only* be available via the Apple Vision Pro. To be fair, it sounds like a great bit of immersive kit that may redefine how filmmakers tell stories. The problem is that I've never heard of it. Admittedly, it's only just launched but it's expensive, with a price tag of around $6000. Given Apple's track record, it might catch on like the iPhone. But for the moment, it's still a niche product. That's going to limit the number of people who actually see the film.

None of this, I decide, is worth worrying about. Right now, all my concentration needs to be on training and the challenge itself. I need to make sure that Apple's film has a happy ending.

CHAPTER 27

In my business class seat on the flight to Reykjavík, I'm so exhausted from all my double training sessions that I sleep for most of the journey, despite the guy in the neighbouring seat, who coughs non-stop.

In Reykjavík, I get an internal flight to Akureyri, a mid-size town in northern Iceland where the attempt is due to take place. There, a driver is waiting to pick me up in a Mercedes van and drive me to my hotel. Sitting in the backseat of the car, it strikes me how different this attempt will be to my slightly shambolic effort in Norway. I've insisted that both Johnny Sunnex and Antero Joki – the most experienced members of that team – will be involved in this challenge. Johnny will lead the safety team while Antero will mastermind the design of the ice track, the placement of holes, and the running of safety lines.

This time round I won't have to worry about team management or logistics. Instead, I'll be able to focus purely on my own performance, which comes as a huge relief. My main problem is that ever since landing in Iceland, I've felt like I'm coming down with something. I've got a scratchy throat and I'm dead tired, but then jet lag always knocks me about.

After a quick shower, I catch up with Johnny in the hotel foyer. It's really good to see him. I've known the man for more than

20 years now and our bond really strengthened after Norway, where he played such a critical role. He's subsequently moved to Maui to expand his photography business after establishing a freediving school in Dominica called Blue Element Freediving. Between his relocation and COVID-19 travel bans, I haven't seen much of him since our last adventure.

Having just endured a 40-hour flight from Hawaii, Johnny is keen to get any available sunlight to try to reset his body clock. Bundled up in giant puffer jackets, we go for an idle stroll around Akureyri, but it's snowing so hard that we can't see much.

'Wow, Iceland is icy, man. Who knew?' Johnny says.

It's reassuring hanging with someone from your homeland. Johnny's New Zealand heritage gives us a shared context and outlook that allows us to communicate almost in shorthand. While highly competent, he wears his expertise lightly. He's no-nonsense and understated, with a 'she'll be right' attitude which is exactly what I need right now. As we trudge through the frozen streets, we joke about how mad it is that two Kiwi boys have ended up on the other side of the planet, trying to break the world record in one of the most niche sports imaginable.

'So what does this opportunity really mean to you?' Johnny asks.

'Well, it's wild to get this opportunity, isn't it? But I also feel that, because I've never had the chance to freedive professionally, I've always flown under the radar and never established much of a name for myself. I guess this is a chance to put myself on the map.'

'Yeah bro, you're going to be an overnight sensation at the age of 53.'

We talk a bit about Apple's involvement and the concern that, given the film will only be released on the Vision Pro, few people will see it. For me, the main thing is that Apple is enabling this whole experience. It's true that right now the Vision Pro is only being used by IT developers and early adopters. But I like the fact that it's fostered a new way of making a film and is genuinely cutting edge. I tell Johnny what Laird Hamilton said to me a few years ago about how the really exciting stuff in any area usually happens on the outer edges.

'This film, I suppose, is the cinematic equivalent.'

Back at the hotel, I meet up with the director, Charlotte Mikkelborg. Given the time constraints, we head straight to Mývatn, a volcanic lake on Iceland's north-eastern shore where the attempt is set to take place. The location scout has done a fine job. Just outside Akureyri, the frozen lake stretches out like a milky sheet, its edges feathered with frost and snowdrifts. Beneath the weak sunlight of a colourless sky, it's piercingly cold, with the temperature hovering around –25°C.

Out on the ice, I'm startled by how many people are already beavering away, given my dive isn't scheduled for another four weeks. There are generators, buses, trucks and huge ice-drilling machines that are being used to create the 'track' that I will swim along. Every 20 metres, a team of men cut triangular-shaped holes that are big enough for a diver and safety diver to exit quickly. If something bad happens and I do have to abort prematurely, these emergency holes represent my escape route. They also let in more light that will help with my navigation while also creating better conditions for the cameras. So far, about 100 metres of the track has been completed.

Some 300 metres away from this, a giant marquee has been set up to cater for the crew. I count ten trestle tables and a kitchen manned by three chefs. Two more adjoining marquees will also be set up and I'm staggered to learn that each will have its own heated spa to enable anyone who's been in the water to warm up quickly. With three spas on a frozen lake, it's clear every precaution is being taken to protect us against the cold. The on-site production team and crew must number about 70 people.

That night over dinner, Charlotte talks me through the plans for the film. Apple Immersive Video, she explains, leverages ultra-high-resolution video to place viewers at the centre of the action. The cameras deliver 7K resolution per eye. 'That's close to our native vision, which means that it's so clear and crisp that a viewer will actually feel like they're under the ice.'

The audio is also special. Whereas the visuals have a 180° field of view, the spatial sound can effectively move around the viewer wearing the headset to further immerse you in the scene. The soundtrack is being scored by the composer Atli Örvarsson, whose credits include *Pirates of the Caribbean* and the Superman reboot *Man of Steel*.

'So this is a pretty big deal,' I say.

'We'll have a decent-sized crew.'

To my ears that's underselling it. A camera crew on a helicopter will capture visuals of the nearby glacier and volcano, while a heavy-lift drone will be used to shoot the track of the ice-dive attempt. The scale of the production is mind-blowing.

'You're doing all this for a 15-minute film?'

'Given the nature of what we're doing, we only get one shot,' Charlotte explains. 'It's not like we can say, "Okay, Anthony: Take 2 – can you please just get back under the ice and swim another 182 metres".'

Fair point.

The next day I wake up feeling even worse. This jet lag is horrific. Maybe my training has made my body clock extra susceptible to the time-zone shift? But I've just got to get on with it. Today is my final day in Iceland before I return home and Charlotte wants me to have a practice dive. There are a few reasons for this. First, she's keen to ensure that I'm happy with the set-up and don't need any adjustments.

Second, Johnny wants to give the safety divers and medics a practice session to see firsthand how the attempt will play out. And third, production-wise, this dive will give the film crew a dummy run at filming under the ice and deliver practical insights into how to make the camerawork flow, the positioning of the close-up rig and various other technical details that I barely understand.

Given how terrible I feel, getting into the icy water is not an attractive proposition. Outside on the lake, it's brutally cold, with the temperature at about –23°C. For some reason, I've only brought a 3-millimetre-thick wetsuit and 1-millimetre-thick gloves, a decision I now regret. I may be attempting a world record, but I'm still pretty naïve about the realities of ice diving.

While the record attempt will be 180 metres, today I've only committed to half that length. When I get into the water, I feel great and strangely relaxed, grateful that I have an elite crew of safety divers around me. I don't feel a hint of discomfort until 10 metres from the end of the dive when it becomes a bit of a struggle. But as soon as I get out of the water I'm suddenly in trouble. My hands and feet are stinging like they've been scorched.

'I need to reheat fast and I need a medic, too. I'm in a bit of bad way here,' I tell my minder.

A snowmobile whisks me straight to the marquee with the spa, where a doctor takes one look at my throbbing fingers and toes before concluding I've got chilblains. I need to warm up, but the contact of the hot spa water is so painful that I can't bear to immerse my fingers or toes. Luckily, within an hour or so, the pain subsides and there's no lasting damage. I've learned a valuable lesson today about how thick my wetsuit and gloves need to be.

CHAPTER 28

What don't subside are my flu-like symptoms. By the time I get back to Australia I feel completely drained of energy, my muscles ache and I'm shivering with a fever. A visit to my doctor reveals dire news: I've got COVID-19. I lay the blame squarely on my neighbour who kept coughing non-stop on the flight over.

The news is a hammer blow to my plans. Freediving requires good lung function because the air sacs are essential for effectively loading your blood with oxygen before a dive and offloading carbon dioxide during the recovery phase. Inconveniently for me, COVID-19 can cause long-term damage to the lungs.

The bottom line is that I have to do whatever it takes to enable my body to fully recover. And that means no training whatsoever for the next two weeks. But if I can't train, do I pull the plug? Swimming 180 metres under the ice was always a stiff challenge within such a narrow time frame. Now I've got COVID-19 it doesn't seem realistic.

But the more I think about it, I realise we've ventured too far down the track to back out now. March is the last month of winter in Iceland. I can't delay my attempt or the ice will start to melt, putting the project on hold for another year. Apple and Charlotte have a production schedule they need to stick to. A 12-month postponement won't cut it and so much costly infrastructure has already been put in place in our remote location on Lake Mývatn. Unless my health takes a nosedive then I simply have to proceed.

I can't deny that thinking about my predicament is unsettling. I haven't trained for two years. I needed every single day of that seven weeks to get myself into shape, and even then I'd have ideally had at least double the preparation time. Prior to the recce trip to Iceland I was feeling reasonably confident. Now the whole mission seems doomed. It's going to be an public failure, too, caught on high-resolution immersive video in front of Apple's vast crew.

Feeling wretched, I'm lying in bed that night freaking out about the humiliation that's surely heading my way. But I haven't got any wriggle room and I don't know what to do. The only shred of comfort I take is that at least I warned Charlotte at the outset that I only had a tiny chance of success. Right now, even that seems optimistic.

I'm bemoaning my fate to Merryn, who listens patiently while trying to gently coax me out of my doom spiral. 'It's not ideal,' she says. 'But you've always said that freediving is more of a mental challenge than a physical one. Maybe the lack of training won't be as disastrous as you think. You've proven you can swim this far before.'

'Not under the ice, though,' I say.

As I lie there in the darkness, I start to realise that Merryn is right. Freediving is mainly about mental fitness; that was what appealed to me when I started more than 20 years ago. Of course I wish I were in better condition for this challenge. But if I can't train my body, I can still train my brain. I can shift the emphasis and concentrate on sharpening my mental edge to compensate for my lack of physical preparation.

Quietly, I slip out of bed and pad into the kitchen. Two hours later, I've scribbled out a tonne of notes and designed a mental boot camp that'll hopefully give me a chance of avoiding total embarrassment, not to mention a freezing death beneath the ice.

I'm now a man with a plan whose working title – until I come up with something better – is the 'Triple R' system. It's based around three key areas: Rehearse, Reframe and Relax. Those are the key strategies that I'll focus on developing in the remaining three weeks. Hopefully, health permitting, I'll be back in the pool in the final week before I head to Iceland. Until then, I'll practise the following mental exercises day in day out, in what I'm envisaging as a *Rocky*-style training montage for the mind.

Rehearse

This training block involves two key elements. The first is to establish a specific goal. The second is to build a crystal-clear plan for game day about how I'm going to nail it.

My overarching goal, of course, is to break the world record for swimming the longest ever distance under the ice. But in order to do that, I need to map out *exactly* what is required on the day. That includes drilling into everything I'll do from the moment I wake up at 7 am until the moment I emerge from the ice hole with my hands held aloft, basking in the applause.

There are a couple of reasons for this granular level of detail. Once I've defined all the components, I can set about trying to optimise them as part of a broader effort to ensure that everything runs smoothly and I'm not ambushed by any nasty surprises (imploding masks, over-heavy weight belts, and so on). In addition, having a step-by-step plan that I know inside-out will provide me with a sense of familiarity and comfort and help make me feel more in control.

The trip to Iceland may have given me a case of COVID-19, but what it also gave me are some vital insights about what to expect. I now know the Berjaya Hotel in Akureyri where I'll be staying and its broader layout. I know how long it will take to drive to the ice hole. I know that it'll be at least –20°C on the lake and that I can get dangerously cold without taking extra precautions. Having that intel allows me to assemble all the pieces of the logistical jigsaw and know exactly what fits where.

When I get out of the car at the foot of the lake, for example, who will help me lug my equipment into the warm-up marquee? Who do I want around me in the final 30 minutes before I dive? What music do I want playing to get in the right state of mind?

My eventual run-list suggests I probably have latent OCD tendencies. But establishing this level of detail will enable me to control the controllables and feel ready and prepared. Figuring out all these technicalities in advance will free up my mental bandwidth, but if I'm feeling particularly nervous, it'll also give me a to-do list to keep me busy.

Run-list

7.00 Get up, shower, shave and dress (indoor clothes – jeans/sweatshirt).

7.45 Breakfast with Johnny Sunnex in hotel restaurant. Food to include one hard-boiled egg, one slice of toast and a fruit bowl.

8.30 Lay out and check all diving gear on the bed. Place warm clothes on chair so everything is ready to go.

9.00 Relax, stretch and visualise the dive. Be careful to breathe naturally.

10.00 Take a 60-minute walk in the park, wearing cold-weather clothes. Schedule two ten-minute stops where I can allow myself to think about the dive.

11.00 Chill in hotel room.

11.30 Take all gear down to foyer, meet Johnny and driver. Brief the driver on playlist, vibe and conversation for drive.

11.40 Head to car, load up and drive to lake.

12.30 Arrive at lake and orient myself to make sure I know where everything is. Find my designated gear supervisor and brief him on exactly what I need and when.

13.00	Go to porta room and lay out and hang gear.
13.10	Attend safety briefing.
13.15	Move to lunch tent – chat, chill and eat. Pick up stereo for music.
14.00	Move to gear porta room. Chill for ten minutes and put reggae playlist on while safety divers get into their wetsuits.
14.10	Safety divers leave for spa tents soon. Focus on starting to relax and centre.
14.30	Take ten minutes to think about the dive and what I have to do. Ask crew for minimal distractions from now.
14.40	Stretch and visualise the dive.
15.15	Move to dedicated spa to get into wetsuit up and warm up. Take radio, soap for monofin, Crocs and bathrobe.
15.35	Take snowmobile ride to ice edge, put on life jacket and spikes.
15.45	Travel out to eskimo tent near ice hole. Focus on staying relaxed, smile and joke around to ward off stress.
15.50	Perform one seated static breath-hold of between two and three minutes. Watch my breathing afterwards – keep it slow and even.
15.55	Transfer outside to ice hole. Put on monofin.
16.00	Send it!

(See page 288 for a QR code to scan for my pre-dive playlist on Apple iTunes.)

The second element of Rehearsal is to mentally visualise success in each element of the day. This involves not just picturing my list of tasks, but the related details, from the music that will be playing to the specific people I'll have around me. Most importantly, I'll be imagining how I'll feel during each step, with a view to tuning my mood to a specific frequency.

The emotional state that I'm targeting is excited yet calm. I want to cultivate a mindset of bullet-proof self-belief, where it's a foregone conclusion that I'm going to succeed. After all, if you definitively knew in advance that you were going to break a world record, why wouldn't you try to enjoy the moment? That's the state of mind that I want to overlay on everything and that will be the dominant headspace of the hyper-confident alter ego I will become on that day.

My visualisation will switch between two perspectives. Some of it will be from my own point of view. I'll imagine, for example, what I'll experience on my morning stroll around the park. The rhythmic crunch of snow under my boots and the trail they leave between the frosted pine trees. The soft blue light under the Arctic sun, the chilly nip of the wind. But the visualisation will also zoom out to a bird's eye perspective in which I'll also watch myself from above.

If at any stage of this visualisation I feel a surge of anxiety, then I'll pause my internal video camera. I'll breathe slowly to relax and allow my physiology to return to its baseline before jumping back in.

The level of detail when I visualise the dive itself will be forensic and take place in real time. I'll imagine myself sitting on the edge of the ice hole, the chill of the water when I slide in, my final breathing exercises to charge up for the final immersion. I'll picture the duck dive, angling me down into the blackness and the single kick to get myself to a depth of 4 metres at which I'll begin to swim.

From there, all I can see is the rope and I'll glide along, watching myself pass the distance markers for 20 metres, 40 metres, then 60 metres. I'll imagine feeling strong with no desire to breathe as I undulate through the water, actually enjoying the swim because it's all going so well. The discomfort from the breath-hold will start at around 70 to 80 metres, but that's just part of the process and I'll accept it and keep plugging on.

Then I'll see the 100-metre mark, and inwardly celebrate because of how comfortably I'm progressing. *Only 50 metres to go*, I'll tell myself because I'm chunking up the swim in a tactical way. While my true aim is to swim 182 metres, if I nail 150 metres then I won't have disgraced myself and Apple will have enough footage to make the film. I've promised myself that at 150 metres, I'll check in to see how I'm feeling and whether I'm game to continue.

At this point, I'll feel the fluttering convulsions in my chest. But they won't bother me because I'm expecting them. In fact, I'll welcome the sensation because I know it's an unavoidable part of the journey to my goal. By familiarising myself with that discomfort, I'm pre-programming my acceptance of it.

When I pass 120 metres, I'll congratulate myself on nailing another sub-goal. Nearly there now and yes, it's getting tough, but I know I can handle it for the final 30 seconds. I'm going to drop the hammer now, speed up and just get it done. At the same time, I'll focus on maintaining perfect technique, partly for the cameras and partly to distract my mind from the mounting desire to breathe.

I hit 150 metres! The discomfort is building exponentially, but I force myself to smile and keep kicking. At 175 metres – the distance set by Arthur Guérin-Boëri in 2017 – I've got someone to wrap red electrical tape around the rope to form a visual candy cane. I picture its bright diagonal stripes. Then I imagine myself swimming past that, until I see another marked stretch of rope that shows Alexey Molchanov's official record of 181 metres.

That's the moment when I switch on my reserve energy boosters. I'm fiercely alert, looking up to see where the ice hole is and checking for the reassuring presence of the safety diver by my side. This is the hardest moment of the dive. I need to breathe now, but it can be hard to see where the hole is. I look up carefully and see it. Then I picture myself coming up smoothly and with controlled precision before I break the surface of the water.

Amid the glare of the light – so bright after the darkness beneath the ice – I'll breathe out to rid my body of CO_2, take in a lungful of oxygen and then repeat the process three times. Then I'll turn my attention to the safety protocol, flashing the okay sign with exaggerated care, signalling to the officials that I'm okay.

I go through that visualisation exercise every single day. By the time I actually dive, I'll have practised it more than 50 times in my head. Getting into the icy water will hopefully feel as natural as brushing my teeth.

Reframe

The second part of my bid to bolster my mental fitness involves confronting the fears and doubts that could otherwise corrupt my internal monologue. I've decided to use the thought-stopping technique that worked so successfully with Shane the cage fighter (see Chapter 3).

This trick involves reframing the nature of my challenge. In a notebook, I divide the page into three columns. In the first column, I acknowledge my greatest fears, delving into the worst-case scenarios that occasionally threaten to send me headfirst down the helter-skelter of panic. The list I write makes for grim reading.

- You've been fooling yourself this whole time.
- You haven't done enough training – you're going to black out for sure.
- It's been two whole years since you've dived properly. There's no way that you're ready for this scale of challenge.
- You've never done this before. What the hell makes you think you'll manage it now?
- You're not going to find the exit hole and you'll be lost under the ice.
- The last two world record holders were full-time professionals. You're way of your depth.
- You're too old to do something like this.
- You're going to suffocate and die.

In the second column, I write the word STOP in huge letters vertically down the page.

Then in the final column I write a list of high-impact positive affirmations.

- This is who I am and this is what I do.
- No one is mentally tougher than me.
- I teach people about how to perform under pressure for a living.
- I've already broken an ice-dive record.
- I always go better in the cold.

Whenever a negative thought from the first column enters my head, it'll trigger the word STOP and prevent it from taking hold. Instead, I'll replace it in my mind with one of the positive statements that I'll repeat several times. I refuse to allow negative thoughts to distract me from my goal or sabotage my efforts. This battle plan will keep me on track.

Relax

To harness the heat of this high-pressure moment, I know that I need to be totally relaxed and confident in my ability. To centre myself in the lead-up to the dive, I'm going to use a number of tactics that will coax my physiology into a calmer state, so that my mind will follow suit.

Part of this comes down to that old chestnut 'fake it till you make it', but in my mind I am deliberately choosing how I show up. I'll consciously modify my posture, walking tall with my shoulders back and my head held high. I'll soften my facial features and smile, thereby triggering a positive feedback loop where the brain starts to release feelgood neurotransmitters, creating a positive mental backdrop despite the strain of the situation. I've read studies that demonstrate the value of this approach, with research showing that laughing or forcing a smile during a stressful task can lead to a lower heart rate and reduced stress when compared to maintaining a neutral expression. My goal with all this is to project an aura of absolute calm and self-belief.

To supplement my body language, I'll also use box breathing, where I inhale for a count of four seconds, hold for four seconds, exhale for four and then hold again for four. The slow, controlled exhales will prompt my vagus nerve to trigger the body's parasympathetic nervous system, which directly counteracts the fight-or-flight stress response, slowing my heart rate and lowering my blood pressure. This simple technique is used by everyone from Navy SEALs to mindfulness gurus to manage stress and enhance mental focus.

I'll also practise a centring technique that slows everything down via a conscious body scan. I'll begin by shifting my focus inwards, observing my breathing rhythm before gradually slowing it down and taking deep breaths from the pit of my diaphragm. As my breaths lengthen, I'll observe a feeling of heaviness like everything is pulling the tension down and away from me.

Gradually, my attention is moving away from my external to my internal reality. As I breathe in, I'm imagining I'm trying to find all the tension in my body from my lower back to my shoulders to my neck. I pinpoint that tension as I'm inhaling, and then visualise myself pulling it up into my shoulders like electricity. Then as I exhale, I shake my arms right down to my fingertips and imagine the tension radiating out of me. At the same time, I feel the weight of my feet on the ground and become aware of the connection I have with the surface I'm standing on. I'm part of this environment now and I'm so anchored to its vast expanse that I can't be affected by the actions of other people.

Finally, when I reach my last breath in this relaxed state, I'll visualise my lungs as two enormous steel oxygen tanks. With that final breath, I imagine a huge torrent of air entering my chest. The quantity is so vast that other people around me start having trouble breathing because I'm taking in so much oxygen from the atmosphere! When they're full, I see the lights on the cylinders go from red to five bars of green. Mentally, I screw the cylinders shut and feel the immense sense of power within. I can now use that energy to propel me forwards to swim 182 metres under the ice.

While recovering from COVID-19, I practise the three parts of the 'Triple R' system several times a day. Now that I have this focus, I no longer feel so powerless. I may not be able to physically train for a fortnight, but at least I can fortify my mind for the task ahead.

When my period of convalescence ends, I'm nervous to see how well I bounce back to the physical rigours of freediving. I've heard worrying tales of how COVID-19 can have a lingering effect on your respiratory and cardiovascular systems. Both are crucial when swimming under the ice of a frozen lake.

Thankfully, when I test myself in the gym and pool, I seem to have escaped relatively unscathed. I suspect the fact that I was in decent nick before contracting the virus may have helped. I'd been eating properly, resting well and training hard, so my immune system may have protected me from too much damage.

In the remaining week before I fly to Iceland, I need to prioritise increasing my breath-hold duration. When I attempt this ice dive, I should be underwater for less than four minutes. In a swimming pool, that would be no problem for me. Yet under the ice it's a very different proposition. In cold water, it's harder to conserve your oxygen because your body burns energy at a far higher rate in a bid to stay warm. The cold also causes your diaphragm and intercostal muscles to contract and tighten, making the act of holding your breath feel more strenuous and fraught.

Nevertheless, I'm still determined to keep within my limits in order not to place too much stress on my system. I practise drills where I grind out a succession of 100-metre swims with my monofin. At the end of that distance – which usually takes me about a minute and 15 seconds – I'll rest for three minutes and then go again, repeating that process about ten times per session.

I also work on trying to increase my CO_2 threshold. Carbon dioxide is essentially a waste product and exhaling is your body's main method of getting rid of it. Essentially, your lungs serve as a sort of biological exhaust pipe. When you're underwater, your cells don't know that you're holding your breath and continue metabolising and producing CO_2 at the same rate. The urge to gasp for air is your brain's direct response to these rising CO_2 levels rather than the actual lack of oxygen.

At home on the sofa I perform one of the main exercises to condition myself to cope better with this CO_2 buildup. Taking a deep breath in, I hold it for 120 seconds. When those two minutes have elapsed, I breathe out and then immediately take in another breath, which I hold for another 120 seconds. I repeat this cycle for up to 20 minutes. Needless to say, it's not a pleasant drill because the build-up of CO_2 is intense, but it works much in the way that track athletes develop their tolerance to lactic acid. Gradually your body is forced to adapt.

The morning of my flight to Reykjavík, Merryn and I take our two dogs Cookie and Louis down to Bells Beach. Watching the waves on this famous point break, I feel ready. Thanks to my preparation, I've given myself a fighting chance. I'm under no illusions about just how tough it'll be, but I've come a long way in seven weeks. Now I just have to deliver.

CHAPTER 29

Johnny Sunnex sinks into the warm water and surfaces with a happy gasp. We're back in Akureyri in northern Iceland, sitting outside by a hot-spring thermal pool fringed with huge boulders. While the water is bath-tub warm, the air is bitterly cold, the contrast kindling a weird buzz that's both calming and mildly invigorating.

'How good it this, eh?' Johnny says.

'Pretty good, mate,' I reply.

And it does feel good. It's just after 5 pm and the winter sun is casting long, golden rays of light, painting everything in a twilight glow. Through the billowing steam of the pool, I can see the slate-grey sea, rolling hills dotted with pine trees and a range of snow-capped mountains in the distance. The topography of this volcanic island nation harbours a strange, elemental power.

'So how are you feeling?' Johnny asks.

'Excited, but apprehensive too. At the end of the day, it's a long swim. Under the ice, I reckon that'll be a real grind. How are you feeling?'

'Great, man. Then again, you're the one who's got to do it.'

Over the following days, I work closely with the director, Charlotte, shooting background scenes. Luckily, because the film is only going to be 15 minutes long, there's not too much to capture, so I also get to do a bit of training with Johnny in an outside pool where the snow comes right up to the water's edge.

The plan is that in two days' time, we'll head to the dive site, where the crew have carved a 200-metre track on a lake selected for the visibility of its water. There, we'll capture some more footage and I'll do a practice dive, with the record attempt due to take place the following day.

Having Apple's production muscle behind us means that all I really have to worry about is my own routine. Aside from the background filming, each day I'm basically free to train and practise my visualisation and mental-fitness exercises. I'd expected the filming to be a hassle, but it actually proves a welcome distraction that stops me from fixating on my dive. More by luck than design, I've hit upon a nice balance and I'm starting to feel quietly optimistic.

Then it begins to snow and it doesn't stop. At first I don't pay much attention – if it's winter in a country called 'Iceland', after all, these are the conditions you expect. But the next afternoon, I get a call from Charlotte.

'Ant, we're going to have to make a change of plan. The weather forecast says 3 feet of snow is set to fall in the coming days. We're going to have to move locations.' Having to work around that much snow, Charlotte explains, will make filming impossible. The production crew is now scrambling to transplant the entire operation down to Reykjavík.

The move is a logistical nightmare. The crew have to uproot tonnes of highly specialised equipment, dismantle the marquees, and shift the whole operation south on a bunch of trucks. But this last-minute switch is also unnerving for me.

For weeks, I've visualised my routine in this Akureyri hotel. I've repeatedly imagined every step of my journey to the lake in microscopic detail. Now we're heading somewhere completely different, a foreign environment that I'm totally unfamiliar with. Will the lake be similar? Could it be darker? The water more murky? What if it's at altitude? An increase of just 300 metres will affect my breath-hold duration. All my carefully laid plans, all that mental preparation, is now largely wasted. I take a deep breath and tell myself not to freak out. Then I call Johnny.

'It's a bummer, no doubt,' he admits. 'But you know it doesn't change anything in real terms, don't you?'

'What do you mean? I've never even been to this lake before.'

'A lake is a lake. It's like playing rugby – teams play home and away. Of course, playing at home gives you an edge because you're on familiar turf. This lake in Akureyri would've given you a home advantage. But good teams also win away.'

'So what you're saying is that we're now going for an away win?'

'That's right. And they're always a little bit sweeter, eh?'

One positive thing about the Reykjavík switch is that we've been upgraded to the Hilton Hotel, where I've somehow wound up with the presidential suite. The room is palatial compared to our last hotel, with a sprawling balcony overlooking the Reykjavík town square and a vast marble bathroom.

At breakfast the next morning, Charlotte greets me with a tired smile. The crew has apparently been working through the night at the nearby Lake Stiflisdalsvatn. Braving the cold and using huge spotlights to illuminate their efforts, they've organised tractors to clear away the snow and carve out a new track punctuated with ice holes every 20 metres. Those holes will allow the safety divers to access each part of the course and provide me with a series of escape routes. Chiselling them out of the 1.2-metre-thick ice in such a narrow time frame would've take a superhuman effort. But somehow they've done it.

'Your new track is ready,' Charlotte beams.

She goes off to deal with one of the countless last-minute tweaks she's now having to figure out. I'm left sitting at breakfast with Johnny. The food on offer at the Hilton buffet is outrageous. There are five different platters of cold meats and smoked salmon, a counter of hot, cooked options, with every form of eggs imaginable, a vast table covered in tropical fruit, a mountain of Danish pastries, plus a selection of multi-coloured juices.

'Bit different from our normal digs,' says Johnny, returning from the buffet with a bowl of fruit and yoghurt.

'It sure is. Do you think that's a problem?'

We talk it over. We usually rough it on freediving trips and stay in no-frills guest houses or cheap hotels. A luxury hotel is a very different proposition. I'm grateful to be here and I'm sure it'll help get me rested for the challenge, but it doesn't feel quite right. Johnny agrees.

'I feel like I'm on holiday, not about to go freediving.'

We decide that from now on, we'll eat breakfast each day at the modest diner down the road.

The next three days are spent filming scenes for the movie that don't require me to be submerged in the lake. Meanwhile I'm hastily trying to get to know my new environment in as much depth as possible to re-establish the step-by-step routine that I'll use for the record attempt.

To minimise surprises on the day, I rehearse every aspect of my run-list. I familiarise myself with the short walk I'll take to get to breakfast until I can pace it out in my mind step by step. I time how long it'll take to be driven to Lake Stiflisdalsvatn and memorise the route until I know every turn. I visit the new track out on the lake and scope the new set-up. My goal is to flesh out a vivid picture of what will happen at each stage of the record-attempt day from the moment I open my eyes until the second I emerge from the lake. Effectively, it's like doing a mental reshoot. Most of the details of my visualisation have to be updated with the change of location.

The day before the attempt, we have a partial dress rehearsal. It's an opportunity for the cameramen and crew to walk through the filming plan and for me to practise my dive-day routine and actually get in the lake. It's long overdue. I haven't done a single ice dive since the recce trip several weeks ago.

Initially, everything proceeds like clockwork. I get up at 7 am to shower, shave and dress. I meet Johnny in the lobby at 7.40 am and we walk down the street for breakfast. Back at the hotel, I lay out and check all my diving gear. My visualisation practice means these steps have become so habitual they now form a well-worn groove in my brain. The familiarity is reassuring and makes me feel in control.

The drive to the lake also goes to plan, with the driver playing the specific reggae playlist I've requested. Out on the ice, the transition goes well, too, and I'm pleased with how accurately the sequence of events coheres to my mental script. The one surprise is that, despite the fact I'm wearing a 5-millimetre wetsuit, it's even colder on the lake than I'd expected, due to the knifing wind. But that's good intel for tomorrow and I make a note to bring additional layers to keep warm ahead of the dive.

I'm planning to do a 100-metre swim beneath the ice today. That's 82 metres less than my intended distance tomorrow, but the cold is so piercing, I tell my safety diver that I'm going to limber up with a 20-metre swim and surface at the second ice hole.

Although it's meant to be an easy warmup, it doesn't go well. When I do my duck dive, the weight around my neck, which I use to counter my buoyancy, rears up to clonk me on the back of the skull. The blow is hard enough to leave a lump. Then, on my first kick, the lanyard that attaches me to my guide rope gets tangled in my monofin, restricting my range of movement. It's a messy introduction to the lake and when I surface at the 20-metre ice hole, I'm not happy. Rather than gloss over this, I decide to start over. I want my final practice dive to boost my confidence, not fill my head with fresh doubts.

'I'm going to reset and go back to the start,' I tell my safety diver.

Walking in a monofin is impossible, so I opt to swim back to the start point under the ice. As it's only a short distance, I just take a couple of semi-deep breaths rather than properly charging my lungs, then duck dive down to 3 metres and start swimming. At that depth, the darkness limits visibility to around 5 metres, making it difficult to see much beyond the guide rope. Making good progress, I feel like I cover the 20-metre distance in a few short kicks. But I can't see the ice hole. Unperturbed, I keep hold of the guide rope and keep swimming. Then I come to the end of the rope.

When I look up there's no ice hole above it.

Momentarily I'm confused until I realise what I've done. The track has been designed for me to swim in one direction. The guide rope is fastened to a wooden stake that's secured to the bottom of the lake, but that stake is positioned *beyond* the first ice hole. What I've accidentally done is swum out *past* the end of the track, which means that I'm now further out, underneath the open ice sheet. As soon as I realise my error, I turn around and start to swim in the opposite direction.

Except I still can't see the first bloody ice hole.

Confounded, I keep swimming, double-checking for the hole. There's no sign of it. Have I passed it again? And that's when it hits me: I'm stuck under the ice and have no idea where to come up.

Don't panic. Just follow the safety rules that Johnny drilled into you. If you get lost under the ice, you stop swimming. You move up to the surface, put both arms up above your head, and you wait for your safety diver to find you.

I follow the instructions until I'm just beneath the surface, arms outstretched. I'm scanning the darkness for my safety diver, but I can't see her anywhere. For a second the primal alarm system in my mind starts to blare, *Oh shit, oh shit, oh shit . . .*

How long have I been under? I swam 20 metres initially and then swam back the same distance. That's not far, but I didn't take a proper lungful of breath. So let's get real. It might take some time for the safety diver to find me. I need to brace myself for at least three and a half minutes down here. That means going into full breath-hold mode and switching off to conserve oxygen. Bloody hell, I'm trapped under the ice! No, don't panic. You're okay. There's a team of safety divers nearby. You're good in the cold. Just relax.

I'm trying to empty my mind and stay calm. Eke everything I can out of this breath-hold. Ignore the fact that the ice is impenetrable and I'm running out of oxygen. Where is the safety diver?

Stay cool, think logically. The safety diver would have swum back with you to the start and then climbed up the first ice hole. She'll have waited there for maybe 20 seconds. Then she'll come back and look for you. But where the hell is she?

Suddenly, she emerges through the darkness and points me in the direction of the exit. After three quick kicks, I punch through to the surface, gasping for breath.

Physically, I'm fine, but mentally I'm rattled. I go to the tent and warm up in the spa, trying to process what went wrong. When Johnny bustles in to check on me, we quickly piece together what happened. The position of each ice hole on the track is indicated on the rope at 20-metre intervals by knotted lengths of hose pipe. Unfortunately, there's one exception. As it's been assumed that I'll start my dive at the first ice hole and swim in one direction, that hole is not marked on the rope like the others. That's why I couldn't find it. If that safety diver wasn't shadowing me, I could've been trapped.

I'm badly shaken up. The fact that I had to be rescued on a 20-metre swim is a demoralising blow that's unsettling at this late stage. Ideally, I'd like to get the hell out of here right now and go back to the hotel to take stock. But I know that I have to exorcise that memory by getting straight back in the water. I can't bring myself to swim any real distance, but I ask the producer if there are any other scenes we need to shoot.

'Actually we do need a set-up shot of you under the open ice sheet with no safety lanyard,' he says. 'We'd like you to go under the ice shelf for a second and then swim back, straight towards the camera.'

'You do realise that's pretty much exactly what I've just done by mistake. Man, it was hideous – I was scared shitless!'

Rationally, I know I've no choice than to get back on the horse, but the prospect fills me with dread. I talk it over at length with the safety team. I may only have to swim about 10 metres, but if I deviate from my path by even 15 per cent – an easy mistake in the dark – then I'll swim straight past the hole and find myself trapped once again. In the end, Johnny comes up with a way to reassure me. He'll tie a rope around my leg so that if I go too far, he can simply reel me back in. Frankly, I still don't like it, but I know it can be done safely. It's only my complete trust in Johnny that persuades me to get back in the water.

In the late afternoon, Johnny and I go for a walk around Reykjavík for a debrief. Thankfully, filming that final dive proved fairly straightforward, but it's still been a bad day for my confidence. I ran into real strife just trying to swim 20 metres. Tomorrow, I'll be attempting four times that distance with the eyes of a 70-person crew and multiple cameras trained on me.

The winter air is crisp as we crunch through streets carpeted with snow in the weakening light. We pass the Icelandic Phallological

Museum that claims to display 'over 300 penises from over 100 species of mammal' including a whale and a polar bear. 'What a load of old pricks,' says Johnny. Turning west, we find ourselves in the shadow of the giant Hallgrímskirkja church, with its concrete tower soaring more than 70 metres above the Reykjavík skyline. We've just got time to climb it to enjoy the view of the city. From the observation deck, Reykjavík unfolds in a tapestry of corrugated-iron roofs in a mad array of reds, blues and yellows. In the distance, the bay is encircled by a range of mountains, a reminder that just past the outskirts of the city is a wild land of lava and ice.

The vista fails to put my troubles into perspective and as we walk back to the hotel, I start gabbling about my experience beneath the ice. I describe my fear as I waited for the safety diver. The sense of creeping panic as I realised I was running out of air.

'It's not great, is it? The day before my attempt . . .'

Johnny turns to face me, his beanie pulled low over his head. 'Listen, bro,' he says. 'You've got to put that out of your mind now, because it doesn't relate to what you're going to do tomorrow. You're not going to have to swim back past the starting hole and you're not going to be in that same situation.'

'So you reckon I just forget it?'

'Every dive gives you data that you can either choose to use or choose to ignore. And I reckon you can ignore today's data because it's completely irrelevant to what you're doing tomorrow. Today wasn't a test of how well you could swim under the ice. It was just about filming a bunch of stuff and trying out your gear. And it was successful in that respect, because you learned a couple of valuable things. You'll take more layers to stay warm beforehand. You'll duck dive more carefully so the neck weight doesn't brain you. You may have had a bad experience, but some really useful stuff came out of it. Overall, today was a success, not a failure.'

Back in my hotel room, I know that Johnny is right and that I need to reframe the experience. Unforeseen events will occur before any performance. The question is whether you allow them to derail you or not.

I'm reminded of a mental trick that I teach my clients. It's something I've shared many times with everyone from golfers to ballet dancers to TED speakers. It's basically how to regain focus when something in your buildup catches you off-guard.

Imagine, I tell the client, that you're a fish swimming happily in the ocean. Suddenly you look up and notice that there are several fishing hooks dangling down into the water. If you swallow one of those hooks, it's game over. But if you refuse to engage with the hooks, then you can just carry on as normal and calmly go about your business without being agitated or disturbed.

In a performance context, those fishing hooks represent all the obstacles and curveballs that can and do happen before you're in action. It might be a nasty message or off-putting sledge that causes you to question your ability. It might be an enforced change of schedule, a missing piece of kit or some freak occurrence that could throw you off your game. But if you stay vigilant and don't let them snare you, those fish hooks don't actually matter at all.

'Dodge the hooks,' I repeat to myself as I double-check my gear before turning in for the night. 'Just make sure you dodge those bloody hooks.'

CHAPTER 30

The next morning, my alarm goes off at 7 am. I feared that I'd be too nervous to get much sleep, but I've somehow managed almost eight hours. Lying there in my supersized bed, I check in with how I'm feeling. Yes, there's a hint of anxiety percolating in my brain, but nothing too debilitating. I get up, go to the bathroom and eye my wind-burned reflection in the mirror.

It's a big day, mate, but you're ready for it. Get excited: you're about to experience 12 hours that you will never forget.

My dive isn't until 4 pm, but I have a run-list that accounts for virtually every minute between now and then. After a shower and shave, I meet Johnny in the foyer and we head off to our local diner for breakfast. On my return, I give myself ten minutes – timed by stopwatch – to think about the dive. During those ten minutes, I allow my inner stress-head free rein.

Will I manage the final exit from the ice hole? What'll happen if I black out . . .?

When the alarm on my phone sounds, I park those concerns and return to my to-do list.

I lay out and check all my diving gear on the bed yet again. Then I take a full hour to relax, stretch and visualise the dive. At 10 am, I get into my big jacket and head out for a 45-minute walk through the nearby botanic gardens. Cloaked with snow, the colours of the flowers have been replaced by a monochrome palette of whites and greys broken only by the deep green of the conifers. It's very quiet apart from the crunch of snow underfoot.

Standing by a small lake, I admire the skeletal forms of the dormant trees. The ice on the lake is broken in patches, allowing a handful of ducks to splash about. Despite it being −20°C, there are still signs of life and vitality in the park, sparks of resilience even in these inhospitable conditions. The weather might be brutal, but living things continue to survive and thrive. They accept the cold and they keep going.

The walk lifts my spirits. I realise, with mild surprise, that I'm actually enjoying myself. That means I must be doing something right. I feel in control and I'm managing the fear.

I have lunch on my own at the Hilton, a simple meal of pumpkin soup with lots of dark rye toast to give me the necessary carbs. Back in my hotel room, I check my gear (again) and then lie on the bed to visualise the dive once more. Afterwards, I can feel my nerves beginning to flicker into life.

It's just excitement. And you should be excited. It's not every day that you get to break a world record.

At 2 pm the driver picks me up. I've met him several times now, so he knows our routine. I hop in the back of his Land Cruiser and he puts on the same reggae playlist. Soon Bob Marley's 'Bad Card' is playing, before segueing into a song by New Zealand's Lomez Brown. I settle in for the 45-minute drive to Lake Stiflisdalsvatn. As we make our way through the snow-clad fields, I'm trying to stay in the moment, reminding myself to appreciate the sights of this strange land on the top of the world that's so different to anywhere I've ever been.

In the final five minutes of the trip, I set my intentions of how I'm going to show up at the dive site. The vibe I'll project through my speech and demeanour will be relaxed, cheerful and self-assured.

I'll walk tall and carry myself with confidence and self-belief. When I get out of the car, I'll become my alter ego, Ant Williams, invincible freediver extraordinaire.

Timing is critical in this final hour. I don't want to have to rush, as that can bring on a state of panic. But nor do I want to get ready too early. If a freediver starts the breathing exercises prematurely and changes their respiratory patterns too soon, it can backfire and increase the chances of a blackout. That's something I obviously want to avoid. It's already dark enough under the ice.

I go into the food marquee and have a chat with some of the crew. Happily, I bump into Antero, who's officiating today's attempt. 'Another record today, yes?' he beams, slapping me hard on the back.

After a brief chat, I walk into the marquee where the safety divers have assembled for Johnny's final briefing. Hearing the clarity and detail of his instructions reminds me that I'm in the best possible hands.

The only thing that's niggling me is that I can't find my regular handler, Victor, whom I've briefed at length on how to look after my equipment. I ask a runner if he's seen him and am told that Victor's not going to be here. Apparently, he's been called away to attend to a job on another film set. Instead, I'm introduced to his replacement, a skinny guy called Gunnar who looks to be in his late teens. This unexpected changeover is aggravating. It means I'll now have to spend 30 minutes getting Gunnar up to speed. There's a lot of detail for him to get his head around. Why wasn't I told about this change in personnel?

Don't swallow the fish hooks. Keep swimming.

Shrugging it off, I talk Gunnar through what's required, emphasising just how critical these details are if the dive is to be successful. His biggest responsibility, I explain, is looking after my monofin. In order to maintain a good sensory connection, my feet will be bare inside the fin.

'So if the monofin gets too cold or freezes up, the dive is basically over before it starts.'

The poor kid looks increasingly anxious as I show him how to keep the monofin warm by wrapping it securely in a towel. Due to the fin's tight fit, I have special soap to grease my feet before inserting them into the foot pockets.

'The soap has to be kept warm, too,' I tell Gunnar who's frantically scribbling down notes.

At 3.30 pm, I put my 5-millimetre wetsuit on, taking care not to tear the neoprene. Then I put on my over jacket, over trousers and boots. Accompanied by my new assistant, we head outside, where a driver is waiting in a Polaris AWD vehicle to escort us to the eskimo tent about 300 metres from the track.

The wind is whistling off the frozen lake, its ferocity making the −12°C air temperature feel much colder. Luckily the tent where I'm to do my final preparation is warmed by a gas furnace and is actually pretty snug. It's important that I maintain a reasonable body temperature. If I'm too cold, I'll start shivering in the water and it'll affect my breath. If I'm too warm, the icy water will be too bracing a shock for my system.

The nerves are really starting to crank up now and I spend a couple of minutes trying to relax and smile, nudging my head into a more positive space.

Yes, of course you're nervous, but mainly you're excited. In ten minutes this will all be done.

I start to do some box breathing to slow my respiratory system down. Gunnar comes in carrying my monofin and soap that he's diligently wrapped in a towel. Right now, he looks more stressed than I do. He carefully positions the monofin in front of the furnace to keep it warm. Then I do a breathe-up and start to hold my breath for two minutes to prime my lungs.

Midway through the breath-hold, I smell something funny. Glancing over, what the hell . . . the furnace is melting my monofin! Layers of rubber are peeling off due to the heat!

Stopping the breath-hold, I rush to grab the fin, desperately trying to smooth down the pieces of rubber that mould it to my feet. I don't have a spare monofin so this has to work. Some of the flakes of rubber won't stick back into place, so I press down harder and then in desperation run outside to the first ice hole and dip the fin in the freezing water to try to seal the rubber. It seems to work. The problem now is that during that mad scramble to save the monofin, I've messed up my breathing and have also got cold having gone outside in only my wetsuit. Having just been dunked in the icy water, the monofin will also now be painfully cold. None of this should have happened.

Don't bite the hooks.

Back in the eskimo tent, poor Gunnar looks even more distraught and keeps apologising.

'Don't worry about it. Here's the fin, it seems okay. Your job now is to try and warm it up as much as possible. I'm going to start my breath-hold again.'

I'm running out of time now. I do another quick breathe-up and return to my breath-hold. During it, I become aware of a slight tingling feeling in my hands and forearms. Unfortunately, I know this sensation only too well. In my eagerness to crack on, I've prepared for my breath-hold too aggressively. This feeling is a sign that I've accidentally lowered my CO_2 levels too much. It can take about ten minutes to get things back to normal and I can't afford not to take some time to reset. If I'm not careful, my anxiety levels will spiral.

'You've got to bring Johnny in,' I tell Gunnar.

Johnny arrives almost immediately. He must have been waiting outside. 'What's going on, bro?'

'Johnny, I just overbreathed on my warm-up and had to abort it.'

'Okay, what do you want to do?'

'I just need to sit and talk naturally for the next three or four minutes before I start over again. Mate, can you just stay with me? Maybe chat and make me laugh? Take my mind off things a bit.'

'No problem.'

There's a long pause. I can't think of a single thing to say because all my effort is going into trying to hold back the panic. Poor Johnny meanwhile is a taciturn guy at the best of times and not one for small talk.

'Did you know that some of the crew are taking bets on whether or not you can do it today? They're running a book on how far you can go.'

'Is that so? What are my odds looking like?'

'Yeah, well, I was actually thinking about that. Maybe we could rig the betting. You and me agree a distance and I'll put on the bet. We'll split the winnings. It'll be 60/40, of course, because I'm fronting the stake . . .'

For some reason, this cracks me up. I can't stop giggling. In fact, I'm soon wiping away tears of laughter, probably more in response to the highly charged situation than Johnny's half-arsed gag. But it's a welcome release from the pressure. Gunnar meanwhile is rubbing the monofin vigorously with the towel to warm it up. It actually seems to be okay. Maybe we're back on track.

'Johnny, one thing I hadn't thought about. Once I've got my fin on, how am I going to get onto the ice? Are they going to carry me out? If so, can you tell the cameras I don't want that to be filmed. It's so undignified.'

'Don't worry, I got you, bro. I sorted something out.'

Johnny pops out the door and returns dragging a kid's toboggan that looks utterly ridiculous. He's clearly delighted with his find. 'We're going to push you out on that.'

'No! You're shitting me. I'm going to look like such a princess. On film!'

'Dude, you *are* a princess.'

So I don't have to raise my heart rate too much, Johnny helps me to put my monofin on – the rubber seems to have held up just fine. My breathing has finally returned to a regular pattern as I ready myself to head out onto the ice.

'You carriage awaits, m'lady,' smirks Johnny gesturing to the sled.

And then I'm being dragged out on this bloody toboggan into the freezing cold. The whole scenario is ludicrous and, coupled with my mounting nerves, makes me start laughing again. The crew chuckle too as I'm pushed out and I smile and give a regal wave. It is pretty funny; I'm wearing a bright red wetsuit and riding a kid's sled. There's about 50 people already out on the ice with 15 cameramen wearing scuba gear underwater. As Johnny pushes me along I can see all the safety crew, the officials and the judges. All these people, all this equipment, all here for me . . .

Then I'm helped off the toboggan and placed on the edge of the ice hole, a yoga mat positioned under my bum so it's not in direct contact with the ice. Now I put my mask on – my final switch – and Johnny checks the seal to make sure it's watertight. Antero comes over in his position as the lead official. Once again, he's eager to hurry me along so I don't get too cold.

'Ready to start your three-minute countdown?'

Not quite. There's been a flurry of drama this last 15 minutes. I've gone from being enclosed in the tent to being out here in this vast, white expanse of ice and wind and snow. I need some time to reorientate. 'Can you just give me 30 seconds? Then we'll start the count.'

You got this, Ant. You've bloody got this. You've just got to kick and count – four double kicks per marker. Let's get this done. Kick and count. This is who you are and this is what you do.

Just before the countdown begins, I look down and notice that my legs are trembling, not with cold but anxiety. My body is trying to shake out the tension, steeling itself for the ordeal ahead.

I'm not thinking about the dive anymore. All my focus is dialled into relaxing my body and preparing my breathing. I don't need to pack my lungs too full, just ensure they're full enough. I've done this so many times now – both in practice and in my mind – that I'm on autopilot. I'm in that magical space where I'm completely in the zone.

Everything goes silent. Now it's just down to me, and me alone, to break the world record. There is no chance to back out and nor do I want one. I welcome this moment of pure discomfort because I am mentally prepared for it and embrace it with total confidence and self-belief.

I take one more breath and lower myself into the ice hole.

The water is insanely cold. As soon as I'm immersed, I angle my body down headfirst to reach a depth of 4 metres. My diving motion is smooth and the neck weight thankfully doesn't bash my head again. But then I feel an unexpected yank. My lanyard has become snagged on my monofin again. Shit! After a couple of kicks, it breaks free. I can see the rope clearly now and I start swimming.

Once again, I'm struck by the profound darkness and how removed I am from the rest of the world. It's like I've entered another planet.

Swimming along, I remind myself this stage is all about staying relaxed. I have no urge to breathe yet. I'm just establishing a smooth rhythm with my monofin. I kick and count. Kick and count. Then I notice a problem. Water is trickling down the right side of my mask.

This is bad news. If too much water enters the mask, I'll have to shut my eyes to stop my eyeballs from freezing. While I don't really need to see for most of the swim, visibility is crucial at the end to navigate the exit hole. If the mask floods, I won't be able to finish the dive or surface through the hole. I could be in big trouble here.

You have to keep going now. Keep swimming. Dodge the hooks.

I'm expecting the breath-hold discomfort to kick in at around the 70-metre mark. But at 35 metres I'm startled by the contractions jerking in my chest. Ugh, I feel atrocious. Seriously? Already?

It's okay. You know that when you attempt a high-stakes dive it's not unusual for the discomfort to come early. It's just a sign of what's at stake. It doesn't mean your breath-hold is going bad.

Except that now there's a chink of self-doubt that my inner critic is trying to prise open.

Your mask is flooding! You're deep under the ice! You don't know where the ice holes are! You're fading! You didn't get enough air in! You are utterly fucked . . .

I think of my notebook. Picture the word STOP. Halt the negative thoughts. Default to my affirmations.

No one is mentally tougher than me. This is who I am and this is what I do.

I pass another marker. But they just signal progression and aren't labelled with the distance. How many have I passed? Would that have been 60 metres or 80 metres? I have no idea and that's a problem. Without knowing how far I've come, I can't calibrate my energy or oxygen supply.

How have I got so disorientated? And those stabbing contractions in my chest are going crazy now. Maybe I should bail? No, I can't do that yet, I haven't even got halfway. They won't have enough footage. I've got to keep swimming. No point in counting the kicks now. Just swim.

I accept that, like it or not, this is my reality. That I'm physically struggling in freezing cold water. That there is still a long way to go. But that's my situation and I just have to swim.

This is who I am and this is what I do.

With that acceptance, things start to become simpler. The contractions ricochet through my chest but I know they won't kill me.

The discomfort isn't unbearable. I can't worry about my mask because there's nothing I can do about it. I don't know how far I have to go, but I just have to swim. The only way out is through.

Gradually, I find my rhythm, the monofin propelling me through the water with greater ease. I'm zipping freely along now like a torpedo through the darkness. I lose myself in the fluid momentum, the hypnotic motion of the kicks. I suddenly realise with surprise that not only am I free from discomfort, I'm actually enjoying the swim. My body is a well-calibrated instrument generating effortless power, slicing through the water with a silken, frictionless ease. I've found my groove and it feels completely sustainable, like I could glide on forever beneath the ice.

This is who I am . . .

Kick and glide.

And this is what I do.

Kick and glide.

Then I see a candy cane on the rope! Already? That's Arthur Guérin-Boëri's distance of 175 metres! I can come up now and it'd be a respectable result. Thank God! I smile with relief, then quickly tell myself not to as it might disrupt the seal of my mask. Plus, I'm not ready to come up just yet. I can keep going. And with one more double kick there's the second candy cane. Just one more metre . . .

Concentrate now, the exit is the hardest part. Turn your body early, give yourself plenty of room, one little kick.

Then I'm piercing the surface of the water. The darkness turns to white. I yank off my mask and flash the okay sign to the officials. My head reels slightly, but I'm totally fine. In fact, I feel great.

'I'm okay,' I say in a faltering voice.

It's not a done deal just yet. The officials will monitor me for 30 seconds, studying my motor control and checking that I don't black out. As I'm waiting, I notice with a pang of horror that there's *another* hole in the ice ahead of me. Did I somehow come up too early? But I counted two candy canes! Have I just made a terrible mistake?

'Congratulations!' Antero cries. 'It's the new world record!'

'But what about the other hole?'

'No, that's for the cameramen.'

Then the euphoria hits. I whoop and splash in the freezing water and a safety diver helps to haul me out. I sit on the edge of the hole, but I'm so buggered that I have to lie down on the cold, cold ice. I stare at the pale sky, trying to get my head around the enormity of what just happened. I'm choking back tears because I can't believe I've done it. I can't believe it's finally over.

Johnny strides over and pulls me to my feet with a gloved hand before engulfing me in a massive bear hug. With his hood pulled up against the cold, only a small section of his face is visible and that's entirely taken up with a huge grin.

'Soak it up, brother,' he says quietly. 'Just soak it all up.'

EPILOGUE

Six months later, I'm standing in Brisbane's Nissan Arena feeling deeply uneasy. Spectators pack the bleachers of this vast sports hall, the crowd's voices forming a collective hum of anticipation and excitement. For this international taekwondo tournament, the space has been divided into multiple rings, each presided over by a panel of judges waiting to scrutinise the athletes. I can already feel a knot of fluttering nerves in my stomach.

But I'm not here as a participant. Nor am I here as a sport psychologist. The reason I'm standing here with a pounding heart is that I'm waiting to watch Chloe, my 16-year-old daughter, compete.

The fact that she's made it to this arena is remarkable, given how her taekwondo career almost ended before it began. Three years ago, when Chloe was barely a teenager, she was due to compete in her first sparring tournament. It didn't go well. Inside the venue she was rattled by the wall of noise – the crack of kicks against chest guards, the wild cheers of the crowd. With multiple battles taking place all around her, the air was thick with nervous energy and the promise of looming violence.

Already jittery, Chloe was unprepared for the pressure and just 20 minutes before her bout, she had a tearful meltdown in the toilets. Not knowing how to regain her composure, she couldn't bring herself to fight. Instead, she withdrew from the competition. She was so unnerved by the whole experience that she suffered a crisis of confidence. Chloe didn't just walk away from her taekwondo fight. For a couple of years, she walked away from the sport altogether.

Today, she's not just participating, she's excelling. She's worked her way up to become a second Dan black belt, winning several national titles in the discipline of Poomsae taekwondo, a contact-free form of the sport where you perform choreographed moves and are judged on your accuracy, power and grace. Next year, Chloe is set to represent Australia at the World Championships in Korea.

I could not be any prouder. Yet my fatherly delight is less bound up in Chloe's achievements than it is in her courage to put that negative experience behind her and be prepared to test herself in this high-pressure crucible once more. It was her own decision to return to taekwondo. But through that willingness to challenge herself, Chloe has evolved in multiple ways. She's learned how to control her emotions when she's feeling the heat. She's learned how to consistently perform when the stakes are high. She's learned how to train her mind to outsmart the belittling voices in her head that previously sabotaged her efforts and trashed her self-worth.

Stepping past a coach barking last-minute instructions to his charges, I head up into the stands and take a seat. Glancing down I can see my daughter warming up with some stretches and tentative kicks. She then starts chatting and laughing with a fellow competitor. That's a good sign. She doesn't look afraid, because she's found ways to manage her fear.

I can't take much credit for this. Chloe discovered these coping tactics largely on her own. And I'm so, so pleased that she's done that, because in modern life, they're becoming dying skills that many kids don't always get the chance to develop.

When I was growing up in New Zealand in the 1970s and 80s, childhood gave us greater scope to test ourselves away from the prying eyes of teachers and parents. We ran around barefoot, we went for long bike rides unsupervised, we spoke to strangers, we fell out of trees. There were casualties: sprained wrists, gashed knees, even the odd broken bone. None of these things was especially valuable in its own right.

But crucially, we were given the opportunity to be independent and to test ourselves through 'micro acts' of bravery. These little tests in turn allowed us to push our limits in a physical realm. Back then, fewer kids were crippled with anxiety and mental health issues. Maybe that's because fewer people were aware of those conditions at the time. But I also wonder whether the greater autonomy we enjoyed made us more resilient.

Today, things are very different. Back when she was in Grade 5, I remember Chloe coming home one afternoon and telling me about a brand-new school rule. Running had been banned in the playground as a safety precaution to stop kids from tripping and hurting themselves.

Appalled, I mentioned it to a mate the next time we went for a surf. 'Doesn't surprise me one bit,' he sighed. 'At my kids' school, they've banned cartwheels and handstands, too.'

I understand that such rules stem from good intentions. Schools want to protect kids from pain, not to mention avoid costly lawsuits. But I worry about the broader implications for a society that puts such an excessive value on protection.

Like it or not, risk, discomfort and suffering are inescapable parts of life. We only get better at dealing with them from cumulative exposure. Of course we want to shield our kids from unnecessary harm. But by trying to insulate them from all forms of jeopardy we leave them ill-prepared for the messy business of real life. We can't treat children like babies and then expect them to magically transform into self-confident adults the moment they hit 18.

Nor is this concern limited to our kids. I constantly see the repercussions in the corporate world too. I work with leaders from a range of professional sectors and am regularly struck by how many of these captains of industry recoil from positive risk-taking, preferring to err on the side of caution, putting safety first.

Yet this meek approach carries its own dangers. Overly cautious managers are often afraid of change because of the inevitable discomfort and disruption that it brings. But clinging to familiarity can hold an organisation back. Risk-averse managers stifle creativity and innovation. They resist the very change that organisations need in order to adapt and survive. Trying out new things always carries an element of risk, but the upside is the huge scope for positive change.

I'm no fan of disruption for the sake of it or indeed of mindless thrillseeking. But there is real value in taking calculated risks. It's impossible to achieve anything significant in life without putting yourself on the line. You'll never meet your soulmate if you don't go on a date. You'll never make it as an entrepreneur if you don't try that side hustle or launch that business. You'll never score a goal if you don't take a shot.

All these opportunities carry risks. The date might end in heartache. Your start-up will probably go bust. You might shank your shot on goal so wide it goes out for a corner. But life isn't about staying on the sidelines as a dispassionate observer. It's about summoning up the courage to have a crack.

I believe that we need to get better at identifying the risks that are genuinely worth taking. Then we need to learn how to manage our emotional state as we tackle them, in order to perform despite the discomfort and the fear. For me, freediving became the vehicle that allowed me to develop those skills. I found a sport that quite literally took me out of my depth. It forced me to find ways to deal with literal pressure.

Down on the arena floor, Chloe's fellow competitors are putting themselves through dynamic warm-ups with leg swings and torso twists to prime their bodies for the explosive moves to come.

One girl looks to be doing a full rehearsal to ingrain the pattern of movements in her mind, calibrating the exact angles of her arms and the precise depth of her stance. Chloe meanwhile is sitting crossed-legged over to one side, eating an energy bar. I take that as a positive sign. If she's able to stomach a few mouthfuls, she must be on top of her nerves.

In ten minutes, she'll be taking the mat to perform. She'll be judged on accuracy and the correctness of each technique and movement. The judges will scrutinise her presentation, looking for the right mix of power, speed and rhythm. They'll dissect her balance through every turn and they'll check that each kick is snapped out with good height and control. The judging process is ruthless and forensically detailed. Even the wrong angle of a thumb can lead to lost points.

Yet watching her sitting quietly on her own, I realise that my nerves are less bound up in her final score. Through her taekwondo I just want Chloe to develop the confidence that she can cope with performance anxiety and silence the inner voice in her head.

Freediving gave me the chance to learn how to do that. I'm well aware my world record of swimming 182 metres under the ice will soon be broken, just as the depth record I set in Norway has also been surpassed. But what freediving taught me was how to master my fear, which in turn allowed me to build the self-confidence and belief to handle other challenges. By taking calculated risks underwater, I learned to trust my judgement in other areas, too. Would I have become emboldened to launch my consultancy business if it hadn't been for freediving? Backed myself to take the leap despite the risk? To be totally honest, I'm not sure I would've dared.

Chloe stands, waiting to be called to the mat. I've no idea what's going through her head. Despite my psychology background, I haven't been allowed to share many tips about how to cope with these moments. No teenager wants advice from their dad, even if he's wangled a couple of world records.

Her name must have been called because I see her shoulders rise as she takes a deep breath and walks over to the competition area with a purposeful stride.

There's nothing I can do to help her now. She's completely on her own. Maybe it's just parental concern, but at this moment she looks so vulnerable, and so terrifyingly young. I get another surge of nerves and start praying that she's coping and that everything goes alright. She looks to be smiling, but is that just a forced expression to hide her fear?

Then I remember our conversation this morning en route to the arena, when I asked how she was feeling about the event. The answer she gave thrilled me more than any medal she'll ever win.

'Dad,' she said. 'I'm not an anxious person anymore. You know I'm an athlete now.'

Sitting here in the stands, I watch as Chloe stops and bows sharply to the judges. And that's when I realise that everything is going to be just fine.

ACKNOWLEDGEMENTS

This book was shaped by many people whose support, expertise and generosity I deeply appreciate.

Ben Ball and the team at Simon & Schuster Australia, thank you for believing in this idea and for bringing the energy, care and steady hands that turned it into a reality. I'm grateful to the editors whose feedback shaped the book and helped it land better than I dreamed to imagine.

Luke, my creative co-conspirator, thank you for the long calls, the powerful questions and the way you took a tangled story and found the clean line through it. Your influence runs through every chapter in the best possible way.

My freediving world has given me more than I can ever repay. Johnny Sunnex, thank you for being the person I want beside me when things get serious. Your calm, your skill and your commitment to making freediving safer have lifted the standard for everyone.

Antero Joki, thank you for opening the door to ice diving and backing me through two world record attempts. You've been the obvious partner to chase records with at the extreme edge of our sport.

To the legendary team of safety divers who came to Iceland – thank you for your extraordinary commitment. Waiting around on the ice in –20°C temperatures was no small ask! My favourite memories were hanging out in the hot pools together and, of course, the great Kiwi reggae tunes that got me in the zone for each dive.

The making of the film *Ice Dive* brought in a different kind of team. Thank you to the amazing people at Apple for trusting me to pull off a world record in one of the most extreme environments on the planet. Charlotte Mikkelborg, your creativity, tireless energy and gift for finding the emotional thread in a story gave this project its heart. You turned an unforgiving environment into something unexpectedly intimate and human. Anthony Geffen at Atlantic Studios, your drive to push filmmaking technology forward is infectious. Thank you for seeing the potential in the project, driving the vision and supporting the team through the challenges that come with filming in such extreme conditions.

My grounding in psychology came from people who mentored me early on and gave me many of the tools I still use today.

Ken Hodge and Alex McKenzie, thank you for shaping the foundations of my understanding of sport psychology and for giving me the tools to help athletes work through the barriers that hold them back. You set me on a path in sport that has been incredibly rewarding.

Associate Professor Dr David O'Hare, thank you for your mentorship during my master's. Your deep knowledge of human factors in high-risk environments was exactly the guidance I needed, and you stretched my thinking in all the right ways.

To my gorgeous wife Merryn, my family and my close friends, thank you for sticking with me through what can only be described as a wildly unconventional life. Chasing world records under the ice in the Arctic is not something most people put on the family calendar, yet you still cheered me on and trusted that I'd stay safe and make it back home. Your unwavering belief has kept me steady through every mad adventure.

And to everyone who played a part, large or small, thank you. I'm grateful.

ABOUT THE AUTHOR

Ant Williams is a two-time world record holder in ice diving, a psychologist, a leadership expert and mental fitness coach who has spent two decades exploring what it means to perform under pressure. Before diving under Arctic ice on a single breath, Ant coached elite athletes, including MotoGP riders, big-wave surfers and extreme sports competitors, helping them master fear, focus and high-stakes performance. But despite his success in the field, he felt something was missing.

To truly understand what it means to operate at the edge, Ant turned to freediving, not because he was born to it, but because it scared him. He trained himself to a world-class level and went on to set multiple world records, including the deepest freedive under ice (70.3 metres) and the longest distance swum under ice (182 metres), performed in darkness in near-zero-degree water.

Today, Ant combines insights from sport psychology and extreme adventure to teach others how to lead through pressure, reframe fear, and perform at their best when it matters most. His immersive dive has been featured in Apple's *Adventure* series on Apple Vision Pro, offering a groundbreaking look at human potential in the world's most unforgiving environments.

Scan here with your phone's camera
for the Mental Fitness Scorecard

Scan here for Ant's video on correct breathing techniques
and his pre-dive playlist on Apple iTunes